Study Guide

HENRY BORNE

Holy Cross College

SOCIOLOGY

FOURTH EDITION

John J. Macionis

Kenyon College

Prentice Hall, Englewood Cliffs, New Jersey 07632

Editorial/Production supervision: **Elaine Price**
Prepress buyer: **Kelly Behr**
Manufacturing Buyer: **Mary Ann Gloriande**
Supplement acquisitions editor: **Sharon Chambliss**
Acquisitions editor: **Nancy Roberts**

 ©1993 by Prentice-Hall, Inc.
A Simon & Schuster Company
Englewood Cliffs, New Jersey 07632

Printed in the United States of America

10 9 8 7 6 5 4

ISBN 0-13-818949-8

Prentice-Hall International (UK) Limited, *London*
Prentice-Hall of Australia Pty. Limited, *Sydney*
Prentice-Hall Canada Inc., *Toronto*
Prentice-Hall Hispanoamericana, S.A., *Mexico*
Prentice-Hall of India Private Limited, *New Delhi*
Prentice-Hall of Japan, Inc., *Tokyo*
Simon & Schuster Asia Pte. Ltd., *Singapore*
Editora Prentice-Hall do Brasil, Ltda., *Rio de Janeiro*

Contents

Preface iv

PART ONE: THE FOUNDATIONS OF SOCIOLOGY

Chapter 1: The Sociological Perspective 1
Chapter 2: Sociological Investigation 15

PART TWO: THE FOUNDATIONS OF SOCIETY

Chapter 3: Culture 30
Chapter 4: Society 45
Chapter 5: Socialization 59
Chapter 6: Social Interaction in Everyday Life 74
Chapter 7: Groups and Organizations 86
Chapter 8: Deviance 100

PART THREE: SOCIAL INEQUALITY

Chapter 9:   Social Stratification 117
Chapter 10: Social Class in America 128
Chapter 11: Global Inequality 142
Chapter 12: Race and Ethnicity 154
Chapter 13: Gender and Sex 170
Chapter 14: Aging and the Elderly 187

PART FOUR: SOCIAL INSTITUTIONS

Chapter 15: Family 199
Chapter 16: Education 216
Chapter 17: Religion 230
Chapter 18: Politics and Government 243
Chapter 19: The Economy and Work 258
Chapter 20: Health and Medicine 271

PART FIVE: SOCIAL CHANGE

Chapter 21: Population and Urbanization 287
Chapter 22: Collective Behavior and Social Movements 303
Chapter 23: Social Change and Modernity 316

Preface

This Study Guide has been written to enhance the foundation of sociological ideas and issues which are presented in the text, _Sociology_, by John J. Macionis. To enable you to review and apply basic sociological concepts, methods, and theories, the Study Guide has been organized into several different sections to accompany each chapter in the text.

A **Chapter Outline** provides a basis for organizing segments of information from each chapter in the text. A section on **Learning Objectives** identifies the basic knowledge, explanations, comparisons, and understandings a student should have after reading and studying each chapter in the text. A section entitled **Chapter Review** consists of a brief review of the chapter in paragraph form, following the outline of each chapter. This is followed by a section entitled **Key Concepts** in which the key terms from the chapter are listed in alphabetical order. Some space is provided for the student to write out the definition for each of these terms. The fifth section for each chapter includes **Study Questions**, including true-false, multiple-choice, definition, and short-answer type questions. The next section provides the **Answers** for the study guide questions, including a listing of the page numbers where answers to these questions can be found. The final section, **Analysis and Comment** provides space for students to raise questions and make comments on the boxes in the text.

This Study Guide is intended to be a concise review and learning tool to accompany _Sociology_. It is complementary to this text and is not intended to stand alone as a brief text. It will provide the student with opportunities to more deeply benefit from the knowledge of sociology which John Macionis offers in his text.

On a personal note, I want to congratulate John Macionis for writing such an excellent text. His text is very clearly written and offers students a very meaningful sociological perspective on a broad range of important contemporary social issues. It has been my pleasure to have had the opportunity to write this Study Guide. I would also like to thank Sharon Chambliss and Millie White for their guidance and assistance during the writing of this Study Guide. It is indeed people like them who make Prentice Hall such a fine publisher. Finally, my love to my family-- Cincy, Ben, and Abby-- for their support and love.

HB

The Sociological Perspective

1

PART 1: CHAPTER OUTLINE

I.   The Sociological Perspective
  A.   Seeing the General in the Particular
  B.   Seeing the Strange in the Familiar
  C.   Putting People in Social Context
      1.   Suicide: The most individual act
  D.   The Importance of Global Perspective
II. The Sociological Perspective in Everyday Life
  A.   Sociology and Social Diversity
  B.   Sociology and Marginality: Race, Gender, and Age
  C.   Sociology and Social Crisis
  D.   Benefits of the Sociological Perspective
III. The Origins of Sociology
  A.   Science and Sociology
  B.   Social Change and Sociology
      1.   A New Industrial Economy
      2.   The Growth of Cities
      3.   Political Change
IV. Sociological Theory
  A.   The Structural-Functional Paradigm
  B.   The Social-Conflict Paradigm
  C.   The Symbolic-Interaction Paradigm
  D.   Sports: Three Theoretical Paradigms in Action
      1.   The Functions of Sports
      2.   Sports and Conflict
      3.   Sports as Interaction
V.   Summary
VI. Key Concepts
VII. Suggested Readings

PART II: LEARNING OBJECTIVES

1. To understand how perspective is shaped and becomes the basis for "reality."
2. To be able to define sociology and understand the basic components of the sociological perspective.
3. To be able to provide examples of the way in which social forces affect our everyday lives.
4. To understand the significance of the research on suicide done by Emile Durkheim, showing the impact of social forces on individual behavior.
5. To recognize the importance of taking a global perspective in order to recognize the how American society fits into the rest of the world.
6. To recognize factors in society which affect how people perceive the world sociologically.
7. To be able to identify important historical factors in the development of sociology.
8. To be able to identify and understand the differences between the three major theoretical paradigms used by sociologists.
9. To be able to provide illustrative questions raised about society using each of the theoretical paradigms.
10. To be able to identify important theorists and researchers who have used the sociological perspective in their study of society, and discuss their respective contributions to the discipline.

PART III: CHAPTER REVIEW

Each of us enter situations with a *perspective*, or point of view. Each perspective identifies different facts as being important and also suggests alternative ways to meaningfully understand the relationship among these facts. The story which is being recounted to begin this chapter concerning the brutal assault and rape of a female jogger in New York's central park by a group of young teenagers illustrates how people in different positions in society will take different perspectives on this case. A basic underlying question though is: What makes people do the things they do? A key feature in taking a sociological perspective is to look beyond *particular* events or people and understand how and why different *categories* of people behavior differently.

THE SOCIOLOGICAL PERSPECTIVE

Sociology is defined as the scientific study of human society. Sociology as a discipline is guided by a distinctive perspective. The qualities of this perspective are outlined, with illustrations for each being presented.

Seeing the General in the Particular

Sociologist Peter Berger made this statement referring to the fact that sociologists see *general* social patterns in the behavior of *particular* individuals. Figure 1-1 (p. 3), which focuses on the variables of homicide, race and sex, illustrates how social forces shape our lives. While not erasing our uniqueness as an individual, these social forces impinge on our lives in many unseen, yet very significant ways.

Seeing the Strange in the Familiar

This refers to the process of detaching oneself from the familiar ways of thinking in order to gain new insights that at first seem strange. The insight gained, according to sociologist Peter Berger, is that "things are not what they seem." Sociology pushes us to question the assumptions we are making about society, and reveals aspects of our social life which most people would not claim to be "obvious" facts. For example, the question, Why did you come to this college? is typically responded to by students with personal answers. The sociological perspective focuses our attention on broader social factors such as family income, age, and government funding as conditions influencing our choice. Again, stepping back from *particular* choices and focusing on *general* patterns. The point is stressed however that our autonomy is not lost using sociology. Rather, it is strengthened as we gain understanding of how our lives are linked to others and to society. The **Social Diversity** box entitled "What's in a Name? How Social Forces Affect Personal Choice" (p. 5) further demonstrates social forces affecting personal choice.

Putting People in Social Context

Sociologists point out that in our individualistic society, we tend to deny our lives are predictable and patterned. The "wilding" case, referred to earlier, addresses the issue of individual responsibility. Sociologists argue that the problem is not simply one of those young males being "evil." There are social forces which must also be studied to understand what happened. A controversy emerges here: Do sociologists minimize the roles of "free will" and "personal choice" too much? Sociologists are suggesting that people must take personal responsibility for their actions, but that an individual's choice and decisions are made within the context of a myriad of social forces. The **Critical Thinking** box (p. 6) entitled "The Wilding Controversy: Are Sociologists Bleeding Hearts?" addresses this issue.

Suicide: The Most Individual Act

Suicide, a seemingly very personal act, is also discussed to demonstrate the effect social forces have on human behavior. The research by Emile Durkheim on suicide clearly shows how impersonal social forces affect personal behavior. Records of suicide in central Europe during the last part of the 19th century were found by Durkheim to show certain social categories as having higher suicide rates than others. It was found that the degree of *social integration*, or how strongly a person is bound to others by social ties, had a significant influence on the patterns of suicide rates. Figure 1-2 (p. 7) provides a contemporary view of suicide rates in the U.S. using the categories of race and sex.

The Importance of Global Perspective

The point is addressed that not only must we study individual experiences in social context, but also study American society as it is affected by the world around us. Data on average per-capita income suggests we are a very wealthy nation when compared to other nations. This fact provides us with certain choices and opportunities not found in other parts of the world. Further, from a practical standpoint, 80 percent of new jobs in America involve some kind of foreign trade. See the **Windows on the World** box presenting global map 1-1: "Wealthy and Poverty: Income in Global Perspective (p. 8).

THE SOCIOLOGICAL PERSPECTIVE IN EVERYDAY LIFE

While Americans tend to understand social life along individualistic lines, there are three situations identified which tend to heighten a person's awareness of the presence of social forces.

Sociology and Social Diversity

Encountering social diversity is one such situation. Confronting unfamiliar social environments tends to broaden our perspective and makes us look for the patterns of behavior which in familiar places tend to be taken for granted. Examples might be visiting a foreign country or going to a strange neighborhood.

Sociology and Social Marginality: Race, Gender, and Age

A second situation is marginality. The term *social marginality* refers to the state of being excluded from social activity as an "outsider." Blacks, women, and the aged are used to illustrate how certain socially significant characteristics can place people on the "outside" of social life, and make them more aware of social patterns others take for granted.

Sociology and Social Crisis

Finally, social crisis can enhance sociological thinking. C. Wright Mills has suggested that certain historical periods have been represented by "social disruption" which has increased sociological awareness. The depression years of the 1930s and the decade of the 1960s are used as examples of historical periods when the influence of social forces became more apparent to members of our society. Our author notes that sociological thinking can also foster social disruption, not merely be a result of it.

Benefits of the Sociological Perspective

Four general benefits of using the sociological perspective are reviewed. These include:

(1)   It challenges familiar understandings about ourselves and others, so that we can critically assess the truth of commonly held assumptions.

(2)   It allows us to recognize both opportunities we have and the constraints that circumscribe our lives.

(3)   It empowers us as active members of our world.

(4)   It helps us to recognize human diversity and to begin to understand the challenges of living in a diverse world.

The **Profile** box on C. Wright Mills (p. 11) focuses on the concept of the "*sociological imagination*." This concept is defined as the quality of mind which enables a person to see the interplay of biography (personal, private life) and history (the broader social structure and social forces impinging upon us).

THE ORIGINS OF SOCIOLOGY

While "society" has been a topic of thought and discussion since the beginning of human history, sociological thinking is a recent historical phenomenon. The discipline of sociology is relatively young, and itself emerged as a product of particular social forces. Auguste Comte coined the term *sociology* in 1838.

Science and Sociology

Emile Durkheim pointed out in the latter 19th century that the great philosophers from antiquity through the first half of the 19th century, using only philosophical and theological perspectives in their studies, concentrated on the qualities of imaginary "ideal" societies rather than on the analysis of what society was really like. Sociology was born when focus was given to understanding how society actually operates.

Auguste Comte argued that the key to achieving this was to use the scientific approach in studying society. He divided the history of the study of society into three distinct eras, which he labeled the *theological*, the *metaphysical*, and the *scientific*. The latter he called *positivism*, or the path to understanding the world based on science. Comte's work is placed within historical context in the **Profile** box (p. 12). He divided sociology into two parts: how society is held together (*social statics*), and how society changes (*social dynamics*).

Social Change and Sociology

Three key factors are identified as reshaping society during the 17th and 18th centuries. These include:

A New Industrial Economy

Rapid technological changes of the 18th century brought people in great numbers to work in factories, thus breaking down established patterns of social life.

The Growth of Cities

As factories spread across Europe, drawing people out of the countryside seeking employment due to the changing nature of the economy, this massive influx of people into cities created many social problems. The crises which emerged stimulated the development of the sociological perspective.

Political Change

The rapid economic and urban growth created a context for change in political thinking. Traditional notions of Divine Law were being replaced by ideas of individual liberty and freedom.

SOCIOLOGICAL THEORY

While the sociological perspective provides us with a unique vantage point from which to observe our social world, theory helps us to meaningfully organize and explain the linkages between specific observations we make. A *theory* is the process of linking facts in order to explain something. There are a number of research methods available to researchers which are used to establish whether a theory is supported by facts. The basis upon which sociologists choose issues to study is called theory building. This is guided by a *theoretical paradigm*, or a set of fundamental assumptions about society that guide sociological thinking and research.

There are three principal theoretical paradigms used by sociologists. Each theory focuses the researcher's attention on particular types of questions about how society is organized, and each provides a different explanation about why certain patterns are found in society.

The Structural-Functional Paradigm

This paradigm is a framework for building theory guided by the assumption that society is a complex system whose parts work together to promote stability. The two basic components of this paradigm are *social structure*, or relatively stable patterns of behavior, and *social functions*, which refer to consequences for the operation of society as a whole. Structural functionalists often liken society to the human body, with different parts of society being interdependent, much like the various organs of the body. The work of Herbert Spencer, one of the first to use structural-functionalism in the analysis of society, is highlighted in the **Profile** box (p. 18). His view of society has been labeled "*social Darwinism.*"

6

Besides Spencer, other early structural-functionalists included Durkheim and Comte. As sociology developed in the United States during the 20th century, researchers Talcott Parsons and Robert K. Merton further applied and developed the thinking of these early social scientists. Merton differentiated between what he called *manifest functions*, or consequences of social structure recognized by people within a society, and *latent functions*, which are unrecognized or unintended consequences of social structure. Merton further points out that elements of social structure may be functional for one aspect of society and not for others. There may be undesirable effects on the operation of society, or *social dysfunctions*. In critically evaluating this paradigm, it is pointed out that it is a conservative approach to the study of society which tends to ignore tension and conflict in social systems.

The Social-Conflict Paradigm

This paradigm is a framework for building theory based on the assumption that society is a complex system characterized by inequality and conflict that generate social change. The unequal distribution of power and privilege is reviewed in the context of educational achievement to demonstrate the insights provided by this view of society. Karl Marx is perhaps the most famous social scientist using this paradigm for the analysis of society. Critical evaluation of this paradigm raises concern that social unity is ignored, and that in focusing on change, objectivity may be lost. Both of these first two paradigms concentrate on broad generalities in society, while failing to study particular people in specific contexts.

The work of W.E.B. DuBois is discussed in the **Profile** box (p. 20) illustrating how theorists using the social-conflict paradigm attempt not only to understand society, but also to reduce inequality.

The contributions to the emergence of sociology by two women, Harriet Martineau and Jane Addams, are briefly introduced (p. 21). While many women contributed to the early development of sociology their work has long been unrecognized.

The Symbolic-Interaction Paradigm

The first two paradigms discussed focus on a *macro-level* orientation, meaning a concern with large-scale patterns that characterize society as a whole. An alternative approach is to take a *micro-level* orientation, meaning a concern with small-scale patterns of social interaction in specific settings. This third paradigm, *symbolic interactionism*, is a theoretical framework based on the assumption that society is continuously recreated as human beings construct reality through interaction. The symbolic-interactionist paradigm was greatly influenced by the work of Max Weber, a German sociologist of the late 18th and early 20th centuries. In the United states, during the 20th century, the work of George Herbert Mead, Erving Goffman, George Homans and Peter Blau was instrumental in the development of this paradigm. Mead's work on socialization, Goffman's work on "*dramaturgical analysis*," and Homan and Blau's work on "*social-exchange analysis*" are discussed in later chapters.

In critically analyzing this view it must be stressed that the focus is on how individuals personally experience society. This approach does not allow us to generalize findings to establish broad general patterns.

Each of the three paradigms provides a unique perspective for the development of greater understanding of society. Table 1-1 (p. 23) reviews the orientation, image of society, and illustrative questions representative of each of the three major theoretical paradigms.

Sports: Three Theoretical Paradigms in Action

Sports in America is discussed as an indispensable part of social life. The question becomes, What insights can the sociological perspective provide us concerning sports?

The Functions of Sports

The structural-functional paradigm reveals many functional consequences which sports has for society. For example, the values sports have in terms of positive application in other arenas of social life.

Sports and Social Conflict

The social-conflict paradigm provides an analysis of sports focusing upon the social inequalities within sports at all levels of competition. Male and female inequalities are addressed, as well as racial inequalities in professional sports. Figure 1-3 (p. 26), for example, illustrates the proportions of white and black players at different positions in professional football and baseball.

Sports as Interaction

The symbolic-interactionists view sports as an ongoing process and not merely as some "system." The individual perceptions of specific participants concerning the reality as each experiences it becomes the focus.

No one paradigm is better than another in analyzing sports, or any other aspect of society. The sociological perspective is enriched by the controversy and debate brought about through the application in research of these different paradigms.

PART IV: KEY CONCEPTS

Define each of the following concepts in the space provided or on separate paper. Check the accuracy of your answers by referring to the key concepts section at the end of the chapter in the text as well as by referring to italicized definitions located throughout the chapter.

latent functions
macro-level orientation

manifest functions
metaphysical stage
micro-level orientation
positivism
seeing the general in the particular
seeing the strange in the familiar
social-conflict paradigm
social dynamics
social dysfunctions
social function
social marginality
social statics
social structure
sociological imagination
sociology
structural-functional paradigm
symbolic-interaction paradigm
theological stage
theoretical paradigm
theory

PART V: STUDY QUESTIONS

True-False

1. T F Blacks are approximately six times more likely to be the victim of a homicide than are whites.
2. T F Approximately 66 percent of eighteen- to twenty-four-year-olds in the United States are enrolled in college.
3. T F Durkheim's research on suicide illustrates the point that not all aspects of life can be meaningfully studied using the sociological perspective.
4 T F Blacks and females have higher suicide rates than whites and males.
5. T F The discipline of sociology first emerged in Europe during the 19th century.
6. T F Positivism is the belief in science as the path to knowledge.
7. T F Sociology emerged and developed more quickly in the 19th century within those countries experiencing the most profound social transformations.
8. T F Latent functions refer to social processes which appear on the surface to be functional for society, but which are actually dysfunctional for society.
9. T F Herbert Spencer's view of society came to be known as "social Darwinism."
10. T F The symbolic-interaction and social-conflict paradigms both operate from a micro-level orientation.

Multiple-Choice

1. Which sociologist linked the incidence of suicide to the degree of social integration of different categories of people?

   (a) Emile Durkheim
   (b) Max Weber
   (c) Herbert Spencer
   (d) C. Wright Mills
   (e) Karl Marx

2. Learning to understand our individual lives in terms of the social forces that have shaped them is a state of mind that C. Wright Mills called:

   (a) positivism
   (b) science
   (c) sociological imagination
   (d) hypothesis testing
   (e) perspective

3. Which one of the following theorists developed the concept of the "sociological imagination"?

   (a) Auguste Comte
   (b) Max Weber
   (c) Emile Durkheim
   (d) Karl Marx
   (e) C. Wright Mills

4. The term "sociology" was coined in 1838 by:

   (a) Emile Durkheim
   (b) Karl Marx
   (c) Herbert Spencer
   (d) Auguste Comte
   (e) Max Weber

5. Positivism is the idea that _____, rather than any other type of human understanding, is the path to knowledge.

   (a) human nature
   (b) religion
   (c) science
   (d) optimism
   (e) intuition

6. A set of fundamental assumptions about society that guides sociological thinking and research is the definition of:

   (a) a research design
   (b) a theoretical paradigm
   (c) the sociological imagination
   (d) an hypothesis
   (e) positivism

7. Consequences of social structure which are largely unrecognized and unintended are called:

   (a) latent functions
   (b) manifest functions
   (c) social marginality
   (d) paradigms
   (e) social dysfunctions

8. Which two sociological theorists using the structural-functional theory came to very different conclusions about whether sociology should guide social reform?

   (a) Peter Berger and C. Wright Mills
   (b) Karl Marx and Robert Merton
   (c) Emile Durkheim and Max Weber
   (d) Herbert Spencer and Auguste Comte
   (e) none of the above

9. Which of the following theoretical perspectives is best suited for analysis using the macro-level orientation?

   (a) dramaturgical analysis
   (b) social exchange theory
   (c) symbolic-interactionism
   (d) social systems analysis
   (e) social-conflict theory

10. The questions, How is society experienced? And, how do individuals attempt to shape the reality perceived by others? are most likely to be asked by a researcher using which of the following theoretical paradigms?

    (a) structural-functionalism
    (b) symbolic-interactionism
    (c) social Darwinism
    (d) social-conflict
    (e) none of the above

Fill-In

1. The scientific study of human society is the general definition for _____.

2. To approach an issue sociologically we must first step back from personal reasons that tell us only about _____ situations and seek more _____ explanations.

3. Journalist _____ contends that sociologists confused the issue of "wilding" by their "dispersal of responsibility into a fog of socio-economic factors."

4. Being excluded from social activity as an "outsider" is termed _____.

5. Auguste Comte termed the study of how society held itself together as _____ _____, and how social changes as _____ _____.

11

6.   Auguste Comte asserted that scientific sociology was a result of a progression throughout history of thought and understanding in three stages, the _____, _____, and _____.

7.   The development of sociology as an academic discipline was shaped within the context of three revolutionary changes in Europe during the 17th and 18th centuries. These included _____, _____, and _____.

8.   A fundamental image of society that guides sociological thinking is called a _____ _____.

9.   An explanation of the relationship between two or more social facts is called a _____.

10. A concern with small-scale patterns of social interaction, such as symbolic-interaction theory, is called _____ orientation.

Definition and Short-Answer

1.   Differentiate between the concepts manifest and latent functions and provide an example for each.
2.   Discuss Emile Durkheim's explanation of how suicide rates vary between different categories of people. Explain how this research demonstrates the application of the sociological perspective.
3.   What three key societal changes during the 17th and 18th centuries were significant for the emergence of sociology as a scientific discipline?
4.   sing the perspectives of a sociologist, a victim, and a psychiatrist, explain the behavior of the male youths who were involved in the "wilding" tragedy in Central Park.
5.   What are the three key aspects of the sociological perspective? Define each.
6.   What are the four basic benefits of using the sociological perspective?
7.   What are the three major theoretical paradigms used by sociologists? Identify the key questions raised by each.
8.   Discuss the contributions to sociology made by the following theorists: Robert K. Merton, Karl Marx, and Max Weber.

PART VI: ANSWERS TO STUDY QUESTIONS

True-False

1.   T (p. 3)   6.   T (p. 14)
2.   F (p. 4)   7.   T (p. 16)
3.   F (p. 7)   8.   F (p. 17)
4.   F (p. 7)   9.   T (p. 18)
5.   T (p. 12)   10. F (p. 20)

Multiple-Choice

1.	a (p. 7)	6.	b (p. 16)
2.	c (p. 11)	7.	a (p. 16)
3.	e (p. 11)	8.	d (p. 17)
4.	d (p. 12)	9.	e (p. 21)
5.	c (p. 13)	10.	b (p. 23)

Fill-In

1. sociology (p. 2)
2. particular, general (p. 3)
3. George F. Will (p. 6)
4. social marginality (p. 9)
5. social statics, social dynamics (p. 12)
6. theological, metaphysical, and scientific (pp. 13-14)
7. rise of the industrial economy, growth of cities, and political changes (pp. 14-15)
8. theoretical paradigm (p. 16)
9. theory (p. 16)
10. micro-level (p. 21)

PART VII: ANALYSIS AND COMMENT

Go back through the chapter and write down in the spaces below key points from each of the following boxes. Then, for each of the boxes identified, write out three questions concerning the issues raised which you feel would be valuable to discuss in class.

Profiles

C. Wright Mills (1916-1962)

Herbert Spencer (1820-1903)

Key Points:

Key Points:

Questions:

Questions:

Auguste Comte (1798-1857)

Key Points:

W.E.B. DuBois (1868-1963)

Key Points:

Questions:

Questions:

Social Diversity

"What's in a Name? How Social Forces Affect Personal Choice"

Key Points:

Questions:

Critical Thinking

"The Wilding Controversy: Are Sociologists Bleeding Hearts?"

Sociological Investigations

2

PART 1: CHAPTER OUTLINE

I. The Basics of Sociological Investigation
    A. Ways of Knowing: Science and "Truth"
    B. Common Sense versus Scientific Evidence
II. The Elements of Science
    A. Concepts, Variables, and Measurement
        1. Reliability and Validity of Measurement
        2. Relationships Among Variables
    B. The Ideal of Objectivity
    C. Some Limitations of Science
    D. The Importance of Subjective Interpretation
    E. Politics and Research
    F. Gender and Research
    G. Research Ethics
III. The Methods of Sociological Research
    A. Experiments
        1. A Laboratory Experiment: The Stanford County Prison
    B. Survey Research
        1. Population and Sample
        2. Questionnaires and Interviews
        3. Surveys at Work: A Study of American Couples
    C. Participant Observation
        1. A Case Study: Street Corner Society
    D. Secondary Analysis
        1. Historical Research: A Tale of Two Cities
    E. The Interplay of Theory and Method
IV. Putting It All Together: Ten Steps in Sociological Investigation
V. Summary
VI. Key Concepts

PART II: LEARNING OBJECTIVES

1. To understand the requirements fundamental to using sociological investigation.
2. To understand how the four ways of knowing facts affect what is considered "true."
3. To become familiar with the basic elements of science and how they are used in sociological investigation.
4. To understand the limitations of the scientific study of our social world.
5. To recognize the importance of subjective interpretation as part of the process of scientific investigation.
6. To see how research is affected by gender and politics.
7. To begin to view ethical considerations involved when studying people.
8. To become familiar with the major research methods used by sociologists, and to be able to compare and contrast the various procedures involved in each.
9. To be able to discuss the relative advantages and disadvantages for each of the different research methods.
10. To be able to discuss each of the four examples of sociological research provided in the text, including research design used, variable identified and studied, findings, and interpretations.
11. To be able to identify and describe each of the ten steps in carrying out a research project using sociological investigation.

PART III: CHAPTER REVIEW

Research by Dorothy Holland and Margaret Eisenhart concerning college women is discussed as an example of *doing sociology*, the process of *sociological investigation*. Their initial observation that few women pursue study and occupations in the sciences led to a systematic scientific study which involved interviewing college women over a number of years.

THE BASICS OF SOCIOLOGICAL INVESTIGATION

There are two basic requirements identified as underlying sociological investigation:

1. Look at the world using the sociological perspective.
2. Be curious and ask questions.

A fundamental issue being raised in this chapter concerns how we recognize information as being true. The requirements identified above are only the beginning of learning about the process of studying society using sociology. The focus now is on how sociologists find answers to questions about society.

Ways of Knowing: Science and "Truth"

How do we come to know something to be true? Four ways of knowing are being identified. These include: faith, recognition of expertise, agreement through consensus, and science. *Science* is the basis of sociological investigation, and is defined as a logical system that bases knowledge on direct, systematic observation. Science is based on *empirical evidence*, meaning evidence that we can verify using our senses.

Common Sense versus Scientific Evidence

Six common sense statements considered to be true by many Americans are identified in the text. However, using scientific evidence these statements are contradicted by empirical facts. For example, the accuracy of the statement that most poor people ignore opportunities to work is seriously brought into question when discovering the empirical evidence that 1/2 of all poor people in the U.S. are either children or the aged.

As a scientific discipline, sociology can provide us with a framework through which to critically evaluate the many kinds of information we are being exposed to, and enable us to more systematically consider the assumptions we are making about social life.

THE ELEMENTS OF SCIENCE

Sociologists see society in a similar fashion to how natural scientists see the physical world. Sociological research is a process of identifying the parts of society and how they are interrelated. The goal of sociological investigation is to use empirical evidence to provide specific answers to questions concerning social life. There are a number of important components of scientific investigation. These include:

Concepts, Variables, and Measurement

Sociologists use concepts to identify elements of society. A *concept* is a mental construct that represents a part of the world, inevitably in a somewhat simplified form. For example, terms like family, society, and social class are concepts sociologists use to help orient us to our social world. A *variable* is a concept whose value changes from case to case. For example, social class varies with some people being identified as middle-class and others as working-class, etc. *Measurement* is the process of determining the value of a variable in a specific case. For example, the factors of family income and occupation can be used to determine what social class a particular person or family is in. The process of creating measurements for variables can be very complicated. Variables can be measured in many different ways, so any measurement used will be arbitrary. Further, we cannot provide a measurement, for example, of every American citizen.

Sociologists must make use of *statistical measures* often called descriptive statistics. The first **Sociology of Everyday Life** box identifies three useful, and often used, descriptive measures *(mean, median, and mode)* using earnings as an illustration (p. 35).

The last example indicates how variables can be operationalized. *Operationalization* of a variable means to specify exactly what is to be measured in assigning a value to a variable. For instance, as mentioned earlier, social class can be measured using income and occupation.

Reliability and Validity of Measurement

Careful and specific operationalization is critical, but there are two other important issues concerning the measurement of variables to be considered. First, there is the issue of *reliability*, or the quality of consistency in measurement. For example, does a person taking several different math achievement tests score equivalently on each? If not, one or more of the tests are not reliable. The second issue is that of *validity*, or the quality of measuring precisely what one intends to measure. The question here is, is the measurement device really measuring what it purports to measure? For example, are math tests truly measuring math skills and knowledge, or are they possibly measuring some other quality in a person like obedience to rules?

Relationships Among Variables

Sociological investigation enables researchers to identify *cause and effect* relationships among variables. In cause and effect relationships we are saying one variable *(independent)* causes a change or effect in another variable *(dependent)*. Determining real cause and effect is a difficult and complex process. While variables may be *correlated*, meaning that two or more variables are related or change together in some way, it does not necessarily mean that one causes the change in the other(s). The concept *spurious correlation* refers to an apparent, although false, association between two (or more) variables caused by some other variable. Figure 2-1 (p. 37) outlines an example using the variables population density, income level, and juvenile delinquency.

Using scientific *control*, meaning the ability to neutralize the effect of one variable in order to assess the relationships among other variables, researchers can check for spuriousness.

In summary, to conclude that a cause and effect relationship exists, at least three conditions must be established:

(1)   a correlation exists between the variables
(2)   the independent variable precedes the dependent variable in time
(3)   no evidence exists that a third variable is responsible for a spurious correlation between the two variables.

The Ideal of Objectivity

Researchers must make every effort to neutralize their personal biases and values. Complete neutrality *(objectivity)* is seen as an ideal rather than as a reality in science, and is defined as a state of personal neutrality in conducting research.

Max Weber argued that research may be *value-relevant*, or of personal interest to the researcher, but the actual process of doing the research must be *value-free*. One way biases are controlled is through *replication*, or repetition of research by others in order to assess its accuracy. The **Critical Thinking** box entitled "The Samoa Controversy" (pp. 38-39) highlights an example of research being replicated, producing inconsistent results

18

and interpretations. The work of Margaret Mead, whose research in Samoa during the 1920s revealed social environmental factors critical in determining the experience of adolescence, is here being criticized by Derek Freeman as being biased and inaccurate.

Some Limitations of Science

To apply the logic of science to our social world several important limitations must be recognized:

(1) Sociologists can rarely make precise determinations of cause and effect. Thus human behavior cannot be predicted with the precision of the natural sciences.

(2) The presence of the researcher can affect the behavior of the people being studied.

(3) Social patterns are constantly changing over place and time.

(4) Objectivity is very difficult because sociologists are themselves part of the social world they are studying.

The Importance of Subjective Interpretation

Some sociologists argue removing all subjectivity from research is undesirable. First, they say, science is more than mere procedures. The elements of imagination and curiosity are critical. Second, science alone cannot grasp the complexity of human motivation and feelings. Third, data gathered through scientific research doesn't speak for itself. *Interpretation* of findings is a quality hard to quantify. Sociology is an art as well as a science.

Politics and Research

Researchers like Alvin Gouldner argue that politics is part of every aspect of our lives. Political neutrality is a myth. Everything social involves power relationships, and science is no exception. He suggests sociologists support certain values.

Gender and Research

Values influence research in terms of gender. Dangers to sound research that involve gender include: androcentricity, overgeneralizing, gender sensitivity, double-standard, and interference. Each of these is briefly discussed.

Research Ethics

Yet another issue concerns how research affects the people being studied. The American Sociological Association has a set of formal guidelines for the conduct of social research, including technical competence, awareness of bias, safety and privacy, discussion with subjects concerning risks involved, accurate presentation of purpose of research, full reporting of findings and identification of any organizational affiliations of the research effort.

THE METHODS OF SOCIOLOGICAL RESEARCH

A *research method* is defined as a strategy for systematically conducting research. Four of the most commonly used methods are presently introduced, each with particular strengths and weaknesses for the study of social life.

Experiments

Experiments study cause and effect relationships under highly controlled conditions. This type of research tends to be explanatory. Experiments are typically designed to test a specific *hypothesis*, or an unverified statement of a relationship between variables. The ideal experiment involves three steps leading to the acceptance or rejection of the hypothesis. The three steps are: measurement of the dependent variable, exposure of the dependent variable to the independent variable, remeasurement of the dependent variable. *Field* and *laboratory* type experimental designs are discussed. The separation of subjects into *control* and *experimental* groups is also discussed.

The issue of the awareness of subjects being studied and how this affects their behavior is reviewed. Distortion in research caused by such awareness is called the *Hawthorne effect*, so labeled after a company in which an experiment was done on work productivity and this effect was first identified.

A Laboratory Experiment: The Stanford County Prison

Philip Zimbardo's classic study focuses on the structural conditions in prisons. The hypothesis being tested was that the character of prison itself, and not the personalities of the prisoners or guards, is the cause of prison violence. Twenty-four volunteers, deemed to be physically and emotionally healthy, participated in this mock prison experiment which was scheduled to run for two weeks. Because of the stress created, the experiment had to be canceled within a week.

Survey Research

A *survey* is a research method in which subjects respond to a series of items in a questionnaire or interview. It is the most widely used of the research methods. Surveys can be used to do explanatory research, but are also useful for descriptive research, or research focusing on having subjects describe themselves or some social setting.

20

Population and Sample

A *population* is defined as the people who are the focus of research. Generally, contacting all members of a population is impossible, so samples are taken from the population to be studied. *Samples* are a part of a population selected to represent the whole. The **Sociology of Everyday Life** box entitled "National Political Surveys" provides an illustration of a particular type of survey, called a poll (p. 46).

The most critical issue concerns how a researcher knows the sample truly is representative of the population, meaning, Does the sample reflect the sample qualities present in the population? *Random selection* techniques are used to help ensure the probability that inferences made from the results of the sample actually do reflect the nature of the population as a whole.

Questionnaires and Interviews

Selection of the subjects is only one step in a survey. Another step requires the researcher to develop a specific plan for asking and recording questions. Two general techniques are used: questionnaires and interviews.

A *questionnaire* is a series of questions presented to subjects. Two basic types of questions asked have *open-ended* and *closed-ended* formats. Generally, surveys are mailed to subjects who are asked to complete a form and return it. This technique is called a self-administered survey. A problem exists however in that many forms do not get returned.

An *interview* is a series of questions administered personally by a researcher to respondents. This strategy has advantages, including more depth, but also involves the disadvantages of extra time and money, and the influence of the researcher's presence on the subjects' responses.

For both questionnaires and interviews, how the questions are asked is extremely important. Poor questions will lead to poor research results and conclusions.

Surveys at Work: A Study of American Couples

Philip Blumstein and Pepper Schwartz completed a large and complex study using both questionnaires and interviews as part of their research. This study is used to illustrate many of the concepts and processes involved in research discussed so far and includes operationalizing variables, sampling strategies (i.e., snowball sampling). Some of the findings of this research are presented in tabular form and focused on in the **Critical Thinking** (p. 50) which also focuses on how to properly read a table.

Participant Observation

Participant observation is a method in which researchers systematically observe people while joining in their routine activities. The approach is very common among cultural anthropologists who use *fieldwork* as the principal method to gather data in the form of *ethnographies*. Sociologists typically use the *case study* approach, a type of participant observation, when doing exploratory research. This is very valuable when there is not a well defined understanding of the social patterns being investigated.

Participant observation has two sides, the participant and observer, sometimes referred to as the insider-outsider roles. These can come into conflict with one another. Field notes, or the daily record kept by researchers, will reveal not only the conclusions of the research, but also the experience of the research itself. Such participant observation is classified as a form of **qualitative research**, or research based heavily on subjective interpretation. Surveys, on the other hand, are examples of **quantitative**, emphasizing the analysis of numerical data.

A Case Study: Street Corner Society

In the 1930s, William F. Whyte conducted what was to become one of the classic participant observation studies. He sought to study a poor, Italian, urban neighborhood of Boston (which he called Cornerville) to determine the true social fabric of the community. His work reveals the conflict between the roles of participant and observer, involvement and detachment. The role of a *key informant* is highlighted as part of this research process.

Secondary Analysis

Secondary analysis is a research method in which researchers utilize data collected by others. Advantages of this approach are the considerable saving of time and money, and the typically high quality of Census Bureau research often used for such purposes. However, problems are also involved, including the possibility that data was not systematically gathered, or not directly focused on the interests of the researcher. Durkheim's research on suicide is an example of using secondary analysis.

Historical Research: A Tale of Two Cities

A study by E. Digby Baltzell using secondary research focuses on the question of the apparent influence of religious doctrine in two different parts of colonial America on achievement orientation. Issues of the application of the sociological imagination, operationalization of variables, and theory building are addressed in this presentation of his research.

We are reminded that sociological investigation is a complex process, involving scientific skills, personal values, and a lively imagination. Table 2-2 (p. 54) reviews the applications, advantages and disadvantages of the four major research methods discussed.

The Interplay of Theory and Method

The obtaining of facts is not the final goal of science. Beyond facts is the issue of the development of theory, or combining facts into meaning. Two processes of logical thought are used by scientists. *Deductive logical thought* is reasoning that transforms general ideas into specific hypotheses suitable for scientific testing. Zimbardo's prison research is a good example of this type of thinking. *Inductive logical thought* involves reasoning that builds specific observations onto general theory. Baltzell's research illustrates this type of thinking. Figure 2-2 (p. 54) diagrams this interplay of theory and method.

PUTTING IT ALL TOGETHER: TEN STEPS IN SOCIOLOGICAL INVESTIGATION

The general guidelines for conducting sociological research follow these steps:

(1) Define the topic you wish to investigate.
(2) Find out what has already been written about the topic.
(3) Assess the requirements for carrying out research on the topic.
(4) Specify the questions you are going to ask.
(5) Consider the ethical issues involved in the research.
(6) Decide what research method you will use.
(7) Put the method to work to gather data.
(8) Interpret the findings.
(9) State your conclusions based on your findings.
(10) Publish your results.

PART IV: KEY CONCEPTS

Define each of the following concepts in the space provided or on separate paper. Check the accuracy of your answers by referring to the key concepts section at the end of the chapter in the text as well as referring to italicized definitions located throughout the chapter.

cause and effect
concept
control
correlation
deductive logical thought
dependent variable
empirical evidence
experiment
Hawthorne effect
hypothesis
independent variable
interview
mean
measurement
median

mode
objectivity
operationalizing a variable
participant observation
population
qualitative research
quantitative research
questionnaire
reliability
replication
research method
sample
science
secondary analysis
spurious correlation
survey
validity
variable

PART V: STUDY QUESTIONS

True-False

1. T F   Research suggests that as we grow older, our personalities change significantly.
2. T F   The mode is the statistical term referring to the value which occurs most often in a series of numbers.
3. T F   When two variables are related in some way, they are said to demonstrate correlation.
4. T F   If two variables are correlated, by definition one is an independent variable and one is a dependent variable.
5. T F   Max Weber argued that people involved in scientific research must strive to be value-free.
6. T F   Margaret Mead's book, *Coming of Age in Samoa*, provides evidence suggesting that the existence of biological forces significantly influences patterns of human behavior.
7. T F   The interview is the most common form of data gathering for researchers using the participant-observation method.
8. T F   Among the findings of the Blumstein and Schwartz study on American couples was that even in loving married relationships "money means power."
9. T F   E. Digby Baltzell's historical study on Boston and Philadelphia supports research linking attitudes toward achievement with religious doctrine.
10. T F   The first step in the scientific research process should be to determine what research design will be used to obtain the data.

Multiple-Choice

1. Specifying exactly what is to be measured in assigning a value to a variable is called:

   (a) validity
   (b) objectivity
   (c) operationalizing a variable
   (d) reliability
   (e) empirical evidence

2. The descriptive statistic which represents the value that occurs midway in a series of numbers is called the:

   (a) mode
   (b) correlation
   (c) mean
   (d) median
   (e) average

3. The quality of consistency in measurement is known as:

   (a) spuriousness
   (b) reliability
   (c) empirical evidence
   (d) objectivity
   (e) validity

4. Measuring what one intends to measure is the quality of measurement known as:

   (a) reliability
   (b) operationalization
   (c) validity
   (d) control
   (e) objectivity

5. Several limitations of scientific sociology are reviewed in chapter 2. Which of the following is **not** identified as a limitation involved in sociological research?

   (a) Sociologists can only rarely make precise determinations of cause and effect.
   (b) We all react to the world around us, so the mere presence of researchers may affect the behavior that is being studied.
   (c) Social patterns are constantly changing.
   (d) Because sociologists are part of the social world they study, objectivity in social research is especially difficult.
   (e) Few quantitative techniques are appropriate for sociologists to utilize in their analysis of data.

6. What is Alvin Gouldner's argument about sociological research?

(a) Sociologists have a choice about which values are worth supporting.
(b) Sociologists must remain completely objective, supporting no particular values.
(c) Values actually play an insignificant role in scientific research.
(d) The only values appropriate within the context of the sociological research process are those which represent the scientific method.
(e) Scientific research has the capacity to test absolute truths about social reality.

7. An unverified statement of a relationship between variables is a(n):

(a) correlation
(b) logical deduction
(c) hypothesis
(d) logical induction
(e) theory

8. The prison research conducted by Philip Zimbardo is an example of the use of which research method?

(a) survey
(b) case study
(c) participant-observation
(d) experiment
(e) secondary analysis

9. Which of the following was not a category used in the research conducted by Blumstein and Schwartz in their study of American couples?

(a) married couples
(b) homosexual couples
(c) cohabitating couples
(d) dual-earner couples

10. E. Digby Baltzell's study of important and successful Americans is an example of which research method?

(a) experiment
(b) participant observation
(c) secondary analysis
(d) survey
(e) case study

11. If a researcher begins a sociological investigation with general ideas about the world which then are used to produce specific hypotheses suited for scientific testing, the process is known as:

(a) inductive logical thought
(b) a qualitative methodology
(c) empirical analysis
(d) deductive logical thought
(e) speculative reasoning

Fill-In

1. _____ evidence we are able to verify with our senses.
2. A(n) _____ is an abstract idea that represents an aspect of the world, inevitably in a somewhat ideal and simplified way.
3. _____ refers to two variables that vary together, such as the extent of crowding and juvenile delinquency.
4. In a cause and effect relationship, the variable which causes the change in the _____ variable is called the _____ variable.
5. The ability to neutralize the effect of one variable so that the relationship among other variables can be more precisely measured is called _____ .
6. The state of complete personal neutrality in conducting research is referred to as _____ .
7. _____ distinguished between value-relevant choice of research topics and value-free conduct of sociological investigation.
8. In survey research, a _____ is defined as the people who are the focus of research.
9. _____ is a method in which researchers systematically observe people while joining in their routine activities.
10. The Zimbardo prison research is an illustration of _____ logical thought.

Definition and Short-Answer

1. What are the two requirements which underlie the process of sociological investigation?
2. What are the four "ways of knowing" discussed in the text? Please describe and provide an illustration for each.
3. What are the three factors which must be determined to conclude that a cause and effect relationship between two variables may exist?
4. Margaret Eichler points out five dangers to sound research that involves gender. Please identify and define each.
5. Define the concept "hypothesis." Further, write your own hypothesis and operationalize the variables which you identify.
6. What are the twin roles of the research involved in participant observation?
7. What are the basic steps of the sociological research process? Please briefly describe each step in the process.
8. What are Alvin Gouldner's points concerning politics and research?
9. Review Max Weber's points concerning objectivity in science.

PART VI: ANSWERS TO STUDY QUESTIONS

True-False

1.	F (p. 34)	6.	F (pp. 38-39)
2.	T (p. 35)	7.	F (p. 49)
3.	T (p. 36)	8.	T (p. 49)
4.	F (pp. 36-37)	9.	T (p. 54)
5.	T (pp. 38-39)	10.	F (p. 56)

Multiple Choice

1.	c (p. 35)	7.	c (p. 43)
2.	d (p. 35)	8.	d (p. 44)
3.	b (p. 35)	9.	d (p. 50)
4.	c (p. 36)	10	c (p. 53)
5.	e (p. 40)	11.	d (p. 55)
6.	a (p. 41)		

Fill-In

1. empirical (p. 33)
2. concept (p. 34)
3. correlation (p. 36)
4. dependent/independent (p. 36)
5. scientific control (p. 37)
6. objectivity (p. 38)
7. Max Weber (p. 39)
8. population (p. 46)
9. participant observation (p. 49)
10. deductive (p. 55)

PART VII: ANALYSIS AND COMMENT

Sociology of Everyday Life

"Three Useful (and Simple) Statistical Measures"

Key Points:

Questions:

"National Political Surveys"

    Key Points:

    Questions:

Critical Thinking

"The Samoa Controversy: The Interplay of Science and Politics"

    Key Points:

    Questions:

"Table Reading: An Important Skill"

    Key Points:

    Questions:

Culture

3

PART I: CHAPTER OUTLINE

I. What is Culture?
    A. Culture and Human Intelligence
II. The Components of Culture
    A. Symbols
    B. Language
        1. Is language uniquely human?
        2. Does language shape reality?
    C. Values
        1. American values
        2. Values: Inconsistency and Conflict
        3. Values in Action: The Games People Play
    D. Norms
        1. Mores and Folkways
        2. Social Control
    E. "Ideal" and "Real" Culture
    F. Material Culture and Technology
III. Cultural Diversity: Many Ways of Life in One World
    A. Subcultures
    B. Multiculturalism
    C. Countercultures
    D. Cultural Change
    E. Ethnocentrism and Cultural Relativity
IV. Theoretical Analysis of Culture
    A. Structural-Functional Analysis
    B. Social-Conflict Analysis
    C. Cultural Ecology
    D. Sociobiology
        1. Sociobiology and Human Evolution
        2. Sociobiology and Human Culture
V. Culture and Human Freedom
    A. Culture as Constraint
    B. Culture as Freedom
VI. Summary
VII. Key Concepts
VIII. Suggested Readings

PART II: LEARNING OBJECTIVES

1. To understand the sociological meaning of the concept culture.
2. To understand the relationship between human intelligence and culture.
3. To know the components of culture and to be able to provide examples of each.
4. To understand the debate concerning multiculturalism in American culture.
5. To explain the current state of knowledge about whether language is uniquely human.
6. To understand the Sapir-Whorf hypothesis.
7. To be able to identify the major American values and to recognize their interrelationships with one another and with other aspects of our culture.
8. To be able to provide examples of the different types of norms operative in a culture.
9. To explain how subcultures and countercultures contribute to cultural diversity.
10. To be able to differentiate between ethnocentrism and cultural relativism.
11. To be able to compare and contrast analyses of culture using structural-functional, social-conflict, ecological, and sociobiological paradigms.
12. To be able to identify the consequences of culture for human freedom and constraint.

PART III: CHAPTER REVIEW

WHAT IS CULTURE?

Culture is defined as the beliefs, values, behavior, and material objects shared by a particular people. The story told at the beginning of the chapter in the text concerning anthropologist Napoleon Chagnon's first visit to the territory of the Yanomamo culture in the tropical rain forest of southern Venezuela illustrates the vast cultural differences which exist around the world. In this instance, the degree of difference was great enough for the researcher that he experienced *culture shock*, or the personal disorientation that may accompany exposure to an unfamiliar way of life.

Sociologists differentiate between *non-material culture*, the intangible creations of human society, and *material culture*, the tangible products of human society. Also, the concepts of *culture* and *society* are understood differently, the latter referring to the interaction among people within geographical boundaries which is guided by culture.

Sociologically, culture is viewed in the broadest possible sense, referring to everything that is part of a people's way of life. Our lives become meaningful to us through culture. Our life-styles are not determined by *instincts*, or biological forces, as is true in large degree for other species. We are the only species whose survival depends on what we learn through culture, rather than by what we are naturally given through biology.

31

Culture and Human Intelligence

The primate order among mammals, of which our species is a part, emerged some 65 million years ago. Humans diverged from our closest primate relatives some 12 million years ago. However, our common lineage remains apparent. This includes, grasping hands, ability to walk upright, great sociability, affective and long-lasting bonds for childrearing and protection.

Fossil records indicate the first creatures with clearly human characteristics lived about 2 million years ago, which is relatively recent in terms of evolutionary time. Our species, *homo sapiens* (meaning thinking person) evolved a mere 40,000 years ago. Civilization based on permanent settlements has existed only for the last 12,000 years.

A major point being made is that human culture and biological evolution are linked. Over evolutionary time, instincts have gradually been replaced by "mental power," enabling us to actively fashion the natural environment. This process of having human nature changed from instinct to culture has allowed great human diversity to be created.

THE COMPONENTS OF CULTURE

Even though considerable cultural variation exists, all cultures share five components: symbols, language, values, norms, and material culture.

Symbols

This component underlies the other four. A *symbol* is anything that carries a particular meaning recognized by members of a culture. Symbols serve as the basis for everyday reality. Often taken for granted, they are the means through which we make sense of our lives. Symbols vary cross-culturally and change over time. To some degree symbols even vary within a single culture. Examples for each type of variation are presented.

Language

The significance of language for human communication is vividly illustrated by the story of Helen Keller recounting the moment she acquired language and a symbolic understanding of the world, through the help of her teacher Ann Sullivan. *Language* is a system of symbols that allows member of a society to communicate with one another. All cultures have a spoken language, though not all have a written language. The Yanomamo, for example, have no written language. The process by which culture is passed, through language, from one generation to the next is our most important form of *cultural transmission*. Like our genes, our language is rooted in our ancestry. It is the key to human imagination. Given the infinite combinations of symbols possible, and hence ideas, human creativity appears to be boundless.

Is language uniquely human?

While virtually all nonhuman animal communication seems largely rooted in instinct, there is some scientific evidence to suggest certain other animals have at least rudimentary ability to use symbols. Research with chimps has found them capable of attaching words to objects and create simple sentences using American Sign Language. While not having the physical ability to form sounds of human speech, nor, at least as yet, being able to demonstrate the capability of transmitting what they learn to other members of their species, it appears they do "experience" culture to some degree.

Does language shape reality?

Two anthropologists specializing in linguistic studies during the first half of this century, Edward Sapir and Benjamin Whorf, have argued that language is more than simply attaching labels to the "real world." They reject the view that language merely describes a single reality. The *Sapir-Whorf hypothesis* holds that we know the world only in terms of our language. Language then determines, to a large degree, our reality. Culture is thereby shaped by language.

Values

Values are defined as the standards by which members of a culture distinguish the desirable from the undesirable, what is good from what is bad, the beautiful from what is ugly. They are broad principles, evaluations, and judgments from the standpoint of a given culture. They are learned through socialization and help shape the development of our personality. Although in our diverse society few cultural values are shared by everyone, there are several central values which are widely accepted in American society.

American Values

Sociologist Robin Williams has identified ten such values, including equal opportunity, achievement, activity and work, material comfort, practicality and efficiency, progress, science, democracy, freedom, and racism and group superiority.

Values: Inconsistency and Conflict

The values people hold vary to some degree by age, sex, race, ethnicity, religion, and social class. Individuals are likely to experience some inconsistency and conflict with their personal values. Further, the dominant values identified above contain certain basic contradictions. Examples of such situations are discussed in the text. Further, values change over time. The traditional value of individual responsibility is apparently in the process of eroding in our society. The **Sociology of Everyday Life** box entitled "A New Culture of Victimization" discusses this trend.

33

Values in Action: The Games People Play

Sociologist James Spates has studied how children's games, like king of the mountain and tag, provide experiences for children which stress basic American values. Lessons are learned about what our culture defines as important, like competition.

Norms

Norms are defined as rules that guide behavior. They can be *proscriptive*, mandating what we must not do, or *prescriptive*, stating what we must do. They can change over time, as illustrated by norms regarding sexual behavior. Some are meant to apply to all situations and all people, while others apply to only certain people and vary situation to situation.

Mores and Folkways

Norms vary in terms of their degree of importance. *Mores* refer to norms that have great moral significance. *Folkways* are norms that have little moral significance.

Social Control

Norms provide for conformity. *Sanctions* are positive and negative responses to the behavior of people that reward conformity and punish deviance. They are an important part of our cultural system of *social control*, or the various means by which members of society encourage conformity to cultural norms. Through socialization we internalize cultural norms and impose constraints on our own behavior, hopefully avoiding *guilt* and *shame*.

"Ideal" and "Real" Culture

Values and norms are not descriptions of actual behavior, but rather reflect how we believe members of a culture should behave. Therefore, it becomes necessary to distinguish between *ideal culture* or social patterns mandated by cultural values and norms, and *real culture* or social patterns that actually occur.

Material Culture and Technology

Material and nonmaterial culture are very closely related. *Artifacts*, or tangible human creations, express the values of a culture. For instance, the Yanomamo value militaristic skill, and devote great care to making weapons. In the U.S. we value independence and individuality, and we have 140 million privately owned automobiles to express these qualities.

Material culture also reflects a culture's *technology*, which is the application of cultural knowledge to the task of living in a physical environment. Technology is the link between culture and nature. The point is made that while we attempt to manipulate our natural environment, most technologically "simple" cultures attempt to adapt to their natural worlds. Also, advances in technology act as double-edged swords, creating both positive and negative effects for the quality of life. Technology also varies within a culture. The Amish in our in the United States illustrate this latter point.

CULTURAL DIVERSITY: MANY MAYS OF LIFE IN ONE WORLD

Cultural variety in the U.S. is described as a "patchwork quilt." We are a land of many peoples.

Subcultures

Sociologists define *subculture* as cultural patterns that distinguish some segment of a society's population. Subcultures can be based on age, ethnicity, residence, sexual preference, occupation, and many other factors.

Ethnicity is perhaps the most recognized dimension with which to identify cultural diversity. While America is considered by many to be a "melting pot" where people from many different racial and ethnic backgrounds blend together, but great diversity still exists, and is perhaps increasing. A problem exists however in that cultural differences involve not only *variety*, but *hierarchy*.

Multiculturalism

This discussion focuses on the debate in our society over whether we as a nation should stress cultural diversity or the common elements of our people. How do we strike a balance within the Latin phrase *E Pluribus Unum* (out of many, one)? For example, an important proposal being addressed in Congress and in state legislatures is whether English should be designated as the official language of the United States.

Multiculturalism is the recognition of past and present cultural diversity in American society coupled to efforts to promote the equality of all cultural traditions. The "singular pattern" focus in our culture is called *Eurocentrism*, the dominance of European (particularly English) cultural patterns. An alternative pattern currently being developed by some multi-culturalists to counter these biases is called *Afrocentrism*, or a view that focuses on the dominance of African cultural patterns.

Multiculturalists are suggesting that their perspective will help us develop a more meaningful understanding of our own *past*, *present*, *ethnic diversity*, and *world interdependence*.

Countercultures

A *counterculture* is defined as cultural patterns that strongly oppose popular culture. Members of countercultures are likely to question the morality of the majority group and engage in some form of protest activities. Typically the majority group will respond with the imposition of varying degrees of social control. The Klu Klux Klan, Black Panthers, and Hippies are examples of counter-cultures in our society.

Cultural Change

Cultural change is continuous, though its rate may vary greatly. Table 3-1 (p. 79) presents data on the changing attitudes of college students, comparing cohorts from 1968 and 1990. Patterns of both change and consistency are found.

The interconnections between elements of culture must be kept in mind. *Cultural integration* is the assertion that various parts of a cultural system are linked together. On the other hand, *cultural lag* refers to disruption in a cultural system resulting from the unequal rates at which different cultural elements change.

Cultural change is set into motion by three different causes invention, discovery, and diffusion. Illustrations for each are presented in the text.

Ethnocentrism and Cultural Relativity

Ethnocentrism is the practice of judging another culture by the standards of our own culture. It creates a biased evaluation of unfamiliar practices. A comparison between the U.S. and the Yanomamo illustrates this concept. Further, Global Map 3-2 entitled "Ethnocentric Images of the World," suggests that people everywhere place their society in the center of the world.

Cultural relativism refers to the practice of judging any culture by its own standards. The issue of cultural sensitivity related to U.S. business ventures overseas is discussed. Tension between these two views of cultural diversity continues to pose difficult problems for Americans abroad, as the **Critical Thinking** box (p. 82) entitled "The Traveler's Dilemma" illustrates.

THEORETICAL ANALYSIS OF CULTURE

Culture is an extremely complex phenomenon. To understand culture and its components requires a macro-level analysis.

Structural-Functional Analysis

Research using this approach draws on the philosophical doctrine of *idealism*, which holds that ideas are the basis of human reality. Stability of a culture, a positive quality, is based on its core values. Cultures are understood as organized systems devised to meet human needs. Therefore, *cultural universals*, or traits found in every culture of the world, are sought and studied. Limitations of this perspective include an underestimation of culture conflict, and downplaying the extent of change in society.

Social-Conflict Analysis

The focus among researchers using this paradigm is the social conflict generated by inequality among different categories of people in a culture. The question of why certain values are dominant in a culture rather than some others is central to this view. Karl

values are dominant in a culture rather than some others is central to this view. Karl Marx, using the philosophical doctrine of *materialism*, argued that the way we deal with the material world (i.e., through capitalism) powerfully affects all other dimensions of our culture. A limitation of this perspective is an underestimation of the extent of integration in society.

Cultural Ecology

Rooted in the natural sciences, this paradigm emphasizes that human culture is significantly shaped by the natural environment. *Cultural ecology* is defined as a theoretical paradigm that explores the relationship of human culture to the physical environment. Marvin Harris' analysis of India's sacred cow provides an informative illustration of the application of this approach. Limitations of this perspective involve oversimplifying the connections between cultural and physical forces.

Sociobiology

Sociobiology is a theoretical paradigm that seeks to explain cultural patterns as a product, at least in part, of biological causes. This view poses an interesting challenge to the sociologist's focus on culture as the dominant force in human life.

Sociobiology and Human Evolution

Sociobiologists argue that Charles Darwin's theory of natural selection, which is based on four basic principles, applies to human evolution as it does to all other species.

Sociobiology and Human Culture

Controversy exists concerning the application of Darwin's insights to humans. Sociobiologists focus on the existence of certain cultural universals as evidence that culture is determined to a significant degree by biology. For example, they point out, our fondness for sweet things is no accident, but is rooted in our primate ancestry. Our distant ancestors who lived in trees primarily ate ripe fruit. This strategy for survival, based on genetic coding, has been passed through the generations to us humans living today. Also discussed is the "double-standard" which exists regarding the sexual activity of males and females. Sociobiologists say that males and females are genetically driven toward different reproductive strategies, "quantity" and "promiscuity" for males, "quality" and "selectivity" for females.

This approach has been criticized, based on historical patterns, of supporting racism and sexism. Also, to date, there is lack of scientific proof of their assertions.

Our author agrees with the suggestion made by one sociobiologist, that the value of this approach will be in illustrating how biological forces make some cultural patterns more common than others. It is doubtful, says our author, that "biological forces will ever be shown to determine human behavior," which he feels is "learned within a system of culture."

37

CULTURE AND HUMAN FREEDOM

Culture as Constraint

Through evolution, culture has become our means of survival. However, it can have negative consequences. For example, by having the ability to symbolically experience the world by attaching meanings to it we are susceptible to alienation and the stress created by inconsistent or conflicting values.

Culture as Freedom

While being dependent on culture and constrained by our particular way of life, the capacity for creating change, or shaping and reshaping our existence, appears limitless. Culture is a liberating force to the extent we develop an understanding of its complexity and the opportunities available within it for change and autonomy.

PART IV: KEY CONCEPTS

Define each of the following concepts in the space provided or on separate paper. Check the accuracy of your answers by referring to the key concepts section at the end of the chapter in the text as well as referring to italicized definitions located throughout the chapter.

Afrocentrism
counter culture
cultural ecology
cultural integration
cultural lag
cultural relativity
cultural transmission
cultural universals
culture
culture shock
discovery
diffusion
ethnocentrism
Eurocentrism
folkways
ideal culture
invention
language
material culture
materialism

mores
multiculturalism
natural selection
nonmaterial culture
norms
prescriptive norms
proscriptive norms
real culture
sanctions
Sapir-Whorf hypothesis
social control
society
sociobiology
subculture
technology
values

PART V: STUDY QUESTIONS

True-False

1. T F According to the author of our text, only humans rely on culture rather than instinct to ensure the survival of their kind.
2. T F Cultural symbols often change over time.
3. T F Social sanctions can be both positive and negative.
4. T F The enforcement of norms always depends directly on the reactions of others.
5. T F The three major sources of cultural change are invention, discovery, and diffusion.
6. T F The practice of judging any culture by its own standards is referred to as ethnocentrism.
7. T F Structural-functionalists argue that there are no cultural universals.
8. T F Marvin Harris uses the cultural ecology perspective to help explain the existence of India's "sacred cow" belief.
9. T F Natural selection refers to the fact that as cultural traits are diffused throughout the world, individual cultures will absorb only those traits which are functional for their particular society.
10. T F According to the author of our text, culture has diminished human autonomy to the point where we are "culturally programmed" much like other animals are "genetically programmed."

Multiple-Choice

1. The Yanomamo are:

    (a) a small tribal group of herders living in Eastern Africa
    (b) a male-dominated horticultural society living in South America
    (c) a seminomadic culture living above the Arctic circle and characterized by warm family relationships
    (d) a small, dying society living as farmers in a mountainous region of western Africa
    (e) a people who until very recently were living in complete isolation from the rest of the world in a tropical rain forest in Malaysia

2. Culture is:

    (a) the process by which members of a culture encourage conformity to social norms
    (b) the beliefs, values, behavior, and material objects shared by a particular people
    (c) the practice of judging another society's norms
    (d) a group of people who engage in interaction with one another on a continuous basis
    (e) the aspects of social life people admire most

3. Studying fossil records, scientists have concluded that the first creatures with clearly human characteristics existed about _____ years ago.

    (a) 2 million   (d) 40 million
    (b) 12,000   (e) 60,000
    (c) 10 million

4. Symbols, a component of culture, can:

    (a) vary from culture to culture
    (b) provide a foundation for the reality we experience
    (c) change over time
    (d) all of the above

5. Which of the following components of culture provides the basis or foundation for the others?

    (a) norms   (d) symbols
    (b) values   (e) material artifacts
    (c) beliefs

6. A system of symbols that allows members of a society to communicate with one another is the definition of:

   (a) values   (d) cultural relativity
   (b) language   (e) cultural transmission
   (c) norms

7. Standards by which members of a culture distinguish the desirable from the undesirable, what is good from what is bad, the beautiful from the ugly, is the definition for:

   (a) norms   (d) mores
   (b) beliefs   (e) sanctions
   (c) values

8. According to the research cited in the text, which of the following is not a central cultural value in American society?

   (a) equal opportunity   (c) science
   (b) racism and superiority   (d) friendship

9. The old adage "Do as I say, not as I do" illustrates the distinction between:

   (a) "ideal" and "real" culture
   (b) subcultures and countercultures
   (c) symbols and language
   (d) folkways and mores
   (e) cultural integration and cultural lag

10. Inconsistencies within a cultural system resulting from the unequal rates at which different cultural elements change are termed:

   (a) cultural lag   (c) counterculture
   (b) culture shock   (d) cultural relativity

11. The theoretical paradigm that focuses upon universal cultural traits is:

   (a) cultural ecology   (c) structural functionalism
   (b) cultural materialism   (d) social-conflict

12. The philosophical doctrine of materialism is utilized in the analysis of culture by proponents of which theoretical paradigm?

   (a) sociobiologists   (d) cultural ecologists
   (b) structural-functionalists   (e) social-conflict
   (c) symbolic-interaction

Fill-In

1. The tangible products of human society are referred to as _____.

2. The history of human life reveals that culture became possible only after _____ diminished and creative mental capacity predominated.

3. The concept _____ is derived from the Latin meaning "thinking person."

4. A _____ is anything that carries a particular meaning recognized by members of a culture.

5. _____ norms tell us what we must do, while _____ norms mandate what we must not do.

6. _____ are rules that guide behavior.

7. _____ _____ is defined as the various means by which members of society encourage conformity to cultural norms.

8. _____ is the recognition of past and present cultural diversity in American society coupled to efforts to promote the equality of all cultural traditions.

9. The practice of judging any culture by its own standards is termed _____.

10. A theoretical paradigm that focuses upon the interrelationship of human culture and the physical environment is _____.

Definition and Short-Answer

1. Three causes of cultural change are identified in the text. Identify these and provide an illustration for each.

2. Discuss the research presented in the text concerning the uniqueness of language to humans. Make specific reference to the research involving the chimps Kanzi and Washoe in your discussion.

3. What are the four basic principles of natural selection?

4. Review the statistics presented in Table 3-1 concerning changing values among college students. What have been the most significant changes? In which areas have values remained consistent? To what extent do your values fit the picture of contemporary college students?

5. What are the basic qualities of the Yanomamo culture? To what extent are you able to view these people from a cultural relativistic perspective? Explain.

6. What is the basic position being taken by sociobiologists concerning the nature of culture? What are three examples used by sociobiologists to argue human culture is determined by biology? To what extent do you agree or disagree with their position? Explain.

7. Define the philosophical doctrine of "idealism."

8. What is the Sapir-Whorf hypothesis? Provide an example.

9. Define the philosophical doctrine of "materialism." How does this doctrine fit into the conflict theory of society?

10. How do cultural ecologists explain the relationship between culture and the physical environment? Using Marvin Harris' analysis of the existence of the sacred cow in India describe this perspective.

11. Identify two limitations for each of the following theoretical perspectives: structural-functionalism, social-conflict, cultural ecology, sociobiology.

PART VI: ANSWERS TO STUDY QUESTIONS

True-False

1.	T (p. 62)	6.	F (p. 82)
2.	T (p. 65)	7.	F (p. 85)
3.	T (p. 73)	8.	T (p. 86)
4.	F (p. 73)	9.	F (p. 86)
5.	T (p. 80)	10.	F (p. 89)

Multiple Choice

1.	b (p. 61)	7.	c (p. 69)
2.	b (p. 62)	8.	d (pp. 69-70)
3.	a (p. 64)	9.	a (p. 74)
4.	d (p. 65)	10.	a (p. 80)
5.	d (p. 65)	11.	c (p. 85)
6.	b (p. 66)	12.	e (p. 85)

Fill-In

1. material culture (p. 62)
2. instincts (p. 62)
3. homo sapiens (p. 64)
4. symbol (p. 65)
5. prescriptive/proscriptive (p. 72)
6. norms (p. 72)
7. social control (p. 73)
8. multiculturalism (p. 76)
9. cultural relativism (p. 82)
10. cultural ecology (p. 86)

PART VII: ANALYSIS AND COMMENT

Critical Thinking

"The Traveler's Dilemma: In the Night Market of Taipei"

Key Points:

Questions:

Sociology of Everyday Life

"A New Culture of Victimization"

    Key Points:

    Questions:

Windows on the World

"Language in Global Perspective"

    Key Points:

    Questions:

"Ethnocentric Image of the World"

    Key Points:

    Questions:

Tables

Table 3-1
"Attitudes Among Students Entering College, 1968 and 1990"

    Key Points:

    Questions:

Society

4

PART I: CHAPTER OUTLINE

I. Gerhard and Jean Lenski: Society and Technology
    A. Hunting and Gathering Societies
    B. Horticultural and Pastoral Societies
    C. Agrarian Societies
    D. Industrial Societies
    E. The Limits of Technology

II. Karl Marx: Society and Conflict
    A. Society and Production
    B. Conflict in History
    C. Capitalism and Class Conflict
    D. Capitalism and Alienation
    E. Revolution

III. Max Weber: The Rationalization of Society
    A. Rationality and Industrial Capitalism
    B. The Roots of Rationality
    C. Rationality and Modern Society
        1. Rational Organization: Bureaucracy
        2. Rationality and Alienation

IV. Emile Durkheim: Society and Function
    A. Social Fact: Society Beyond Ourselves
    B. Function: Society in Action
    C. The Individual: Society in Ourselves
    D. Evolving Societies: The Division of Labor

V. Critical Evaluation: Four Visions of Society
        1. How do societies of the past and present differ?
        2. How and why do societies change?
        3. How are societies united and divided?
        4. Are human societies improving or not?

VI. Summary
VII. Key Concepts
VIII. Suggested Readings

PART II: LEARNING OBJECTIVES

1. To give answers to the questions "How do societies differ?", "What do societies have in common?" and "How and why do societies change?"
2. To be able to differentiate between the four "visions" of society discussed in this chapter.
3. To explain the sociocultural evolution from hunting and gathering societies to industrial societies as developed by Gerhard and Jean Lenski.
4. To contrast the different types of societies described by the Lenksis on the basis of their historical period, productive technology, population size, settlement pattern and social organization.
5. To explain the model of society based on conflict and change developed by Karl Marx.
6. To be able to discuss the perspective of Marx on the concepts of capitalism, communism, revolution, alienation, and materialism.
7. To explain the role of rationality in modern society developed by Max Weber.
8. To be able to identify Weber's qualities of rationality in modern society.
9. To describe Emile Durkheim's functional view of society, including his analyses of the influence of social facts and the role of the division of labor in society.

PART III: CHAPTER REVIEW

We are introduced in the preface of this chapter to the great accomplishments we have made in regard to our modes of travel. But, as technological power of humankind continues to increase, we simultaneously improve our lives and threaten our very existence.

The concept *society* refers to people who interact within a limited territory and who share a culture. In this chapter four separate visions of society are discussed; each addresses questions which concern forces that shape human life. The visions include: (1) Gerhard and Jean Lenskis' focus on the importance of technology, (2) Karl Marx's understanding of the key role social conflict plays in society, (3) Max Weber's illustration of the significance of human ideas, and (4) Emile Durkheim's analysis of the patterns of social solidarity.

GERHARD AND JEAN LENSKI: SOCIETY AND TECHNOLOGY

Until about 10,000 years ago the hunting and gathering type of society was the only one in existence. Comparing present day hunting and gathering type societies with modern technologically "advanced" societies raises many interesting questions. The Lenskis analyze human society using the *sociocultural evolution* approach which focuses on the process of social change that results from gaining new cultural information, particularly technology. The relationship of society to the physical environment is studied, with society being understood as being like a living organism. A key variable determining the rate of change in a society is the amount of technological information available. The

46

Lenskis and their approach are highlighted in the **Profile** box (p. 95). Their perspective is compared to the cultural ecological approach of Marvin Harris. Based on their view, four general types of societies are distinguished.

Hunting and Gathering Societies

Hunting and gathering societies are defined as those which use simple technology to hunt animals and gather vegetation. Only a very small number of such societies are still in existence today. Examples include the Tasaday of the Philippines and the Aborigines of Australia. Typical characteristics of people using this subsistence strategy include small bands of people, a nomadic lifestyle over large territories, stratification based only on age and sex, and characterized by few positions of leadership. Social organization tends to be simple and equal, being organized around the family. Life expectancy at birth is relatively low, however in environments with ample food supplies the quality of life is good, with much leisure time.

Horticultural and Pastoral Societies

Approximately 10-12,000 years ago plants began to be cultivated. *Horticultural* societies are those that use hand tools to cultivate crops. This strategy first appeared in the Middle East and Southeast Asia, and through diffusion spread through Europe and Asia. Some societies, like the Yanomamo, combine horticulture with hunting and gathering strategies.

In regions where horticulture was impractical societies based on *pastoralism* emerged. These societies livelihood were based on the domestication of animals. Settlements using horticultural subsistence become linked through trade roots, with many having populations in the thousands. Both horticultural and pastoral societies tend to have a more complex social organization and have increased specialization. *Material surpluses* become possible with these lifestyles, and this is often linked to greater social inequality. These societies given their increased technological development are more productive than hunting and gathering societies. However, the Lenksis suggest this was often accompanied by ethical regression.

Agrarian Societies

Agrarian societies emerged about 5,000 years ago and are based on *agriculture*, or the technology of large-scale farming using plows powered by animals or advanced energy. Technological change during this period was so dramatic that the Lenksis have argued it was the era of the "dawn of civilization." The use of the plow increased soil fertility as well as made agriculture more efficient. This also greatly increased the surplus of food available. Irrigation was developed at this time. The power of the elite greatly increased, supported by religious beliefs and the expanding political power structure. The **Social Diversity** box (p. 99) discusses factors in sociocultural evolution, such as the development of metal, which helped propel men into an even stronger position of social dominance.

47

Industrial Societies

Industrialism is the technology that powers sophisticated machinery powered by advanced fuels. The muscle power of humans and animals are no longer the basis of production and tools and machinery become more complex and efficient owing to the incorporation of metal alloys, such as steel. Figure 4-1 (p. 100) shows the increasing rate of technological innovation during the 19th century, bringing about vast social changes. A major shift occurring was from production within families to production within factories. Great population increases occurred as health conditions began to improve. Occupational specialization became even more pronounced and cultural values became more heterogeneous.

As sociocultural evolution continues economic, social, and political inequality is decreasing. Table 4-1 (pp. 102-103) summarizes basic points concerning the social stages in societal evolution, including the historical period for each, their productive technologies, population size, settlement patterns, and social organization.

The Limits of Technology

The point is made that while the technological abilities of industrial societies are unparalleled in history they offer no "quick fix" for social problems. Further, advances in our technological level cause some problems, for example, loss of personal freedom, loss of community, and pollution.

KARL MARX: SOCIETY AND CONFLICT

Marx's thinking focused on a fundamental contradiction of industrial society, How could vast social inequality exist given the new industrial technology with its phenomenal productive capability? The central focus of Marx's work was on the idea of *social conflict*, which means struggle between segments of society over valued resources. For Marx, the most significant type of social conflict results from the manner in which society produced material goods. The **Profile** box (p. 104) discusses some of the controversy surrounding Marx's research and theory.

Society and Production

Marx designated a very small part of the population as *capitalists*, or those who owned factories and other productive enterprises. Their goal was profit. The vast majority of people however were termed the *proletariat*, meaning those who provided the labor necessary for the operation of factories and other productive enterprises. Labor is exchanged by these people for wages. Fundamental conflict exists between the competing needs of these two groups.

Marx's analysis of society followed the philosophical doctrine of *materialism* in asserting that the system of producing material goods can shape all of society. He labeled the economic system the *infrastructure* and all other social institutions as the *super-structures*. Figure 4-2 (p. 106) illustrates this philosophical viewpoint.

Marx seriously questioned the supposed "truths" of capitalist society which he saw as being based on the operation of the marketplace. He believed capitalism promoted *false consciousness*, or the belief that the shortcomings of individuals, rather than society, are responsible for many of the personal problems people have.

Conflict in History

Marx understood historical change in society as operating in both gradual evolutionary and rapid revolutionary processes. He believed early hunting and gathering societies to be represented by communism, or the equal production of food and other material as a common effort shared more or less equally by everyone. He saw horticultural, pastoral, agrarian, and industrial societies as based on systems of inequality and exploitation. The concepts *bourgeoisie* (French, meaning "of the town") and proletariat are discussed further within the framework of social history during the period of industrialization.

Capitalism and Class conflict

Marx viewed all social history as one of *class conflict*, or the struggle between social classes over the distribution of wealth and power in society. Social change involved workers first becoming aware of their shared oppression and then organizing and acting to address their problems. The process involved replacing false consciousness with *class consciousness*, or the recognition by workers of their unity as a class in opposition to capitalists and, ultimately, to capitalism itself.

Capitalism and Alienation

For Marx, *alienation* meant the experience of separation resulting from powerlessness. Workers perceive themselves as a mere commodity. Four ways industrial capitalism alienates workers are identified: (1) alienation from the act of working, (2) alienation from the products of work, (3) alienation from other workers, and (4) alienation from humanity. The **Sociology of Everyday life** box (p. 108) entitled "Alienation and Industrial Capitalism" provides illustrations.

Revolution

Marx viewed revolution as the only way to change the nature of society. The type of system he saw as replacing industrial capitalism was socialism, which he believed was a more humane and egalitarian type of productive system.

MAX WEBER: THE RATIONALIZATION OF SOCIETY

Weber made many contributions to sociology, perhaps more than any other sociologist. One of the most significant was his understanding about how our social world differs from societies of early times. His work reflects the philosophical approach of *idealism* which emphasizes the importance of human ideas in shaping society. New ways of thinking, not merely technology and materialistic relationships was the major force in social change.

Weber's life and times are briefly reviewed in the **Profile** box (p. 111). A conceptual tool used by Weber in his research was the concept *ideal-type*, defined as an abstract statement of the essential characteristics of any social phenomenon.

Rationality and Industrial Capitalism

Weber differentiated between two types of societies in terms of how people thought. The first is characterized by *tradition*, or sentiments and beliefs about the world that are passed from generation to generation. The other is characterized by *rationality*, or deliberate, matter-of-fact calculation of the most efficient means to accomplish any particular goal. This process of change from tradition to rationality he termed the *rationalization of society*, denoting the change in the type of thinking characteristic of members of society. Industrialization was an expression of this process. The **Global Map** (p. 112) shows expenditures on the sciences for the world's nations. Great difference are revealed.

Roots of Rationality

Weber points out that industrial capitalism developed where Calvinism was widespread. This is discussed as an example of how the power of ideas shapes human social development. A central doctrine of this religion was *predestination*, creating visions of either damnation or salvation, but in the hands of God not the people. Anxious to know their fate people looked for signs of God's favor. Some reassurance was to be found in personal success and achievement.

Rationality and Modern Society

Weber believed rationality shaped modern society in various ways. This included: (1) creating distinctive *social institutions*, or major spheres of social life organized to meet basic human needs, (2) specialization, (3) personal discipline, (4) awareness of time, (5) technical competence, (6) impersonality, and (7) large-scale organizations. Each of the seven are described.

Rational Organization: Bureaucracy

While traditional societies had such systems, they were not based on rationality. Modern day society becomes characterized by a type of social organization called *bureaucracy*. Weber viewed this as the clearest expression of a rational world.

Rationality and Alienation

Weber, like Marx, was critical of modern society, but for different reasons. For Weber, economic inequality was not the major problem, rather dehumanization and alienation were what troubled society most. Weber saw individuality being constricted by modern rationality.

EMILE DURKHEIM: SOCIETY AND FUNCTION

Emile Durkheim's work is briefly introduced to us in the **Profile** box (p. 116).

Social Fact: Society Beyond Ourselves

Central to the work of Durkheim is the concept of *social fact*, or any part of society that is argued to have an objective existence apart from the individual and is therefore able to influence individual behavior. Examples are values and norms of a society. Further, Durkheim observed society as being characterized by three elements. The first is that society is structured. Second, these structural patterns shape our thoughts and actions. Third, these patterns can be viewed as "facts" because they have an objective existence apart from any individual's subjective experience of them. Society is something which is more than the sum of its parts. The power of society is experienced as morality for the individual.

Function: Society in Action

Function is another concept important in the understanding of Durkheim's view of society. The significance of social facts is to be discovered in the functional contribution to the general life of society, not in the experience of individuals. His perspective leads us to view the functional consequences of any social phenomenon, even crime for example.

The Individual: Society in Ourselves

According to Durkheim, society exists not only beyond us, having a life of its own, but also within us. Personalities are built through the internalization of social facts. Suicide, discussed in chapter 1, illustrates this point. The diminishing regulation of people by society creates individualism and creates *anomie*, a condition in which society provides individuals with little moral guidance.

Evolving Societies: The Division of Labor

Durkheim differentiated between two types of solidarity which gave characterized societies over history. For most of history human societies were dominated by a collective conscience, or moral consensus. Durkheim termed this *mechanical solidarity*, meaning

51

social bonds, common to preindustrial societies, based on shared moral sentiments. Likeness was the rule in society. As this type declined it was replaced by *organic solidarity*, or social bonds, common to industrialized societies, based on specialization. So Durkheim saw history in terms of a growing *division of labor*, or specialized economic activity.

Durkheim, like Weber and Marx had concern about modern society and its effect on the individual. The dilemma for Durkheim was the fact that the positive benefits of modern society, such as technical advances and personal freedoms, were accompanied by diminishing morality and the danger of anomie.

CRITICAL EVALUATION: FOUR VISIONS OF SOCIETY

The concluding section focuses on the four questions raised at the beginning of this chapter using each of the four visions provided by the Lenskis, Marx, Weber, and Durkheim. These questions include:

How have societies changed?

The sociocultural evolution model used by the Lenskis focuses on technology in answering this question. Marx's conflict approach focuses on historical differences in the productive system. And, while Weber focused on characteristics of human thought, Durkheim concentrated on how societies differ in terms of how they are bound together.

Why do societies change?

The Lenskis see change occurring through technological innovation. Marx saw class struggles as the "engine of history." Weber's idealist approach focused on how ideas contribute to social change. Finally, Durkheim believed the expanding division of labor was the main force behind the increasing complexity of society.

How are societies united and divided?

The Lenskis would answer by focusing on cultural patterns. Marx argued that only through cooperative enterprise could a united society develop. Weber saw unity created through a society's distinctive world view. Durkheim focused on the factor of social integration.

Are societies improving?

The views of the Lenskis and Marx are mixed on this point. Weber had a rather pessimistic view, while Durkheim had the most optimistic view of this group of theorists.

PART IV: KEY CONCEPTS

Define each of the following concepts in the space provided or on a separate paper. Check the accuracy of your answers by referring to the key concepts section at the end of the chapter in the text as well as referring to italicized definitions located throughout the chapter.

agriculture
alienation
anomie
bourgeoisie
bureaucracy
capitalists
class consciousness
class conflict
collective consciousness
division of labor
false consciousness
horticultural society
hunting and gathering society
idealism
ideal-type
infrastructure
materialism
material surplus
mechanical solidarity
organic solidarity
pastoralism
proletariat
rationalization of society
rationality
social fact
social institutions
society
sociocultural evolution
superstructure
tradition

PART V: STUDY QUESTIONS

True-False

1. T F   As used sociologically, the concept of society refers to people who interact with one another within a limited territory and who share a culture.

2. T F While both the cultural ecological and sociocultural evolution perspectives emphasize that the natural environment can shape cultural patterns, the latter shows that this is more true for some societies than others.
3. T F Hunting and gathering societies are typically nomadic.
4. T F Hunting and gathering societies tend to be characterized by social inequality more so than horticultural or agrarian societies.
5. T F Agrarian societies emerged about 5,000 years ago.
6. T F For Karl Marx, the most significant form of social conflict arises from the way society produces material goods.
7. T F According to Durkheim, a social fact is defined as anything that can be quantitatively measured.
8. T F Durkheim argued that the significance of social facts is discovered not in the experience of individuals, but in the functional contributions they have for the general life of society itself.
9. T F Organic solidarity characterizes preindustrial societies.
10. T F Unlike Marx and Weber, Durkheim was relatively optimistic about industrialization and the development of modern society.

Multiple-Choice

1. Gerhard and Jean Lenski focus on which factor as a major determinate of social change:

    (a) human ideas   (d) social solidarity
    (b) technology   (e) religious doctrine
    (c) social conflict

2. Which of the following was a small hunting and gathering society living on the southern most tip of South America?

    (a) the Nayar   (d) the Enta
    (b) the Ituri   (e) the Netsilik
    (c) the Ona

3. A settlement of several hundred people who used hand tools to cultivate plants, was family-centered, and existed about 10,000 years ago is:

    (a) a hunting and gathering society
    (b) a horticultural society
    (c) a pastoral society
    (d) an agrarian society

4. Which of the following qualities is/are more characteristic of horticultural and agrarian societies as compared to hunting and gathering societies?

   (a) greater social inequality
   (b) greater material surplus
   (c) greater specialization
   (d) all of the above

5. Agrarian societies first emerged about _____ years ago.

   (a) 5,000   (d) 50,000
   (b) 12,000   (e) 1,000
   (c) 25,000

6. The development of metal for use in agriculture about 5,000 years ago:

   (a) increased the status of women in society
   (b) lowered the status of males in society
   (c) had little effect on the status of either men or women
   (d) lowered the status of females in society

7. For Karl Marx, ideas, values and social institutions like religion, education and the family were part of the _____ of society.

   (a) infrastructure   (d) superstructure
   (b) predestination   (e) ideal type
   (c) rationality

8. Marx concept of the "bourgeoisie" is a word derived from the French meaning:

   (a) to be exploited   (d) to be revolutionary
   (b) to be alienated   (e) to be above the law
   (c) to be of the town

9. In order for exploited classes to take political action to improve their situation, Marx proposed they must:

   (a) become aware of their shared oppression
   (b) organize to take collective action
   (c) replace false consciousness with class consciousness
   (d) all of the above

10. Max Weber's analysis of society reflects the philosophical approach known as:

    (a) materialism   (d) egalitarianism
    (b) idealism   (e) radicalism
    (c) cultural ecology

11. Weber argued that modern society is characterized by:

    (a) conflict   (d) ambiguity
    (b) harmony   (e) rationality
    (c) indecision

12. Max Weber's theory of the rationalization of society is based upon:

    (a) modes of human thought   (d) social conflict
    (b) ideal versus real culture   (e) none of the above
    (c) functional interrelationships

Fill-In

1. A _____ society is one whose members use hand tools to raise crops.
2. Marx referred to those who own the means of production as the_____, and those who provide the labor for its operation as the _____.
3. _____ _____ refers to the belief that the shortcomings of individuals themselves rather than society are responsible for social problems that people experience.
4. The foundation, or _____, of society is the economic system according to Karl Marx.
5. The experience of powerlessness in social life is termed_____ using Marx's theory of social conflict.
6. Max Weber demonstrated the importance of _____ in shaping social change and development.
7. An abstract description of a social phenomenon on the basis of its essential characteristics Weber called an _____.
8. Any part of society that is argued to have an objective existence apart from the individual Durkheim called a_____ _____.
9. _____ refers to a condition in which society provides individuals with little moral guidance.
10. Social bonds, common in industrial society, based on specialization, Durkheim called _____ _____.

Definition and Short-Answer

1. How do the Lenskis define sociocultural evolution?
2. What are the basic types of societies identified by the Lenskis? What are the basic characteristics of each?

3. What does our author mean by the "limits of technology"?
4. What is the meaning of the philosophy of materialism?
5. How does Marx understand the role of social conflict through history?
6. According to Marx, what are the four ways in which industrial capitalism alienates workers?
7. According to Weber, what are the roots of rationality in modern society?
8. For Weber, what are the components of rationality in modern society?
9. What is the meaning of the term "social fact" as discussed by Durkheim?
10. Define the two types of solidarity according to Durkheim?

PART VI: ANSWERS TO STUDY QUESTIONS

True-False

1.	T	(p. 93)	6.	T	(p. 103)
2.	T	(p. 95)	7.	F	(p. 116)
3.	T	(p. 95)	8.	T	(p. 116)
4.	F	(p. 98)	9.	F	(p. 117)
5.	T	(p. 98)	10.	T	(p. 119)

Multiple-Choice

1.	b	(p. 93)	6.	d	(p. 99)
2.	c	(p. 94)	7.	d	(p. 104)
3.	b	(p. 96)	8.	c	(p. 106)
4.	d	(pp. 97-99)	9.	d	(p. 107)
5.	a	(p. 98)	10.	b	(p. 110)

Fill-In

1. horticultural (p. 96)
2. capitalists/proletariat (p. 103)
3. false consciousness (p. 105)
4. infrastructure (p. 106)
5. alienation (p. 108)
6. ideas or rationality (p. 110)
7. ideal type (p. 110)
8. social fact (p. 116)
9. anomie (p. 117)
10. organic solidarity (p. 114)

PART VII: ANALYSIS AND COMMENT

Profiles

"Gerhard Lenski and Jean Lenski"

    Key Points: Questions:

"Karl Marx" (1818-1883)

    Key Points: Questions:

"Max Weber" (1864-1920)

    Key Points: Questions:

"Emile Durkheim" (1858-1917)

    Key Points: Questions:

Social Diversity

"Technology and the Changing Status of Women"

    Key Points: Questions:

Sociology of Everyday life

"Alienation and Industrial Capitalism"

    Key Points: Questions:

Socialization

5

PART I: CHAPTER OUTLINE

I.   The Importance of Social Experience
      A.   Human Development: Nature and Nurture
      B.   Social Isolation
            1.   Effects of Social Isolation in Nonhuman Primates
            2.   Effects of Social Isolation on Children
II.   Understanding the Socialization Process
      A.   Sigmund Freud: The Elements of Personality
            1.   Basic Human Needs
            2.   Freud's Model of Personality
      B.   Jean Piaget: Cognitive Development
            1.   The Sensorimotor Stage
            2.   The Preoperational Stage
            3.   The Concrete Operations Stage
            4.   The Formal Operations Stage
      C.   George Herbert Mead: The Social Self
            1.   The Self
            2.   The Looking-Glass Self
            3.   The I and the Me
            4.   Development of the Self
III. Agents of Socialization
      A.   The Family
      B.   Schooling
      C.   Peer Groups
      D.   The Mass Media
      E.   Public Opinion
IV.   Socialization and the Life Course
      A.   Childhood
      B.   Adolescence
      C.   Adulthood
            1.   Early Adulthood
            2.   Middle Adulthood
      D.   Old Age and Dying
V.   Resocialization: Total Institutions
VI.   Socialization and Human Freedom
VII. Summary
VIII. Key Concepts
IX.   Suggested Readings

PART II: LEARNING OBJECTIVES

1. To understand the "nature" versus "nurture" debate regarding socialization.
2. To explain the effects of social isolation on humans and other primates.
3. To identify the key components in Sigmund Freud's model of personality.
4. To identify and describe the four stages of cognitive development in the theory of Jean Piaget.
5. To explain the contributions of George Herbert Mead to the process of socialization.
6. To be able to compare and contrast the theories of Freud, Piaget and Mead concerning socialization and human development.
7. To compare and contrast the spheres of socialization (family, schooling, etc.) in terms of their effects on an individual's socialization experiences.
8. To compare and contrast the modes of socialization in childhood, adolescence, adulthood, and old age.
9. To describe the social experience of life within a total institution.
10. To discuss the issue of the extent to which socialization constrains human freedom.

PART III: CHAPTER REVIEW-KEY POINTS

THE IMPORTANCE OF SOCIAL EXPERIENCE

We are told the story of Anna, a young girl who was raised in a context devoid of meaningful social contact. Kingsley Davis, a sociologist, studied the six year old girl, and described her as being more an object than a person. What Anna had been deprived of was *socialization*, or lifelong social experience by which individuals develop human potential and learn the patterns of their culture. Socialization is the foundation of *personality*, referring to a person's fairly consistent pattern of thinking, feeling, and acting. In Anna's case, personality just did not develop.

Human Development: Nature and Nurture

Naturalists during the later 19th century, applying Charles Darwin's theory of evolution, claimed that all human behavior was instinctive. By the end of the 19th century this was clearly the dominant mode through which human behavior was understood. Sociologists, however, see human nature itself as being shaped by cultural context.

Psychologist John Watson challenged the naturalistic perspective and developed an approach called behaviorism, claiming that all human behavior was learned within particular social environments. The work of anthropologists illustrating the great cultural variation existing around the world supports Watson's view.

Contemporary sociologists do not argue that biology plays no role in shaping human behavior. At the very least, human physical traits are linked to heredity. Also, certain characteristics such as intelligence, potential to excel in music and art, and personality characteristics seem to be influenced by heredity. The current position on this issue among sociologists is that nature and nurture are not so much in opposition as they are inseparable.

Social Isolation

For obvious ethical reasons research on the effects of social isolation has been limited to the study of animals. A few rare cases, like Anna's, of human isolation have been investigated.

Effects of Social Isolation on Nonhuman Primates

Classic research by Harry and Margaret Harlow using rhesus monkeys has illustrated the importance of social interaction for other primates besides humans. Using various experimental situations with artificial "mothers" for infant monkeys they determined that while physical development occurred within normal limits, emotional and social growth failed to occur. One important discovery was that monkeys deprived of mother-infant contact, if surrounded by other infant monkeys, did not suffer adversely. This suggested the importance of social interaction in general rather than specifically a maternal bond. A second conclusion was that monkeys who experienced short-term isolation (3 months or less) recovered to normal emotional levels after rejoining other monkeys. Long-term separation appears to have irreversible negative consequences.

Effects of Isolation in Children

The cases of Anna, Isabelle, and Genie, all of whom suffered through years of isolation and neglect as young children are reviewed. Each case suggests that while humans are resilient creatures, extreme social isolation results in irreversible damage to emotional, cognitive and behavior domains of personality development.

UNDERSTANDING THE SOCIALIZATION PROCESS

Sigmund Freud: The Elements of Personality

While trained as a physician, Freud's most important contribution became the development of psychoanalysis and the study of personality development.

Basic Human Needs

Freud saw biological factors having a significant influence on personality, though rejected the argument that human behavior reflected biological instinct. He conceived instincts as general urges and drives. He claimed humans had two basic needs. One he labeled *eros*, or a need for bonding. Another be called the death instinct, or *thanatos*, which related to an aggressive drive.

Freud's Model Of Personality

Freud's perspective combined both these basic needs and the influence of society into a unique model of personality. He argued the personality is comprised of three parts. One is the *id*, rooted in biology and representing the human being's basic needs, which are unconscious and demand immediate satisfaction. Another, representing the conscious attempt to balance innate pleasure-seeking drives of the human organism and the demands of society, he labeled the *ego*. Finally, the human personality develops a *superego* which is the presence of culture within the individual. There is basic conflict between the id and the super-ego which the ego must continually try to manage. If the conflict is not adequately resolved personality disorders result.

The controlling influence on drives by society is referred to as *repression*. Often a compromise between society and the individual is struck, where fundamentally selfish drives are redirected into socially acceptable objectives. This process is called *sublimation*.

While being controversial, Freud's work highlights the internalization of social norms and the importance of childhood experiences in the socialization process and the development of personality.

Jean Piaget: Cognitive Development

A prominent psychologist of the 20th century, Piaget's work centered on human *cognition*, or how people think and understand. He was concerned with not just what a person knew, but how the person knows something. He identified four major stages of cognitive development which he believed were tied to biological maturation as well as social experience.

The Sensorimotor Stage

The *sensorimotor stage* is described as the level of human development in which the world is experienced only through sensory contact. This stage lasts for about the first two years of life. A critical event during this stage is the development of *object permanence*, or the ability to know something exists even without direct sensory contact. The understanding of symbols does not exist during this period. The child experiences the world only in terms of direct physical contact.

The Preoperational Stage

The *preoperational stage* was described by Piaget as the level of human development in which language and other symbols are first used. This stage extends from the age of two to the age of seven. Children continue to be very egocentric during this time, having little ability to generalize concepts. An experiment is discussed illustrating this point.

The Concrete Operational Stage

The third stage in Piaget's model is called the *concrete operational stage* and is described as the level of human development characterized by the use of logic to understand objects or events. This period typically covers the ages of seven to eleven. Cause and effect relationships begin to be understood during this period. The ability to take the perspective of other people also emerges.

The Formal Operational Stage

The fourth stage is the *formal operational stage* and is described as the level of human development characterized by highly abstract thought and the ability to imagine alternatives to reality. This stage begins about age twelve. The ability to think in hypothetical terms is also developed.

Piaget viewed the human mind as active and creative. Research now is focusing on the cross-cultural relevance of this model and to what extent males and females develop differently through these stages. Further, some evidence suggests that almost one-third of the adults in the U.S. do not reach stage four.

George Herbert Mead: The Social Self

Questions such as, What exactly is social experience? And, How does social experience enhance our humanity? were central to Mead's research on the socialization process. Mead's analysis is often referred to as *social behaviorism*. This view is similar to Watson's behaviorism, however Mead's work was not limited to the study of behavior only. Mead's work also concerned mental processes. Mead's life and career are reviewed in the **Profile** box (p. 131).

The Self

Mead understood the basis of humanity to be the *self*, a dimension of personality composed of an individual's self-conception. For Mead, the self was a totally social phenomenon, inseparable from society. The connection between the two was explained in a series of steps, the emergence of the self through social experience, based on the exchange of symbolic intentions, and occurring within a context in which people take the role of the other, or take their point of view into account during social interaction.

The Looking-Glass Self

The process of taking the role of the other can be more meaningfully understood using Charles Horton Cooley's concept of the *looking-glass self*. This term focuses on the ideas that a person's self-conception is based on the response of others.

The I and The Me

An important dualism is suggested by Mead's idea that the self thinks about itself. The two components include: (1) the self as subject by which we initiate social action. This subjective part of the self Mead labeled the "*I*". And, (2) the self as object, concerned how we perceive ourselves from the perspective of others. This objective aspect Mead called the "*Me*." All social interaction is seen as the continuous interplay of these two aspects of the self.

Development of the Self

Mead minimized the importance of biology in personality development. Further, while seeing early childhood experiences as significant, he did not see developmental stages closely linked to age. The key was social experience, not maturation. Mead also saw infants as responding to others only in terms of imitation. As the use of symbols emerges the child enters a "*play*" stage, in which role-taking occurs. Initially, the roles are modeled after significant others, especially parents. Through further social experience children enter the "*game*" stage where the simultaneous playing of many roles is possible. The final stage involves the development of a "*generalized other*," or widespread cultural norms and values used as a reference in evaluating ourselves.

The **Sociology of Everyday Life** box (p. 133) provides examples of the differences between the play and game stages. Figure 5-1 (p. 134) illustrates the development of the self as a process of gaining social experience.

AGENTS OF SOCIALIZATION

The Family

The family is identified as the most important agent of socialization. The process of socialization within this institution is discussed as being both intentional and unconscious. While parenting styles vary, the most important aspect in parent-child relations seems to be *attention* paid by parents to their children. The family is the initial source for transmission of culture to the child.

The social class of the family has been shown to have a considerable bearing upon the values and orientations children learn. This point is elaborated using the research of Melvin Kohn who found that middle-class and working-class parents stress different values for their children.

Schooling

It is within the context of school that children begin to establish contact with people from a diversity of social backgrounds. The expressed objective purpose of the school experience is the imparting of knowledge, math, reading, etc. However, there exists a "*hidden curriculum*" which also teaches children important cultural values.

It is within the educational environment that evaluations are made of children based on universal standards on *how they perform* instead of *who they are*. Schooling is critical for obtaining the knowledge and skills necessary for adult roles.

Peer Groups

Peer group socialization typically occurs outside the context of adult supervision. A *peer group* is defined as a social group whose members have interests, social position, and age in common. Some research provides evidence suggesting that the conflict between parents and their adolescent children is more apparent than real. A major feature operative during adolescence is referred to as *anticipatory socialization*, or the process of social learning directed toward gaining a desired position.

The Mass Media

The *mass media* are impersonal communications directed to a vast audience. This includes television, newspapers, radio, etc.. While it attempts to be factual, many sociologists have argued that the mass media offers a biased perspective on society, presenting the established elites in a favorable light. The influence of television on thought and behavior is discussed. Also, **Global Map** 5-1 (p. 138) provides a look at how common television sets are around the world.

The **Social Diversity** box (p. 139) illustrates an example of advertising involving racial and ethnic biases.

Public Opinion

Public opinion is defined as the attitudes of people through-out society about one or more controversial issues. What we as individuals perceive others believe significantly influences us.

SOCIALIZATION AND THE LIFE COURSE

While focus is given to childhood in terms of the significance of socialization this process is lifelong. Social experience is viewed in this section as being structured during different stages
of the life course.

Childhood

The novel by Charles Dickens about Oliver Twist is briefly discussed to provide a portrait of Oliver's life, one very different from contemporary American childrens' experience.

Childhood in American culture lasts roughly the first twelve years of life. It is a period characterized by freedom from responsibilities. It is an expanding period in technologically advanced societies. However, some research, especially on affluent families, suggests it actually may be getting shorter as a period. The "hurried child" pattern reflects this idea. In primitive societies less differentiation is made between childhood and adulthood. **Global Map** 5-2 shows how commonplace work is for children in the poorer societies of the world.

An interesting example of how differences between childhood and adulthood is understood in primitive cultures is provided by comparing sex among children in the **Cross-Cultural Comparison** box (p. 142). Such research is used to suggest that childhood is far from just being an inevitable consequence of biological maturation.

65

Adolescence

This period emerged as a distinct life cycle stage during industrialization. This period corresponds roughly to the teen years. The social turmoil often associated with this stage appears to be the result of inconsistences in the socialization process as opposed to being based on physical changes. Examples concerning the status of teens in relation to voting and drinking are discussed. Margaret Mead's cross-cultural research suggests this point.

Adulthood

Eleanor Roosevelt's life is briefly reviewed to illustrate two major characteristics of this stage of life. First, it is a period when most of our life's accomplishments occur. Second, especially toward the end of this stage, people reflect upon what they have accomplished.

Early Adulthood

This period lasts approximately from the early 20's to age 40. While personality is largely set by this time, certain transitions, life unemployment, divorce, or a serious illness can result in significant personality changes. This period is dominated by meeting day-to-day responsibilities and achieving goals set earlier in life. The juggling of conflicting priorities also characterizes this period.

Middle Adulthood

This period lasts roughly between the ages of 40 to 60. A distinctive quality of this period is reflection on personal achievements in light of earlier expectations. Certain differences between men and women are discussed, including family roles and attractiveness.

Old Age and Dying

This period begins during the mid-60s. The status of the aged varies greatly cross-culturally. In rapidly changing modern societies the aged tend to be defined as marginal or even obsolete. This period is quite different from previous ones as it is characterized by the leaving of roles instead of entering new ones.

Elizabeth Kubler-Ross has written extensively on the process of death as an orderly transition involving five distinct stages, denial, anger, negotiation, resignation, and acceptance. As society
changes, particularly with more people living into old age, our conception of both old age and death are changing.

In summarizing the vast amount of research on socialization discussed in this chapter, our author makes four general conclusions: (1) although linked to the biological process of aging, the essential characteristics of each stage of socialization are constructions of society, (2) each period provides different problems and transitions, (3) the process varies by social background, and (4) experiences during the life course must be understood within the context of past historical periods.

RESOCIALIZATION: TOTAL INSTITUTIONS

A *total institution* is defined as a setting in which individuals are isolated from the rest of society and manipulated by an administrative staff. Erving Goffman has identified three distinct qualities of such institutions: (1) they control all aspects of the daily lives of the residents, (2) they subject residents to standardized activities, and (3) they apply formal rules and rigid scheduling to all activities. This structure is designed to achieve the policy of *resocialization*, or deliberate control of an environment to radically alter an inmates personality. This is understood as a two part process - the destruction of the individual's self-conception, and the systematic building of another one. A process known as *institutionalization* often occurs whereby residents become dependent on the structure of the institution and are unable to function outside the institution.

SOCIALIZATION AND HUMAN FREEDOM

While society affects both our outward behavior and inner-most feelings, we are not merely puppets. Even though we are further influenced by biological forces, our existence as humans provides tremendous opportunity for freedom, spontaneity, and creativity. The process of socialization affirms the capacity for choice. The sociological perspective can help us overcome an *"oversocialized"* view of ourselves.

PART IV: KEY CONCEPTS

Define each of the following concepts in the space provided or on separate paper. Check the accuracy of your answers by referring to the key concepts section at the end of the chapter in the text as well as by referring to italicized definitions located throughout the chapter.

adolescence
adulthood
anticipatory socialization
behaviorism
childhood
cognition
cohort
concrete operations stage
ego
eros
formal operations stage
game stage

generalized other
I
id
looking-glass self
hidden curriculum
institutionalized
mass media
me
object permanence
old age
peer group
personality
preoperational stage
public opinion
resocialization
repression
self
sensorimotor stage
significant other
social behaviorism
socialization
sublimation
superego
taking the role of the other
thanatos
total institution

PART V: STUDY QUESTIONS

True-False

1. T F John Watson was a 19th century psychologist who argued that human behavior was largely determined by heredity.
2. T F As defined by our author, the concept of personality does not concern behavior.
3. T F The Harlows' research on rhesus monkeys concerning social isolation illustrates that while short-term isolation can be overcome, long-term isolation appears to cause irreversible emotional and behavioral damage to the monkeys.
4. T F The cases of Isabelle, Anna, and Genie support the arguments made by naturalists that certain personality characteristics are determined by heredity.
5. T F Freud envisioned biological factors as having little or no influence on personality development.

6. T F According to Piaget, object permanence occurs during the preoperational stage.
7. T F George Herbert Mead argued that biological factors played little to no role in the development of the self.
8. T F Mead's concept of the generalized other refers to widespread cultural norms and values used as a reference in evaluating ourselves.
9. T F The concept "hidden curriculum" relates to the important cultural values being transmitted to children in school.
10. T F Childhood in technologically advanced societies is much more similar to adulthood than it is in pre-industrialized societies.

Multiple-Choice

1. The story of Anna illustrates the significance of _____ in personality development.

   (a) heredity   (d) ecological forces
   (b) social interaction   (e) historical processes
   (c) physical conditions

2. Which of the following is representative of Freud's analysis of personality:

   (a) biological forces play only a small role in personality development
   (b) the term instinct is understood as very general human needs in the form of urges and drives
   (c) the most significant period for personality development is adolescence
   (d) personality is best studied as a process of externalizing social forces

3. Culture existing within the individual Freud called:

   (a) thanatos   (d) the id
   (b) eros   (e) the superego
   (c) the ego

4. Freud's model of personality does not include which of the following elements:

   (a) superego   (c) self
   (b) id   (d) ego

5. According to Piaget, which of the following best describes the preoperational stage of cognitive development:

   (a) the level of human development in which the world is experienced only through sensory contact
   (b) the level of human development characterized by the use of logic to understand objects and events
   (c) the level of human development in which language and other symbols are first used
   (d) the level of human development characterized by highly abstract thought
   (e) none of the above

6. G. H. Mead's perspective has often been described as:

   (a) psychological pragmatism   (d) behaviorism
   (b) psychoanalysis   (e) naturalism
   (c) social behaviorism

7. The concept of the looking-glass self refers to:

   (a) Freud's argument that through psychoanalysis we can uncover our unconscious
   (b) Piaget's view that through biological maturation and social experience individuals become able to logically hypothesize about thoughts without relying on concrete reality
   (c) Watson's behaviorist notion that one can see through to a person's mind only by observing their behavior
   (d) Cooley's idea that a person's self-conception is based on responses of others

8. Melvin Kohn's research on social class and socialization of children within the family found that compared to middle-class parents, working-class parents were more likely to stress the value of _____ for their children.

   (a) conformity   (d) achievement
   (b) affection   (e) success
   (c) independence

9. The process of social learning directed toward assuming a desired status and role in the future is called:

   (a) resocialization   (c) socialization
   (b) looking-glass self   (d) anticipatory socialization

70

10. Latest statistics show that the average American family has a television on in the house how many hours per day:

(a) 7   (c) 13
(b) 3   (d) 10

Fill-In

1. A _____ is defined as a person's fairly constant pattern of thinking, feeling, and acting.
2. The approach called _____ developed by John Watson in the early 20th century provided a perspective which stressed learning rather than instincts as the key to personality development.
3. According to Freud, the _____ represents the conscious attempt to balance the innate pleasure-seeking drives of the human organism and the demands of society.
4. Freud termed society's controlling influence on the drives of each individual as _____, whereas he called the process of transforming fundamentally selfish drives int more socially acceptable objectives as _____.
5. Piaget's work centered on human _____.
6. Jean Piaget's model of cognitive development focused not on what children knew about the world but _____ they understood the world.
7. George Herbert Mead defined _____ as the individual's awareness of being a distinct entity in the midst of society.
8. The process of social learning directed toward gaining a desired position is called _____.
9. The attitudes of people throughout a society about controversial ideas is termed _____.
10. A prison or mental hospital is an example of a _____.

Definition and short-Answer

1. Briefly review the history of the nature-nurture debate concerning human development.
2. Review the cases of social isolation described in the text. What are the effects of social isolation on nonhuman primates? What are the effects of social isolation on children?
3. According to Freud, what are the basic components of personality? What stages of human development does Freud's identify?
4. According to Piaget, what are the stages of cognitive development? What are the characteristics of each stage?
5. What is Mead's theory of personality development? What are the stages identified in his model? What is the "self" and how does it develop?

6. What are the major agents of socialization? Briefly describe how each influences human development.
7. What are the two major characteristics of adulthood?
8. According to Kubler-Ross, what are the stages of death?
9. What is a total institution? Provide an example.
10. Discuss the similarities and differences between the developmental theories of Freud, Piaget, and Mead.

PART VI: ANSWERS TO STUDY QUESTIONS

True-False

1.	F (p. 124)	6.	F (p. 129)
2.	F (p. 124)	7.	T (p. 131)
3.	T (p. 126)	8.	T (p. 133)
4.	F (p. 127)	9.	T (p. 135)
5.	F (p. 127)	10.	F (p. 140)

Multiple-Choice

1.	b (p. 123)	6.	c (p. 131)
2.	b (p. 127)	7.	d (p. 132)
3.	e (p. 128)	8.	a (p. 135)
4.	c (p. 128)	9.	d (pp. 136-37)
5.	c (p. 129)	10.	a (p. 137)

Fill-In

1. personality (p. 124)
2. behaviorism (p. 124)
3. ego (p. 128)
4. repression/sublimation (p. 128)
5. cognition (p. 129)
6. how (p. 129)
7. self (p. 131)
8. anticipatory socialization (pp. 136-37)
9. public opinion (p. 139)
10. total institution (p. 146)

PART VII: ANALYSIS AND COMMENT

Profile

"George Herbert Mead" (1863-1931)

Key Points: Questions:

Sociology of Everyday Life

"Play and Games: Taking the Roles of Others"

Key Points: Questions:

Social Diversity

"When Advertising Offends: The Death of the Frito Bandito"

Key Points: Questions:

Cross-Cultural Comparison

"Sex Among Children? The Social Construction of Childhood"

Key Points: Questions:

Social Interaction In Everyday Life

6

PART I: CHAPTER OUTLINE

I.   Social Structure: A Guide To Everyday Living
    A.   Status
        1.   Ascribed Status and Achieved Status
        2.   Master Status
    B.   Role
        1.   Role Conflict and Role Strain
        2.   Role Exit
II.   The Social Construction of Reality
    A.   The Thomas Theorem
    B.   Reality-Building in Global Perspective
    C.   Ethnomethodology
III. Dramaturgical Analysis: "The Presentation of Self"
    A.   Performances
    B.   Nonverbal Communication
    C.   Gender and Personal Performances
        1.   Demeanor
        2.   Use of Space
        3.   Staring, Smiling, and Touching
    D.   Idealization
    E.   Embarrassment and Tact
IV.   Interaction in Everyday Life: Two Illustrations
    A.   Language: The Gender Issue
        1.   The Control Function of Language
        2.   The Value Function of Language
        3.   The Attention Function of Language
    B.   Humor: Playing with Reality
        1.   The Foundation of Humor
        2.   The Dynamics of Humor: "Getting It"
        3.   The Topics of Humor
        4.   The Functions of Humor
        5.   Humor and Conflict
V.   Summary
VI.   Key Concepts
VIII. Suggested Readings

PART II: LEARNING OBJECTIVES

1. To identify the characteristics of social structure.
2. To explain the relationship between social structure and individuality.
3. To distinguish between the different types of statuses and roles and the interconnection between them.
4. To describe the importance of role in social interaction.
5. To explain the social construction of reality.
6. To understand the theoretical approach within the symbolic-interaction paradigm known as ethnomethodology.
7. To know the importance of performance, nonverbal communication, idealization, and embarrassment to the "presentation of self."
8. To describe dramaturgical analysis.
9. To be able to use gender and humor as illustrations of how people construct meaning in everyday life.

PART III: CHAPTER REVIEW

We are asked at the beginning of this chapter to question some of our assumptions about everyday social patterns in society. The example given concerns contrasts in language used for advertising burial plots versus those used for advertising cars. This chapter focuses on *social interaction*, or the process by which people act and react in relation to others. Social meaning is created through such activity.

SOCIAL STRUCTURE: A GUIDE TO EVERYDAY LIVING

The point is again stressed, as it has been in each chapter, that we tend in our society to emphasize individual responsibility for behavior, highlighting our uniqueness. But the argument that we act in patterned ways based on social influences is not meant to suggest our behavior is rigidly determined by social structure. Rather, social structure is seen as *guiding* behavior, not *rigidly determining* it, and individuality is viewed as something actually encouraged.

Status

A *status* refers to a recognized social position that an individual occupies within society. Each involves certain rights, privileges, obligations and expectations that are widely recognized. Statuses guide the behavior of people in different social situations, and are an important part of how people define themselves. *Status set* refers to all statuses a particular person holds at a given time. An example would include being a father, accountant, male, and husband. Status sets are both complex and changeable.

Ascribed Status and Achieved Status

Sociologists distinguish between two ways in which statuses are obtained. An *ascribed status* is a social position that is received at birth or involuntarily assumed later in the life course. In contrast, an *achieved status* refers to a social position that is assumed voluntary and that reflects a significant measure of personal ability and effort. Most often there is a combination of ascribed and achieved factors in each of our statuses.

Master Status

A *master status* is defined as a status that has an exceptional importance for social identity, often shaping a person's entire life. In our society, one's occupation often comprises this position. The **Social Diversity** box (p. 154) points out that physical disability becomes the master status for many people. Ascribed statuses such as race and sex are discussed as other examples of positions which act as a person's master status.

Role

The concept *role* refers to patterns of expected behavior attached to a particular status. Ralph Linton describes it as the dynamic expression of a status. However, sociologists differentiate between actual role performance and role expectations society attaches to a role.

Like statuses, roles are *relational*, meaning they organize our behavior toward other people. Generally, a person has many more roles than statuses, as each status typically has multiple roles attached. Robert Merton defines a *role set* as a number of roles attached to a single status. Figure 6-1 (p. 155) provides an illustration of a status set and role set.

Conflict and Strain

The concept *role conflict* refers to incompatibility among the roles corresponding to two or more statuses. Even the roles attached to a single status can create problems for an individual. *role strain*, referring to incompatibility among roles corresponding to a single status, describes this situation. Prioritizing roles is one strategy used to resolve this condition. Another way to deal with role strain is by insulating roles from one another, limiting involvement in particular roles to only certain specific times of the day or week.

Role Exit

Role exit is the process by which people disengage from social roles that have been central to their lives. Helen Ebaugh, herself an ex-nun, discusses the process of becoming an "ex."

THE SOCIAL CONSTRUCTION OF REALITY

While statuses and roles structure our lives, we as individuals have considerable ability to shape patterns of interaction with others. The phrase *social construction of reality* refers to the process by which individuals creatively shape reality through social interaction. Social interaction is understood as a process of negotiation which generates a changing reality. Examples from literature are discussed to illustrate this process.

The Thomas Theorem

One observation made by sociologists is that situations that are defined as real are real in their consequences. This has become known as the *Thomas theorem*.

Reality-Building in Global Perspective

Human creativity draws on what is available in the surrounding culture. Variation exists between subcultures in any given society, and cross-culturally in terms of how reality is fashioned. A question raised in the **Cross-Cultural Comparison** box (p. 160-61) concerns whether basic human feelings are universal.

Ethnomethodology

One approach to understanding the ways humans shape reality is called *ethnomethodology* which is based on the symbolic-interaction paradigm. Harold Garfinkel coined the term, which is defined as the study of everyday, common-sense understandings that people have of the world around them. Garfinkel did research in which he had students deliberately refuse to "play the game." This approach highlights awareness of many unnoticed patterns of everyday life.

DRAMATURGICAL ANALYSIS: "THE PRESENTATION OF SELF"

Another approach to understanding the social interaction of everyday life is *dramaturgical analysis* developed by Erving Goffman. This approach is defined as the analysis of social interaction in terms of theatrical performances. Goffman theorized that statuses and roles are used to create impressions. Central to this analysis is the process called the *presentation of self*, meaning the ways in which individuals, in various settings, attempt to create specific impressions in the minds of others. This process is also referred to as *impression management*.

Performances

Goffman referred to the conscious and unconscious efforts of people in conveying information about themselves as *performances*. These would include dress, tone of voice, objects being carried, etc. An interesting analysis of physicians and their offices is discussed to illustrate this idea.

Nonverbal Communication

Novelist William Sansom's description of a fictional character named Mr. Preedy walking across a beach in Spain is used to illustrate the process of *nonverbal communication*. This concept refers to communication using body movements, gestures, and facial expressions rather than spoken words. Types of smiles, eye contact and hand movements are reviewed to further highlight this concept.

The **Sociology of Everyday Life** box (p. 162-63) reviews examples of nonverbal clues which can be identified to suggest if a person is telling a lie. A distinction is made between messages "given" and nonverbal signals "given off." This section of the chapter concludes with a review of examples of how the meanings of gestures varies cross-culturally.

Gender and Personal Performances

How societies link human traits to being female or male is very important to take into account when studying personal performances.

Demeanor

Demeanor refers to general conduct or deportment. It tends to vary by an individual's power. Given that men are more likely than women to be in positions of dominance it is suggested that women must craft their performances to maintain subordinance.

Use of Space

Power is a key here as well. Masculinity has been traditionally associated with greater amounts of *personal space*, or the surrounding area over which a person makes some claim to privacy. Also, men tend to intrude on a woman's space more often than women intruding on a man's space.

Staring, Smiling, and Touching

While women tend to maintain interactions through sustaining eye contact longer than men do, men tend to stare more. Meanings associated with smiling also seem to vary with gender. Touching patterns also vary, with men tending to touch women more than women touch men. Various rituals are created in which men tend to express their dominance over women.

Idealization

Goffman suggests that we attempt to idealize our intentions when it comes to our performances. The context of a hospital involving physicians making their rounds with patients is used to illustrate how people, in this case doctors, try to convince people they are abiding by ideal cultural standards.

Embarrassment and Tact

As hard as we may try to craft perfect performances, slip-ups do occur and may cause embarrassment, or the recognition that we have failed through our performance to convince our audience. Oftentimes audiences will ignore flaws in performances, using tact to enable the performance to continue. This is because embarrassment causes discomfort for all present.

While life is not a scripted play, Shakespeare's "All the world's a stage" idea does portray our relationships within social structure to some extent.

INTERACTION IN EVERYDAY LIFE: TWO ILLUSTRATIONS

Language: The Gender Issue

The content of communication is both manifest, or what is explicitly stated, and latent, which conveys much more information. One such latent message concerns the relative social definitions of men and women. Language functions to define the sexes in at least three ways.

The Control Function of Language

One example of this is that males tend to attach female pronouns to valued objects, consistent with the concept of possession. Another illustration is women changing their name when they marry.

The Value Function of Language

Language conveys different levels of status in many subtle ways. Typically, the masculine terms carry higher status.

The Attention Function of Language

The English language seems to almost ignore what is feminine. This is reflected in our pronoun usage.

Humor: Playing With Reality

Another example of the sociological importance of everyday interaction is in the analysis of humor. The issue of why something is funny is virtually never analyzed critically by people.

The Foundation of Humor

Humor emerges out of ambiguity and double meanings involving two differing definitions of the situation, a contrasting of the *conventional* and the *unconventional*. Examples of this are given to illustrate this idea. The key to a good joke seems to lie in the opposition of realities.

The Dynamics of Humor: "Getting It"

To get the joke the listener must understand the two realities, the conventional and the unconventional. Examples of different levels of complexity of jokes on this dimension are provided. People derive satisfaction and even "insider status" by being able to "piece together" the realities to "get the joke."

Topics of Humor

While humor is universal, what is viewed as funny is not. Yet, humor is everywhere closely tied to what is controversial. There is also a fine line between what is funny and what is "sick."

Functions of Humor

The universality of humor reflects its function as a safety-valve. Sentiments can be expressed that might be dangerous to relationships if taken seriously. Humor also allows us to explore alternatives to the status quo.

Humor and Conflict

Humor is often used by different groups in society to question the interests of those they oppose.

Finally, humor allows some freedom as with it we are never prisoners of the present.

PART IV. KEY CONCEPTS

Define each of the following concepts in the space provided or on separate paper. Check the accuracy of your answers by referring to the key concepts section at the end of the chapter in the text as well as by referring to italicized definitions located throughout the chapter.

achieved status
ascribed status
demeanor
dramaturgical analysis

ethnomethodology
humor
idealization
master status
nonverbal communication
performance
personal space
presentation of self
role
role conflict
role exit
role expectations
role performance
role set
role strain
social interaction
status
status set
social construction of reality
Thomas theorem

PART V: STUDY QUESTIONS

True-False

1. T F A status refers to a pattern of expected behavior for individual members of society.
2. T F A status set refers to all statuses a person holds during his or her lifetime.
3. T F Both roles and statuses are "relational" concepts.
4. T F Role strain refers to incompatibility among roles corresponding to a single status.
5. T F The phrase, "the social construction of reality" relates to the sociologists view that statuses and roles structure our lives along narrowly delineated paths.
6. T F According to Goffman, performances are rigidly scripted, leaving little room for individual adaptation.
7. T F The dramaturgical concept "gave off" relates to nonverbal information available to the observer.
8. T F Research suggests virtually all nonverbal communication is universally understood among humans.
9. T F According to Goffman's research, tact is relatively uncommon in the U.S.
10. T F The essence of humor lies in the contrast between two incongruous realities, the conventional and the unconventional.

Multiple-Choice

1. The relationship between social structure and human behavior is one of:

    (a) providing guidelines
    (b) no relationship
    (c) rigid determination

    (d) ideal vs. real culture
    (e) predestination

2. Which of the following is not a structural component of social interaction:

    (a) master status
    (b) role
    (c) value

    (d) role set
    (e) ascribed status

3. Ralph Linton described _____ as the dynamic expression of a status.

    (a) master status
    (b) role
    (c) performance

    (d) dramaturgy
    (e) nonverbal communication

4. The incompatibility among the roles corresponding to two or more statuses refers to:

    (a) role conflict
    (b) role strain
    (c) status overload

    (d) status inconsistency
    (e) role set

5. Methods of reducing role strain include which of the following:

    (a) discarding one or more roles
    (b) compartmentalizing roles
    (c) emphasizing some roles more than others
    (d) all of the above
    (e) none of the above

6. The Thomas theorem states:

    (a) roles are only as important as the statuses to which they are attached
    (b) statuses are only as important as the roles to which they are attached
    (c) the basis of humanity is built upon the dual existence of creativity and conformity
    (d) common sense is only as good as the social structure within which it is embedded
    (e) situations defined as real are real in their consequences

7. The methodology used by ethnomethodologists to study everyday interaction involves:

(a) conducting surveys   (d) breaking the rules
(b) unobtrusive observation   (e) experimentation
(c) secondary analysis

8. The fictional character Mr. Preedy was introduced in the text to provide an example of:

(a) role conflict   (d) nonverbal communication
(b) role strain   (e) status inconsistency
(c) role exit

9. The example of doctors "making the rounds" in a hospital and reading the patients' charts is an illustration of Goffman's concept:

(a) idealization   (d) embarrassment
(b) role conflict   (e) the Thomas theorem
(c) role exit

10. Which of the following is not an example provided in the text to illustrate how language functions to define the sexes:

(a) the attention function   (d) the control function
(b) the value function   (e) none were used
(c) the affective function

Fill-In

1. The process by which people act and react in relation to others is termed _____.

2. A _____ is a recognized social position that an individual occupies within society.

3. An _____ status is a social position that is received at birth or involuntarily assumed later in the life course.

4. _____ refers to incompatibility among the roles corresponding to a single status.

5. The phrase _____ _____ __ _____ refers to the process by which individuals creatively shape reality through social interaction.

6. The _____ theorem states that situations that are defined as real are real in their consequences.

7. _____ is the study of the everyday, common-sense understandings that people have of the world around them.

8. _____ analysis is defined as the analysis of social interaction in terms of theatrical performance.

9. _____ _____ refers to the area around a person over which some claim to privacy is made.

10. The essence of humor lies in the contrast between two incongruous realities, the _____ and the _____.

Definition and Short-Answer

1. Read the "Sociology of Everyday Life" box (p. 162-63). Using it as an example, select a social situation you have been involved in and do a dramaturgical analysis to describe its context.

2. What are the four types of information provided by a "performer" in terms of nonverbal communication which can be used to determine whether or not the person is telling   the truth?

3. Refer to Figure 6-1 (p. 155) and using it as a model diagram your own status and role sets. Identify points of role conflict and role strain.

4. What are the three ways in which language functions to define the sexes differently? Provide an illustration for each.

5. What is ethnomethodology? Provide an illustration of how a researcher using this approach would study social interaction.

6. Define the concept idealization.

7. Discuss the issue of gender and role performances as reviewed in the text. Provide illustrations from your own experience to demonstrate the points being made about the respective patterns of male and female social interaction.

8. What are the basic characteristics of humor? Write a joke and analyze how it manifests the characteristics discussed.

PART VI: ANSWERS TO STUDY QUESTIONS

True-False

1. F (p. 152)
2. F (p. 152)
3. T (p. 154)
4. T (p. 155)
5. F (p. 156)
6. F (p. 159)
7. T (p. 162)
8. F (p. 164)
9. F (p. 166)
10. T (p. 168)

Multiple-Choice

1. a (p. 152)
2. c (pp. 152-53)
3. b (pp. 153-54)
4. a (p. 155)
5. d (p. 155)
6. e (p. 158)
7. d (p. 159)
8. d (p. 162)
9. a (p. 165)
10. e (p. 167)

Fill-In

1. social interaction (p. 151)
2. status (p. 152)
3. ascribed (pp. 152-53)
4. role strain (p. 155)
5. social construction of reality (p. 156)
6. Thomas (p. 158)
7. ethnomethodology (p. 159)
8. dramaturgical (p. 159)
9. personal space (p. 164)
10. conventional/unconventional (p. 168)

PART VII: ANALYSIS AND COMMENT

Social Diversity

"Physical Disability as Master Status"

    Key Points: Questions:

Cross-Cultural Comparison

"Human Emotions in Global Perspective"

    Key Points: Questions:

Sociology of Everyday Life

"Telling Lies: Clues to Deceit"

    Key Points: Questions:

Groups And Organizations

7

PART I: CHAPTER OUTLINE

I. Social Groups
    A. Groups, Aggregates, and Categories
    B. Primary and Secondary Groups
    C. Group Leadership
    D. Group Conformity
        1. Asch's Research
        2. Milgrim's Research
        3. Janis's Research
    E. Reference Groups
        1. Stouffer's Research
    F. Ingroups and Outgroups
    G. Group Size
    H. Social Diversity
    I. Networks
II. Formal Organizations
    A. Types of Formal Organizations
        1. Normative Organizations
        2. Coercive Organizations
        3. Utilitarian Organizations
    B. Origins of Bureaucracy
    C. Characteristics of Bureaucracy
    D. Bureaucracy Versus Small Groups
    E. The Informal Side of Bureaucracy
    F. Limitations of Bureaucracy
        1. Bureaucratic Waste and Incompetence
        2. Bureaucratic Ritualism
        3. Bureaucratic Inertia
    G. Oligarchy
    H. Gender and Race in Organizations
    I. Opportunity and Power: Effects on Employees
    J. Humanizing Bureaucracy
    K. Organizational Environment
    L. Formal Organizations in Japan
III. Groups and Organizations in Global Perspective
IV. Summary
V. Key Concepts
VI. Suggested Readings

PART II: LEARNING OBJECTIVES

1. To explain the differences among primary groups, secondary groups, aggregates, and categories.
2. To identify the various types of leaders associated with social groups.
3. To compare and contrast the research of Asch, Milgram and Janis on group conformity.
4. To explain the importance of reference groups to group dynamics by understanding Stouffer's research on soldiers.
5. To distinguish between ingroups and outgroups.
6. To explain the relevance of group size to the dynamics of social groups.
7. To identify the types of formal organizations.
8. To identify the primary characteristics of bureaucracy
9. To compare and contrast the small group and the formal organization on the basis of their respective activities, hierarchies, norms, criteria for membership, relationships, communications, and focuses.
10. To identify the outcomes of the informal side of bureaucracy.
11. To explain the limitations of bureaucracy.
12. To understand the effects of power and opportunity on employees and the effects of "humanizing" bureaucracy.
13. To compare and contrast formal organizations in the U.S. and Japan and to understand formal organizations in a more global perspective.

PART III: CHAPTER REVIEW-KEY POINTS

The introduction to this chapter relates a story to us in order to illustrate the extent to which we are using lawyers and the courts to handle problems in our social relationships. The U.S. has 70 percent of the world's lawyers. Is this an indication that our society is becoming too complex and impersonal? This chapter gives insight into the extent to which *social groups*, from families to *formal organizations*, have meaning in our lives.

SOCIAL GROUPS

A *social group* is defined as two or more people who identify with one another and have a distinctive pattern of interaction. While we each have our own individuality, the "we" feeling that can only be achieved in social groups is central to our existence as human beings.

Groups, Aggregates, and Categories

Not all collections of individuals are social groups. The term *aggregate* refers to people who are in the same place at the same time but who interact little, if at all. People who share a status in common are defined as a *category*. Potentially, members of categories and aggregates could become social groups given certain circumstances.

Primary and Secondary Groups

Charles Horton Cooley studies the extent to which people have personal concern for each other in social interaction settings. He distinguished between primary and secondary groups. *Primary groups* are defined as a typically small social group in which relationships are both personal and enduring. They are characterized as ends in and of themselves. They are critical in the socialization process. Members are considered unique and not interchangeable. *Secondary groups* are defined as large and impersonal social groups usually based on a specific interest or activity. They are typically short-term with narrowly-defined relationships and are seen as a means to an end. The distinction in real life is not always as clear as these definitions might suggest. Table 7-1 (p. 177) provides a summary of the key differences between primary and secondary groups.

Group Leadership

Leadership plays a critical role in group dynamics. Research shows that leadership has less to do with individual traits and more to do with the needs of the group itself. Research also reveals that there are usually two types of leaders in social groups held by separate individuals. *Instrumental leadership* refers to group leadership that emphasizes the completion of tasks. *Expressive leadership* emphasizes collective well-being. This differentiate is also linked to gender, with men typically taking the instrumental role and women taking the expressive role in leadership positions. Leaders also vary in the ways in which they include others in the decision-making process. Three decision-making styles are identified. One is *authoritarian* leadership which focuses on instrumental concerns. This type of leader makes decisions on their own, demanding strict compliance from subordinates. Another type is the *democratic* leader who takes a more expressive approach, seeking to include all members in the decision-making process. A third type is labeled *laissez-faire*. Leaders using this approach tend to downplay their power, allowing the group to function on its own.

Group Conformity

Group conformity is another dimension of group dynamics in which members seek the satisfaction of being like other members. Three research projects illustrate the importance of group conformity to the sociological understanding of group processes.

Asch's Research

Solomon Asch conducted an experiment in which "naive" subjects were asked to answer questions concerning the length of lines. Five to seven secret accomplices of the experimenter comprised the rest of the group. They purposely gave incorrect answers. Often the naive subject would give a "wrong" answer in order to conform. Figure 7-1 (p. 179) illustrates an example of the lines used in this experiment.

Milgram's Research

Stanley Milgram conducted an experiment which naive subjects believed was about learning and memory. The naive subject played the role of a "teacher" and the accomplice played the role of a "learner." If learners failed to correctly remember word pairs given by the teacher, the teacher was instructed by Milgram (a legitimate authority figure) to electrically shock the learner. His research suggests that people comply with almost blind obedience to authority figures. Further, if encouraged by others in a group situation, subjects were likely to administer even higher voltage shocks. The learners were not actually being shocked at all, but were play-acting as if they were. Naive subjects involved in this research found it to be a very stressful experience and this type of research remains very controversial.

Janis's Research

Irving Janis researched the actions of high government offi-cials by examining historical documents. He theorized that people in groups can be led to engage in behavior that violates common sense. Janis discusses three factors which affect decision-making processes and create *groupthink*, a reduced capacity for critical thinking caused by group conformity. The Kennedy administration's decision to invade Cuba is used as an example of this phenomenon.

Reference Groups

The term *reference group* signifies a social group that serves as a point of reference for people making evaluations and decisions. These groups can be primary or secondary. They are a major factor involved in anticipatory socialization processes.

Stouffer's Research

Stouffer conducted research on the morale and attitudes of soldiers in World War II in order to investigate the dynamics of reference groups. Stouffer found what appeared to be a paradox: Soldiers in branches with higher promotion rates were more pessimistic about their own chances of being promoted than soldiers in branches with lower rates of promotion. This is explained however by the identification of the groups against which the soldiers measured their progress. In relative terms, those soldiers in branches with higher rates felt deprived.

Ingroups and Outgroups

Two other kinds of groups provide us with standards against which we evaluate ourselves. People tend to perceive certain groups as more attractive to belong to than others. An *ingroup* is an esteemed social group commanding a member's loyalty. This group exists in relation to *outgroups*, or a scorned social group toward which one feels competition or opposition. This dichotomy allows us to sharpen boundaries between groups and to highlight their distinctive qualities. The operation of the group dynamics created by these distinctions affect broader social patterns in society, such as social inequality between blacks and whites.

Group Size

Group size significantly influences how members socially interact. As a group's membership is added to arithmetically, the number of possible relationships increases in a geometric progression. Figure 7-2 (p. 183) provides an illustration.

Georg Simmel studied social dynamics in small social groups. He differentiated between the *dyad*, a social group with two members, and the *triad*, a social group with three members. Each is identified as having certain unique qualities resulting in particular patterns of stability, intensity, and other socially significant variables.

Social Diversity

This section focuses on the research by Peter Blau who identifies four ways in which the structure of social groups regulates intergroup association. The four factors include group size, heterogeneity of group members, social parity within the group, and physical space.

Networks

The term *network* refers to a web of social ties that links people, often with little common identity and social interaction. Little sense of membership is felt by individuals in the network and only occasionally do they come into contact. Some can be operating at a primary level, but most are secondary in nature. Demographic characteristics, such as age, education, and residence patterns influence the likelihood of a person's involvement in networks.

FORMAL ORGANIZATIONS

Today our lives seem focused around *formal organizations*, or large, secondary groups that are formally organized to facilitate achieving their goals.

Types of Formal Organizations

Amitai Etzioni uses the variable of how members relate to the organization as a criteria for distinguishing three types of formal organizations.

Normative Organizations

People join *normative organizations* to pursue some goal they consider morally worthwhile. Voluntary associations like the PTA, the Red Cross, and the Lions Club would be examples. Traditionally, because women had been excluded from the labor force they have had higher participation rates in such organizations than men.

Coercive Organizations

Coercive organizations serve as a form of punishment (prisons) and treatment (mental hospitals). People are separated from the rest of society within distinct physical boundaries and are labeled as inmates or patients.

Utilitarian Organizations

Utilitarian organizations provide material benefits for members in exchange for labor. Most people must join at least one such organization in order to "make a living."

Origins of Bureaucracy

Formal organizations date back thousands of years. The type of formal organization called **bureaucracy** emerged as a result of changes occurring in societies in Europe and North America during the industrial revolution. A bureaucracy is an organizational model rationally designed to perform complex tasks efficiently. Our telephone system is illustrated to show examples of the scope and capacity of bureaucracies. Global map 7-1 (p. 188 shows an example (facsimile machine distribution by nation) of the extent of bureaucratic organization in the world today.

Characteristics of Bureaucracies

Max Weber identified six basic characteristics or elements of the ideal bureaucracy. These include: specialization, heirarchy or offices, rules and regulations, technical competence, impersonality, and formal, written communications.

Bureaucracy Versus Small Groups

In contrast to small groups, like a family, which have intrinsic value for its members, the organizational model of bureaucracy has at its heart a goal-oriented approach. It works to promote efficiency. Table 7-2 (p. 190) differentiates between the qualities of bureaucracies and small groups.

The Informal Side of Bureaucracy

While in principle bureaucracy has a highly formal structure, in reality not all behavior in bureaucracies fits precisely the organizational rules. While it is the position or office which is supposed to carry the power, the personalities of the occupants are important factors. Also, "grapevines" become an important source of information and interaction within such systems.

Limitations of Bureaucracy

Bureaucracy is not without its problems, and can be very unresponsive to individual needs. Being fair to the system of bureaucracy, some problems are the result of the fact organizations are not truly bureaucratic. Bureaucracies due tend to dehumanize those it serves through its impersonal operation. It also often alienates those who work within them. The **Critical Thinking** box (p. 192) discusses the question whether bureaucracy is a threat to personal privacy. Other problems are discussed below.

Bureaucratic Waste and Incompetence

Waste and incompetence are also features of bureaucracies. Parkinson's law, for example, states that "work expands to fill the time available for its completion." Also, the Peter principle states that bureaucrats are promoted to their level of incompetence. Both seem evident in bureaucratic systems to some degree.

Bureaucratic Ritualism

The image of red tape is closely tied to bureaucracies. *Bureaucratic ritualism* signifies a preoccupation with rules and regulations as ends in themselves rather than as means to organizational goals. This process tends to reduce performance and stifle creativity of members.

Bureaucratic Inertia

Bureaucracies seem to have lives of their own. *Bureaucratic inertia* refers to the tendency of bureaucratic organizations to persist over time.

Oligarchy

Robert Michels observed the fact that *oligarchy*, or the rule of the many by the few, was a typical outgrowth of bureaucracy. He suggested that individuals in high levels within a bureaucratic hierarchy tend to accumulate power and use it to promote their own objectives.

Gender and Race in Organizations

Rosabeth Moss Kanter, who is introduced in the **Profile** box (p. 195), points out that ascribed statuses such as gender and race often determine who holds power in bureaucratic hierarchies. Such stratification in term dramatically affects a person's on-the-job performance. Widely shared responsibility and opportunities for advancement in the company seem to be highly correlated with worker performance and creativity. Table 7-3 (p. 196) summarizes Kanter's findings comparing "advantaged" and "disadvantaged" employees.

"Humanizing" Bureaucracy

Humanizing bureaucracy means fostering an organizational environment that develops human resources. This seems to produce happier employees and better profits. Humanized organizational environments have certain basic characteristics which fall into three broad categories. These include: social inclusiveness, a sharing of responsibilities, and expanding opportunities for advancement.

Organizational Environment

Organizational environment refers to a range of factors outside an organization that affect its operation. This would include technology, politics, the economy, demographics, and other organizations. Each of these factors is briefly discussed.

Formal Organizations in Japan

Japan's economic success during the past few decades has raised great interest among Americans. Their formal organizations reflect their culture's collective identity and social solidarity. Americans, on the other hand, have stressed individuality. Japan's approach to constructing organizations makes bureaucracies remarkably personal. Five distinctions between Japanese and Western formal organizations are highlighted by William Ouchi. These include: hiring and advancement, lifetime security, holistic involvement, nonspecialized training, and collective decision-making. The Critical Thinking box (p. 198-99) addresses the issue of whether worker participation strategies similar to Japan's model will work in the U.S.

FORMAL ORGANIZATIONS AND SOCIETY

In recent years there has been a shift in focus from organizations themselves to organizational environments in which they operate. The Japanese success with more humanized and personal organizational environments has illustrated that organizations need not be impersonal. Collective identity and responsibility seems to be compatible with high organizational productivity.

PART IV: KEY CONCEPTS

Define each of the following concepts in the space provided or on a separate paper. Check the accuracy of your answers by referring to the key concepts section at the end of the chapter in the text as well as by referring to italicized definitions located throughout the chapter.

aggregates
authoritarian leader
bureaucracy
bureaucratic inertia
bureaucratic ritualism
category
coercive organization
democratic leader
dyad
expressive leadership
formal organizations
groupthink
humanizing bureaucracy
ingroup
instrumental leader
laissez-faire leader
network
normative organization
oligarchy
organizational environment
outgroup
Parkinson's law
Peter principle
primary group
secondary group
social group
triad
utilitarian organization

PART V: STUDY QUESTIONS

True-False

1. T F While members of aggregates could potentially become transformed into a social group, by definition members of categories cannot be transformed into groups.
2. T F Expressive leadership emphasizes the completion of tasks.

3. T F Stanley Milgram's research on group conformity patterns illustrated that most individuals are skeptical about the legitimacy of authority for people in positions of power.

4. T F Stouffer's research on soldier's attitudes toward their own promotions during World War II demonstrates the significance of reference groups in making judgments about ourselves.

5. T F According to research by Georg Simmel, larger groups tend to be more stable than small groups, such as dyads.

6. T F Networks tend to be more enduring and provide a greater sense of identify than most other types of social groups.

7. T F Normative organizations are defined as those which impose restrictions on people who have been labeled as deviant.

8. T F Bureaucracy is being defined in the text as an organi- zational model rationally designed to perform complex tasks.

9. T F Parkinson's Law and the Peter Principle relate to processes of bureaucratic waste and incompetency.

10. T F Kanter's research on hierarchies in organizations demonstrates that those members of a bureaucracy who have restricted opportunities often are the people who demonstrate the most creativity and have the highest aspirations to achieve.

Multiple-Choice

1. A social group characterized by long-term personal relationships usually involving many activities is a _____.

   (a) primary group   (d) aggregate
   (b) secondary group   (e) normative organization
   (c) category

2. Which of the following is not true of primary groups:

   (a) they provide security for their members
   (b) they are focused around specific activities
   (c) they are valued in and of themselves
   (d) they are viewed as ends in themselves

3. Which of the following theorists differentiated between primary and secondary groups:

   (a) Max Weber   (d) Charles Horton Cooley
   (b) Amitai Etzioni   (e) George Herbert Mead
   (c) Emile Durkheim

4. Which of the following is not identified in the text as a type of leadership decision-making style:

   (a) laissez-faire
   (b) democratic
   (c) authoritarian
   (d) utilitarian

5. Promoting group goals in social groups is least adequately accomplished when the leader is _____ in terms of decision-making style.

   (a) instrumental
   (b) democratic
   (c) authoritarian
   (d) laissez-faire

6. Which researcher concluded that people are not likely to question group opinion even when common sense dictates that they should:

   (a) Irving Janis
   (b) Hans Windler
   (c) Stanley Jacobson
   (d) Charles Kanter

7. The Kennedy administration's decision of invade Cuba is used as an example of:

   (a) ingroups and outgroups
   (b) reference groups
   (c) bureaucracy
   (d) oligarchy
   (e) groupthink

8. Amitai Etzioni constructed a typology of formal organizations. Organizations such as the PTA, Red Cross and United Way illustrate the type of organization he called:

   (a) utilitarian
   (b) coercive
   (c) normative
   (d) oligarchical

9. Which of the following is not a type of formal organization as identified by Amitai Etzioni:

   (a) coercive
   (b) normative
   (c) hierarchial
   (d) utilitarian

10. Bureaucratic ritualism is:

    (a) the process of promoting people to their level of incompetence
    (b) the tendency of bureaucratic organizations to persist over time
    (c) the rule of the many by the few
    (d) a preoccupation with rules and regulations as ends in themselves rather than as means toward organizational goals

11. Robert Michels identified one of the limitations of bureaucracy which involves the tendency of bureaucracy to become an oligarchy because:

    (a)   technical competence cannot be maintained
    (b)   bureaucrats abuse organizational power
    (c)   bureaucrats get caught up in rule-making
    (d)   specialization gives way to generalist orientations

12. According to Kanter's research:

    (a)   proper application of technology is the most significant factor in the success of bureaucracies
    (b)   oligarchy actually is the most effective bureaucratic structure during times of rapid technological change
    (c)   people are the company's most important resource
    (d)   humanizing bureaucracies would diminish productivity
    (e)   none of the above

Fill-In

1.   A _____ is defined as two or more people who identify with one another and have a distinctive pattern of interaction.
2.   Political organizations are examples of _____ groups.
3.   _____ leadership refers to group leadership that emphasizes the completion of tasks.
4.   _____ leaders focus on instrumental concerns, make decisions on their own, and demand strict compliance from subordinates.
5.   Irving Janis studied the group process he called _____ that reduces a group's capacity for critical reflection.
6.   A social group that consists of two members is a _____.
7.   A _____ is an organizational model rationally designed to perform complex tasks efficiently.
8.   Preoccupation with rules and regulations as ends to themselves rather than as a means to organizational goals is called _____.
9.   _____ is the term used to describe the tendency for bureaucratic organizations to persist over time.
10.   The cultural emphasis on individual achievement in our society finds its parallel in Japanese _____.

Definition and Short-Answer

1.   Differentiate between the qualities of bureaucracies and small groups. In what ways are they similar?

2. What are the three factors in decision-making processes in groups that lead to "groupthink?"

3. What are the major limitations of bureaucracy? Provide an example for each.

4. In what ways do bureaucratic organizations in Japan differ from those in the U.S.? What are the consequences of these differences?

5. Provide two examples of a coercive organization.

6. Differentiate between the concepts "aggregate" and "category."

7. Identify the basic types of leadership in groups (in terms of both "styles" and "decision-making" approach) and provide examples of the advantages and disadvantages for each type.

8. What are the three "paths" to a more humane organizational structure? How does Rosabeth Kanter's research relate to the humanizing of bureaucracy?

9. Review Peter Blau's research concerning how the structure of social groups regulates intergroup association.

10. Review the research by Janis, Milgram, and Asch concerning group conformity.

11. What are factors relating to the "organizational environment?" Provide an example for each.

PART VI: ANSWERS TO STUDY QUESTIONS

True-False

1.	F (p. 176)	6.	F (p. 185)
2.	F (p. 178)	7.	F (p. 186)
3.	F (p. 180)	8.	T (p. 187)
4.	T (p. 182)	9.	T (p. 191)
5.	T (p. 183)	10.	F (p. 194)

Multiple-Choice

1.	a (p. 176)	7.	e (p. 181)
2.	b (p. 176)	8.	c (p. 186)
3.	d (p. 176)	9.	c (p. 186)
4.	d (p. 178)	10.	d (p. 192)
5.	d (p. 178)	11.	b (pp. 193-94)
6.	a (p. 179)	12.	c (pp. 194-95)

Fill-In

1. social group (p. 176)
2. secondary (p. 177)
3. instrumental (p. 178)
4. authoritarian (p. 179)
5. groupthink (p. 181)

6.   dyad (p. 183)
7.   bureaucracy (p. 187)
8.   bureaucratic ritualism (pp. 192-93)
9.   bureaucratic inertia (p. 193)
10. groupism (p. 200)

PART VII: ANALYSIS AND COMMENT

Profiles

"Charles Horton Cooley" (1864-1929)

    Key Points: Questions:

"Rosabeth Moss Kanter"

    Key Points: Questions:

Critical Thinking

"Bureaucracy and the Information Revolution: A Threat to Privacy?"

    Key Points: Questions:

Cross-Cultural Comparison

"The Japanese Model: Will It Work In the United States?"

    Key Points: Questions:

Deviance

8

PART I: CHAPTER OUTLINE

I.   What Is Deviance?
     A.   Social Control
     B.   The Biological Context
          1.   Early Research
          2.   Delinquency and Body Structure
          3.   Recent Research
     C.   Personality Factors
     D.   The Social Foundations of Deviance
II. Structural-Functional Analysis
     A.   Emile Durkheim: The Functions of Deviance
          1.   An Illustration: The Puritans of Massachusetts Bay
     B.   Robert Merton: Strain Theory
     C.   Deviant Subcultures
     D.   Hirschi's Control Theory
III. Symbolic-Interaction Analysis
     A.   Labeling Theory
          1.   Primary and Secondary Deviance
          2.   Stigma
          3.   Retrospective Labeling
          4.   Labeling and Mental Illness
     B.   The Medicalization of Deviance
     C.   Sutherland's Differential Association Theory
IV. Social-Conflict Analysis
     A.   Deviance and Capitalism
     B.   White-Collar Crime
V.   Deviance and Gender
VI. Crime
     A.   Types of Crime
     B.   Criminal Statistics
     C.   The "Street" Criminal: A Profile
     D.   Crime In Global Perspective
VII. The Criminal Justice System
     A.   The Police

B.   The Courts
C.   Punishment
VIII. Summary
IX.   Key Concepts
X.   Suggested Readings

PART II: LEARNING OBJECTIVES

1.   To explain how deviance is interpreted as a product of society from the sociological perspective.
2.   To explain the historical and recent biological explanations for deviance.
3.   To evaluate the explanatory views of biological theories of deviance.
4.   To explain the psychological explanation of deviance.
5.   To evaluate the explanatory views of psychological theory of deviance.
6.   To explain the sociological explanations of deviance focusing upon the main sociological paradigms.
7.   To compare and contrast different theories representative of these main paradigms.
8.   To evaluate empirical evidence used to support these different sociological theories of deviance.
9.   To distinguish among the types of crime.
10.   To know the limitations of criminal statistics
11.   To identify the elements of our criminal justice system.

PART III: CHAPTER REVIEW

This chapter addresses a number of questions concerning deviance. For instance, How do societies confront what is "offensive and disagreeable"? How and why does deviance occur? And, do all people who violate norms become labeled as deviants? The introduction to this chapter discusses the Rodney King incident. The questions raised involve the issues of whether or not excessive force was used and whether this case involves racism.

WHAT IS DEVIANCE?

Deviance is the recognized violation of cultural norms. It is a very broad concept. Many characteristics are used by members of society in identifying deviance. One familiar type of deviance is *crime*, or the violation of norms formally enacted into criminal law. A special category of crime is *juvenile delinquency*, or the violation of legal standards that apply to the young.

It is pointed out that deviance can be negative or positive, but that it stems from *difference* that causes us to react to another person as an "outsider."

Social Control

Social control is defined as attempts by society to regulate the behavior of individuals. Like deviance, it takes many forms, both positive and negative, and involves a complex process. A very structured form is called the *criminal justice system*, or a formal system that responds to alleged violations of the law through using police, courts, and punishment.

The Biological Context

Early Research

During the latter part of the 19th century Caesare Lombroso, an Italian physician who worked in prisons, suggested that criminals have distinctive physical traits. He viewed them as "evolutionary throwbacks to lower forms of life." Lombroso's research was scientifically flawed. Several decades later, Charles Giring, a British psychiatrist, more scientifically conducted a comparison of prisoners and people living in society and found no overall physical differences.

Delinquency and Body Structure

During the middle of this century William Sheldon suggested that body structure was a critical link to criminal behavior. He identified three distinctive body types, *ectomorphs*, *endomorphs*, and *mesomorphs*. He reported a positive correlation between mesomorphs, or the muscular, athletic body type and criminality. Subsequent research by Sheldon and Eleanor Glueck has supported this argument; however, they argue that the body structure is not the cause of the delinquency. They stress the importance of social processes in provoking certain types of people to become delinquent.

Recent Research

Since the 1960s new knowledge in the field of genetics has rejuvenated interest in the study of biological causes of criminality. The connection between a specific pattern of chromosomes, the *XYY* structure, has been shown to be related to deviant behavior. In its attempt to explain crime in terms of physical traits alone, this approach provides a limited understanding of its causes. Further, genetic research is so recent, effects of genes on behavior are still very speculative. Further, how it is that specific behavior comes to be defined as deviant cannot be answered using this biological perspective. Overall, research findings lead us to the understanding that the interaction of genetic and social influences is significant in affecting the patterns of deviant behavior in society.

Personality Factors

Psychological explanations of deviance concentrate on personality abnormalities, and so like biological theories are focused on "individualistic" characteristics.

Containment theory posits the view that juvenile delinquency (among boys) is a result of social pressure to commit deviant acts in the absence of moral values and a positive self-image. The presence of morality and good self-image is theorized to contain deviance. Longitudinal research conducted by Walter Reckless and Simon Dinitz during the 1960s supported this conclusion.

Our author points out that there are weaknesses to psychological research, however. First, most serious crime is committed by people who are not psychologically abnormal. Second, cross-cultural differences in what is deemed normal and abnormal tends to be ignored. And three, the fact that people with similar psychological qualities are not equally as likely to be labeled deviant is not considered.

The Social Functions of Deviance

Deviance is not simply a matter of free choice or personal failings. Both conformity and deviance are shaped by society. Our author points out this is evident in three ways. Deviance exists only in relation to cultural norms; people become deviant as others define them that way, and both rule-making and rule-breaking involve social power.

STRUCTURAL-FUNCTIONAL ANALYSIS

Emile Durkheim: The Functions of Deviance

While on the surface deviance may appear to be harmful only for society, Emile Durkheim asserted that deviance is an integral part of all societies and serves four major functions. These include affirming cultural values and norms, clarifying moral boundaries, promoting social unity, and encouraging social change. An interesting illustration of this last point is presented in the **Sociology of Everyday Life** box (p. 211) entitled "Rock and Roll: From Deviance to Big Business."

An Illustration: The Puritans of Massachusetts Bay

Kai Erikson's historical research on this highly religious society supports Durkheim's theory concerning the functions of deviance. For these people deviance helped clarify various moral boundaries. Over time, he noted, what was defined as deviant changed as social and environmental conditions changed. However, what remained constant was the proportion of people viewed as deviant.

Robert Merton: Strain Theory

According to Merton, deviance is encouraged by the day-to-day operation of society. Analysis using strain theory points out imbalances between socially endorsed "means" available to different groups of people and the widely held goals and values in society. As a result of this structured inequality of opportunity, some people are prone to anomie. This leads to higher proportions of deviance in those groups experiencing anomie. Four adaptive strategies, or deviant responses, are identified by Merton: innovation, ritualism, retreatism, and rebellion. Table 8-1 (p. 212) outlines the components of this theory. Conformity, or the acceptance of both cultural goals and means is seen as the result of successful socialization and the opportunity to pursue these goals through socially approved means. The **Social Diversity** box (p. 213) discusses Al Capone's life as an example of Merton's "innovation" mode of adaptation for those experiencing social marginality.

As insightful as Merton is in recognizing the importance of social structural elements in causing deviance, there are some inadequacies of this approach. First, it is difficult to measure precisely how much deviance is actually caused by strain. Second, some kinds of deviance, like mental illness and homosexuality, are not adequately explained using this perspective. Third, Merton is not precise about why one response to strain is chosen over another by an individual. And fourth, the extent to which the variability of cultural values creates different concepts of personal success is not incorporated into this model very well.

Deviant Subcultures

Researchers Richard Cloward and Lloyd Ohlin have attempted to extend the work of Merton utilizing the concept of relative opportunity structure. They argue criminal deviance occurs when there is limited opportunity to achieve success and also limited availability of illegitimate opportunities. They further suggest that criminal subcultures emerge to organize and expand systems of deviance. Al Capone's life is an example. In poor and highly transient neighborhoods "conflict subcultures" (i.e., violent gangs) are more often the form this process takes. Those who fail to achieve success using legitimate means are likely to fall into "retreatist subcultures" (i.e., alcoholics).

Albert Cohen found that deviant subcultures occur more often in the lower classes and are based on values that oppose the dominant culture. Walter Miller, while agreeing that deviant subcultures are more likely to develop in the lower classes, suggests that the values which emerge are not a reaction against the middle-class way of life. Rather, he suggests that their values emerge out of daily experiences within contexts of limited opportunities. He described six focal concerns of these delinquent subcultures, trouble, toughness, smartness, excitement, fate, and autonomy.

Hirschi's Control Theory

Hirschi's point is that what really requires explanation is conformity. He suggests conformity results from four types of social controls: attachment, commitment, involvement, and belief. Once again, a person's position in the social structural system is important in determining one's likelihood of being involved in subcultural deviance.

Structural-functional analysis focuses our attention on the linkage between deviance and social norms and structures. However, three limitations to this approach are pointed out. First, functionalists assume a single, dominant culture even though research reveals American society to be comprised of a variety of cultural patterns with competing ideas about what constitutes deviance. Second, the assumption that deviance occurs primarily among the poor is a weakness of the subcultural theories of deviance. Third, the view that the definition of being deviant will be applied to all who violate norms is inadequate.

SYMBOLIC-INTERACTION ANALYSIS

The symbolic-interaction paradigm focuses attention on the creation of different social realities in society and the extent to which these create distinguishable understandings of what deviance is.

Labeling Theory

Labeling theory, the assertion that deviance and conformity result from the response of others, stresses the relativity of deviance. Of critical significance to proponents of this perspective is the process by which people label others as deviant.

Primary and Secondary Deviance

Edwin Lember has distinguished between the concepts of *primary deviance*, relating to activity that is initially defined as deviant, and *secondary deviance*, corresponding to a person who accepts the label of deviant.

Stigma

Erving Goffman suggested secondary deviance is the beginning of a "deviant career." This typically results as a consequence of acquiring a *stigma*, or a powerful negative social label that radically changes a person's social identity and self-concept. Some people may go through a "*degradation ceremony*," like a criminal prosecution, where a community formally condemns the person for deviance allegedly committed.

Retrospective Labeling

Retrospective labeling is the interpretation of someone's past consistent with present deviance. In this case, other people selectively rethink the "deviant's" past, arguing all the evidence was there that would inevitably become a problem.

Labeling and Mental Illness

Theorist Thomas Szaz has argues the concept "mental illness" should stop being applied to people. He says that only the "body" can become ill, and mental illness is therefore a myth. Szaz suggests the label mental illness is attached to people who are different and who concern the status quo of society. It acts as a justification for forcing people to comply with cultural norms.

Erving Goffman concurs with this perspective to the extent that he feels oftentimes a person is sent to a mental institution for the benefit of the status quo. The label of mental illness becomes an extremely powerful stigma and can act as a self-fulfilling prophecy.

The Medicalization of Deviance

Over the last fifty years the field of medicine has had a tremendous influence on how deviance has been understood and explained. The *medicalization of deviance* relates to the transformation of moral and legal issues into medical matters. Instead of seeing conformity and deviance as matters of "bad" and "good," we conceive the dichotomy as one of "well" versus "sick." The general view of alcoholism in our society is a good illustration of this process in recent years.

There are cases however that are more complex. Homosexuality, for example, has historically been viewed as deviance from a moral perspective, medical perspective, and as merely a "form of sexual behavior."

Whichever approach is used, moral or medical, will have considerable consequences for those labeled as deviant. Questions concerning the effects of who responds to deviance, how people respond to deviance, and the personal competence of the person labeled as deviant are also addressed.

Sutherland's Differential Association Theory

Edwin Sutherland suggests that deviance is learned through association with others. Accordingly, a person's likelihood of violating norms is dependent upon the frequency of association with those who encourage norm violation. This perspective is known as differential association theory. A survey research study is reviewed supporting this view. However, limitations concern a lack of focus on why society defines certain behavior as deviant and other behavior as not deviant. Unlike other theories which focus on the act of deviance, the focus of labeling theory is on the reaction of people to perceived deviance. Limitations on this very relativistic view of deviance include an overlooking of certain inconsistencies in the actual consequences of deviant labeling for people, the assumption that all people resist the deviant label, and limited research on actual response of members of society to people labeled deviant.

SOCIAL-CONFLICT ANALYSIS

Social inequality serves as the basis of social-conflict theory as it relates to deviance. Certain less powerful people in society tend to be defined as deviant. This pattern is explained in three ways. First, the norms of society generally reflect the interests of the status quo. Second, even if the behavior of the powerful is questioned they have the resources to resist deviant labels. And third, laws and norms are usually never questioned, being viewed as "natural."

Deviance and Capitalism

Steven Spitzer has suggested that deviant labels are attached to people who interfere with capitalism. These people he refers to as "problem populations." Four qualities of capitalism are critical to recognize in order to understand who is labeled as deviant. These are: private ownership, production labor, respect for authority, and acceptance of the status quo. He differentiates between two types of problem populations. One, represented by nonproductive, but nonthreatening members of society he labels as "*social junk*." Another, characterized by people perceived as directly threatening to the capitalist system he calls "*social dynamite*." Spitzer says that capitalism itself creates these groups, though the individuals themselves are blamed for their own problems.

White-Collar Crime

The concept *white-collar crime*, or crimes committed by persons of high social position in the course of their occupations, was defined by Edwin Sutherland in the 1940s. This type of crime involves powerful people taking illegal advantage of their occupational position. While it is estimated that the harm done to society by white-collar crime is greater than street crime, most people are not particularly concerned about this form of deviance. This is in part illustrated by the fact that violators who are caught are typically dealt with in civil court rather than criminal court.

Social-conflict theory focuses our attention on the significance of power and inequality in understanding how deviance is defined and controlled. However, several weaknesses of this approach have been identified. The assumption that the rich and powerful directly create and control cultural norms is questionable given the nature of our political process. Further, the approach seems to overgeneralize the cost of white-collar crime relative to street crime. Finally, the approach suggests that only when inequality exists is there deviance, yet all societies exhibit types of deviance, and as Durkheim has pointed out deviance can be functional.

Table 8-2 (p. 223) summarizes the major contributions of each of the sociological explanations of deviance.

Deviance and Gender

The significance of gender in the study of deviant behavior has historically been ignored in sociological research. The behavior of males and females has tended to be evaluated using different standards and the process of labeling has been sex-biased. The **Critical Thinking** box (pp. 224-25) takes a look at the issue of date rape, exposing some dangerous myths threatening to women.

CRIME

What is viewed as criminal varies over both time and place. What all crime has in common is that perceived violations bring about response from a formal criminal justice system. Crime contains two elements, the act and the intent. The latter is a variable concept.

Types of Crime

Two major types of crime are recorded by the FBI in its statistical reports as "index crime." One, *crimes against the person,* or violent crimes, are defined as crimes against people that involve violence, or the threat of violence. Examples are murder, rape, aggravated assault, and robbery. And two, *crimes against property*, or property crimes, defined as crimes that involve theft of property belonging to others. Examples are burglary, larceny-theft, auto theft, and arson.

A third category, *victimless crime*, is defined as violations of law in which there are no readily apparent victims. Examples are gambling, prostitution and the use of illegal drugs.

Criminal Statistics

The FBI statistics indicate that crime dramatically rose during the 1970s, declined during the early 1980s, and since has been rising again. Figure 8-1 (p. 227) shows the trends and relative frequencies for types of both violent and property crime.

It is pointed out that these official statistics are far from accurate. First, they only include cases known by the police. People sometimes may not know they have been victimized, or may be reluctant to report a crime to the police. Victimization surveys suggest that the actual crime rate may be three times higher than official statistics show.

The "Street" Criminal: A Profile

The likelihood of engaging in crime increases sharply during adolescence and declines thereafter. While only 16% of the population is between the ages of 15-24, this age group accounts for over 50% of all arrests.

Statistics indicate crime to be predominantly a male activity. Males are four times more likely than women to be arrested. However, recent evidence suggests the disparity is shrinking.

While most people believe that poor people simply commit more crime, the situation is actually more complex. Research suggests crime rates across social strata are relatively equivalent; it is the types of crimes committed which vary. Variation also exists in the victimization of people of different social strata by different types of crime.

The relationship between race and crime is also discussed as being very complex. While blacks, proportionally speaking, are arrested for "index crime" more than whites, three factors make this connection between race and crime very tenuous. First, arrest records are not statements of proven guilt. Second, race is closely related to social class. And third, white-collar and other crimes more representative of the white population are not counted in the statistics.

Crime in Global Perspective

Relative to European societies, America has a very high crime rate. Figure 8-2 (p. 230) compares rates of rape and robbery in societies around the world.

Several reasons for the relatively high rates in the U.S. have been offered. First, our culture emphasizes individual economic success. Second, families are weakened without guaranteed family incomes and child care. Third, the high levels of unemployment and underemployment create chronically poor categories of people. Finally, our society encourages private ownership of guns. All of these factors, says Elliot Currie, combine to encourage criminality.

Global Map 8-1 (p. 232) looks at prostitution worldwide. Rates for prostitution by society seem to vary with the relative status of women in the societies.

THE CRIMINAL JUSTICE SYSTEM

The criminal justice system is comprised of three component parts. These are:

The Police

The police represent the point of contact between the public and the criminal justice system. They are responsible for maintaining public order by uniformly enforcing the law. However, particularly because of the relatively small number of police in our population, they must exercise much discretion about which situations receive their attention. Seven "external clues" used by police to help them decide how to carry out their duties are discussed.

The Courts

It is within this component of the system where guilt or innocence is determined. *Plea bargaining* is a major practice in resolving cases. It is defined as a legal negotiation in which the prosecution reduces a charge in exchange for a guilt plea. This saves both time and expense, but it is a very controversial element within our court system.

Punishment

Four justifications for using punishment as part of our criminal justice system are given. These include: *retribution*, or subjecting an offender to suffering comparable to that caused by the offense; *deterrence*, or the attempt to discourage criminality through punishment; *rehabilitation*, or reforming the offender to preclude subsequent offenses; and *social protection*, or rendering an offender incapable of further offenses either temporarily during a period of incarceration or permanently by execution. These justifications of punishment are summarized in Table 8-3 (p. 235).

While these justifications are widely recognized, demonstrating their consequences is very problematic. Their relative effectiveness is questioned given the high *criminal recidivism* rates, or subsequent offenses by people previously convicted of crimes.

PART IV: KEY CONCEPTS

Define each of the following concepts in the space provided or on separate paper. Check the accuracy of your answers by referring to the key concepts section at the end of the chapter in the text as well as by referring to italicized definitions located throughout the chapter.

civil law
containment theory
conflict subculture
conformity
control theory
crime
crimes against property
crimes against the person
criminal justice system
criminal law
criminal recidivism
criminal subculture
deterrence
deviance
differential association
ectomorph
endomorph
index crime
juvenile delinquency
labeling theory
medicalization of deviance
mesomorph
plea bargaining
primary deviance

rebellion
rehabilitation
retreatism
retreatist subculture
retribution
retrospective labeling
secondary deviance
social control
social junk
stigma
white-collar crime
victimless crime
victimization survey
XYY chromosome pattern

PART V: STUDY QUESTIONS

True-False

1. T F   Social sanctions can be either positive or negative.
2. T F   Containment theory focuses our attention on how certain behaviors are linked to or contained in genetic structures within our biological make up.
3. T F   Deviance exists and varies according to cultural norms.
4. T F   In Robert Merton's strain theory the concept anomie is applied by linking deviance to certain social imbalances.
5. T F   Walter Miller's subcultural theory of deviance points out that delinquent boys tend to have no "focal concerns" in life.
6. T F   Primary deviance tends to be more harmful to society than secondary deviance.
7. T F   Thomas Szaz argues that mental illness is a myth and is a label used by the powerful in society to force people to follow dominant cultural norms.
8. T F   Our author suggests that during the last fifty years there as been a trend away from what is known as the "medicalization of deviance."
9. T F   Sutherland's differential association theory suggests that certain individuals are incapable of learning from experience and therefore are more likely to become deviant.
10. T F "White-collar crime" is defined as crime committed by persons of high social position in the course of their occupations.
11. T F Most "index crimes" in the U.S. are committed by white people.
12. T F Using "index crimes," the crime rate in the U.S. is relatively high compared to European societies.

111

Multiple-Choice

1. Which of the following is not a social foundation of deviance according to our author:

    (a) deviance exists in relation to cultural norms
    (b) people become deviant in that others define them that way
    (c) both norms and the way people define social situations involve social power
    (d) all are identified as foundations of deviance
    (e) none are identified as foundations of deviance

2. Containment theory is an example of a(n) _____ explanation of deviance.

    (a) biological   (d) sociological
    (b) psychological   (e) none of the above
    (c) anthropological

3. Which of the following theories is not derived from Durkheim's analysis of anomie:

    (a) Hirschi's control theory
    (b) Merton's strain theory
    (c) Cloward and Ohlin's deviant subculture theory
    (d) Becker's labeling theory

4. Emile Durkheim theorized that all but which of the following are functions of deviance:

    (a) it clarifies moral boundaries
    (b) it affirms cultural values and norms
    (c) it encourages social stability
    (d) it promotes social unity

5. Which contribution below is attributed to the structural-functional theory of deviance:

    (a) deviance always has negative consequences for society
    (b) deviance is inherent in the operation of society
    (c) the reactions of others to deviance are highly variable
    (d) laws and other norms reflect the interests of the powerful in society

6. Kai Erikson's historical research on the Puritans of Massachusetts Bay supports:

   (a) Durkheim's structural-functional perspective concerning the functions of deviance
   (b) the psychological theory of containment
   (c) the genetic inbreeding theory of deviance
   (d) the body structure theory of deviance
   (e) the social conflict theory of deviance

7. A theory of deviance that explains deviance in terms of the relative opportunity structure available to various categories of young people is called:

   (a) containment theory   (d) labeling theory
   (b) strain theory   (e) The XYY theory
   (c) differential association theory

8. Which of the following is not an example of a factor in Hirschi's control theory of conformity:

   (a) attachment   (c) ritualism
   (b) belief   (d) commitment

9. When Joan, an overweight child of six, is first taunted by other children as a "fatty" and "pig" she is experiencing what sociologists call:

   (a) recidivism   (c) degradation ceremony
   (b) primary deviance   (d) secondary deviance

10. The statements: While what is deviant may vary, deviance itself is found in all societies. Deviance and the social response it provokes serve to maintain the moral foundation of society. Deviance can direct social change. All of these help summarize which sociological explanation of deviance:

    (a) structural-functional   (d) social-conflict
    (b) symbolic-interaction   (e) labeling
    (c) exchange

11. Which of the following are included as part of the FBI report on crime in The U.S.:

    (a) white-collar crime and property crime
    (b) victimless crime and federal crime
    (c) crime against the state and civil crime
    (d) crime against the person and crime against property
    (e) violent crime and white-collar crime

Fill-In

1. The _____ _____ _____ is a formal reaction to alleged violations of the law through the use of police, courts, and punishment.
2. Tall, thin, and fragile individuals would be characterized as having the _____ body type.
3. A psychological explanation of deviance which posits the view that if boys have developed strong moral values and a positive self-image they will not become delinquents is called _____ theory.
4. The strain theory of deviance is based on the _____ paradigm.
5. For Hirschi, what requires explanation is not deviance, but _____.
6. Activity that is initially defined as deviant is called _____ deviance. On the other hand, a person who accepts the label of deviant may then engage in _____ deviance, or behavior caused by the person's incorporating the deviant label into their self-concept.
7. _____ law refers to general regulations involving economic losses between private parties.
8. _____ surveys show that the actual level of crime is three times as great as that indicated by official reports.
9. The American criminal justice system consists of three elements: _____, _____, _____.
10. Subsequent offenses by people previously convicted of crimes is termed _____.

Definition and Short-Answer

1. According to Hirschi's control theory there are four types of social controls. What are these? Provide an example of each.
2. According to Merton's strain theory, what are the four deviant responses by individuals to dominant cultural patterns?
3. What are the functions of deviance according to Durkheim?
4. What characteristics are likely to have people labeled as being a member of a "problem population" according to Spitzer?
5. How do researchers using the differential association theory explain deviance?
6. What is meant by the term "medicalization of deviance"?
7. According to Elliot Currie, what factors are responsible for the relatively high crime rates in the U.S.?
8. What are the four justifications for the use of punishment against criminals?
9. What are the social foundations of deviance? Illustrate each.
10. Summarize the basic explanations of deviance using each of the following perspectives: social-conflict, symbolic-interactionism, and structural-functionalism.

PART VI: ANSWERS TO STUDY QUESTIONS

True-False

1.	T (p. 207)		7.	T (p. 217)	
2.	F (p. 209)		8.	F (p. 217)	
3.	T (p. 209)		9.	F (p. 218)	
4.	T (p. 212)		10.	T (p. 221)	
5.	F (p. 214)		11.	T (p. 229)	
6.	F (p. 216)		12.	T (p. 230)	

Multiple-Choice

1.	d (pp. 209-10)		7.	b (p. 212)	
2.	b (p. 209)		8.	c (p. 215)	
3.	d (pp. 210-15)		9.	b (p. 216)	
4.	c (p. 210)		10.	a (p. 223)	
5.	b (p. 210)		11.	d (p. 226)	
6.	a (p. 211)				

Fill-In

1. criminal justice system (p. 207)
2. ectomorph (p. 208)
3. containment (p. 209)
4. structural-functional (p. 212)
5. conformity (pp. 214-15)
6. primary/secondary (p. 216)
7. civil law (p. 222)
8. victimization (p. 226)
9. the police, the courts, punishment (p. 231)
10. criminal recidivism (p. 235)

PART VII: ANALYSIS AND COMMENT

Sociology of Everyday Life

"Rock and Roll: From Deviance to Big Business"

Key Points:

Questions:

Social Diversity

"Al Capone: Crime and Marginality"

    Key Points:

    Questions:

Critical Thinking

"Date Rape: Exposing Dangerous Myths"

    Key Points:

    Questions:

Social Stratification

9

PART I: CHAPTER OUTLINE

I.   What is Social Stratification?
II.   Caste and Class Systems
    A.   The Caste System
        1.   Illustrations: India and South Africa
    B.   The Class System
    C.   Caste and Class Together: Great Britain
        1.   The Estate System
        2.   Great Britain Today
    D.   Another Example: Japan
        1.   Feudal Japan
        2.   Japan Today
    E.   The Former Soviet Union
        1.   A Classless Society?
        2.   The Second Soviet Revolution
    F.   Ideology
III.   The Functions of Social Stratification
    A.   The Davis-Moore Thesis
    B.   Stratification and Conflict
        1.   Marx's View of Social Class
        2.   Why No Marxist Revolution?
        3.   Max Weber: Class, Status, and Power
IV.   Stratification and Technology in Global Perspective
V.   Social Stratification: Facts and Values
VI.   Summary
VII.   Key Concepts
VIII. Suggested Readings

PART II: LEARNING OBJECTIVES

1. To understand the four basic principles of social stratification.
2. To differentiate between two systems of stratification: caste and class, and to be able to provide historical and cross-cultural examples of each.
3. To know the relationship between culture and stratification.
4. To differentiate between the structural-functional and social-conflict perspectives of stratification.
5. To understand the views of Max Weber concerning the dimensions of social class.
6. To know the synthesis approach to understanding social stratification put forward by the Lenskis.

PART III: CHAPTER REVIEW

WHAT IS SOCIAL STRATIFICATION?

Social inequality, referring to the unequal distribution of valued resources, is found in every society. Some of the inequality is the result of individual differences in ability and effort. However, it also relates to society. *Social stratification* refers to a system by which categories of people in society are ranked in a hierarchy. This chapter opens with an illustration of the sinking of the *Titanic* to show the consequences of social inequality in terms of who survived the disaster and who did not. Four principles are identified which help explain why social stratification exists. First, social stratification is a characteristic of society and not merely of individuals. Second, social stratification is universal but variable. Third, it persists over generations. And, fourth, it is supported by patterns of belief.

CASTE AND CLASS SYSTEMS

Sociologists distinguish between two general systems of social stratification based on the degree of social mobility representative of the system.

The Caste System

A *caste system* is a system of social stratification based on ascription. Pure caste systems are "closed" with no social mobility. Two different stratification systems representing elements of a caste are discussed.

Illustrations: India and South Africa

The Hindu social system of rural India and racial apartheid in South Africa are used to illustrate caste systems. In such systems three factors underlie the fact that ascription determines virtually everything about a person's life. First, birth determines one's occupation. Second, marriage unites people of the same social standing through the rule of endogamy. And, third, powerful cultural beliefs underlie such systems. The **Cross-Cultural Comparison** box (pp. 242-43) discusses the situation in South Africa where apartheid has created a caste type system based on race.

The Class System

Representative of industrial societies, *class systems* are defined as systems of social stratification based on individual achievement. Social categories are not as rigidly defined as in the caste system. Individual ability, promoted by open social mobility, is critical to this system. Other factors characteristic of industrial economies which are central to such a system are high levels of migration to cities, democratic principles, and high immigration rates. *Status consistency*, or the consistent ranking across various dimensions of social standing, also distinguishes between caste and class systems. Class systems tend to have less status consistency.

Caste and Class Together: Great Britain

England represents a society where caste qualities of its agrarian past still are interwoven within the modern day industrial class system.

The Estate System

Great Britain's agrarian past, with deep historical roots, was based on a caste-like estate system. Three estates, the first (nobles), the second (primarily clergy), and the third (commoners) comprised this system. The law of *primogeniture* by which property of parents could only be inherited by the eldest son helped maintain this system.

Great Britain Today

Aspects of their feudal past persist today. For example, a monarch still stands as Britain's head of state, and descendants of traditional nobility still maintain inherited wealth and property. However, power in government resides in the House of Commons, which is comprised of people who have achieved their positions. Today, about 25% of Great Britain's population falls into the middle-class, and 50% into the working-class. Almost 25% are "poor." Their system reflects a class system, with an unequal distribution of wealth, power, and prestige. Though opportunities for social mobility are present they are not as numerous as those which represent the United States. Their class system is reflected in different linguistic patterns between social classes.

Another Example: Japan

Like Great Britain, Japan mixes both the traditional and contemporary in their social stratification system.

Feudal Japan

For many centuries of agrarian feudalism, Japan was one of the most rigidly stratified cultures in the world. An imperial family maintained a network of regional nobility *shoguns*, or powerful warlords of the nobility, who fought each other for control of the land. A warrior caste, called *samurai*, fell just below the nobility. The majority of people were commoners, like serfs in feudal Europe. However, there was an additional ranking, called *burakumin*, or outcasts, who were below the commoners.

Japan Today

Industrialization, urbanization, and intercultural contact have dramatically changed Japan over the last century. The nobility lost its legal standing after World War II. For many though, tradition is still revered and family background continues to remain important in determining social status. Male dominance, as an example, continues to be more extreme than in the West.

The Former Soviet Union

The "new Commonwealth," formally the Soviet Union, has experienced great changes during the last few years. We are perhaps seeing a second Russian revolution

A Classless Society?

The Soviet Union, created through the 1917 revolution, has claimed itself to be a classless society because of the elimination of private ownership of the productive components of society. Yet, it remains socially stratified as occupations generally fall into four major categories: high government officials, the intelligentsia, manual laborers, and rural peasantry.

The Second Soviet Revolution

The reforms spurred by Mikhail Gorbachev's economic program known as *perestroika*, or "restructuring", has been significant. But, economic reform has been complicated by a number of factors, including the need to acquire advanced technology and to cut military spending.

Interestingly, research has suggested that there has been more upward social mobility in the Soviet Union than in Japan, Great Britain, or the United States over the last century. A major reason for this is what sociologists call *structural social mobility*, or social mobility by large numbers of people that is due to changes in society and the economy rather than to efforts of individuals.

Ideology

For the ancient Greek philosopher Plato, a people's sense of stratification formed the basis of justice. For Marx, it created social injustice. In any event, social institutions ensure that systems of social stratification endure. Generally, members of society tend to accept their system of social stratification as fair. The role of culture in promoting values that support the system is critical in ensuring acceptance. *Ideology*, or ideas that reflect and support the interests of some portion of society, is the link between culture and stratification. However, over time people inevitably begin to question cultural "truths." The example of American women questioning the assumptions of their "place in society" over the last three decades is evidence of this fact. The **Critical Thinking** box (p. 251) discusses the issues of justice and inequality by putting things into historical perspective.

THE FUNCTIONS OF SOCIAL STRATIFICATION

The Davis-Moore Thesis

The Davis-Moore thesis asserts that some degree of social stratification actually serves society, and is even a social necessity. They theorize that certain tasks in society are of more value than others, and in order to ensure the most qualified people fill these positions they must be rewarded better than others. As society approaches a *meritocracy*, or a system linking rewards to personal merit, it becomes more productive. Melvin Tumin, a critic of this view, argues that certain highly rewarded occupations seem no more intrinsically important than other less valued jobs. The **Critical Thinking** box (p. 253) illustrates a few examples. He also points out ascribed statuses still remain as significant factors in our society. Further, social stratification creates conflict as well, so it is not merely functional.

Stratification and Conflict

Marx's View of Social Class
Marx's view of social stratification is based on his observations of industrialization in Europe during the second half of the 19th century. He saw a class division between the *capitalists* (owners of the means of production) and the *workers* (proletariat). This resulted in separation and inevitable conflict. As influential as Marx's thinking has been for sociological understanding of social stratification, it does overlook its motivating value. The insight provided by the Davis-Moore thesis perhaps explains, in part, the low productivity characteristic of Eastern Europe under socialism.

Why no Marxist Revolution?

The overthrow of the capitalist system has not occurred for at least four central reasons. First, the capitalist class has become fragmented over the last century. A larger managerial class with numerous stockholders has also developed. Second, the proletariat

121

has been significantly changed by the "white-collar revolution." A century ago the vast majority of workers in America had *blue-collar occupations*, or work involving mostly manual labor. Today, most members of the labor force hold *white-collar occupations*, or work that involves mostly mental activity and nonmanual skills. Most of this change has occurred through structural social mobility. A third factor involves the fact that the workers' conditions have improved and they are not as "desperate" as Marx envisioned them in his time. Finally, legal protection has been widely expanded for workers.

The value of Marx's perspective is still significant. There continues to be exploitation of workers, and a small percentage of people control the vast majority of wealth in our society. Table 9-1 (p. 256) compares and contrasts the structural-functional and social-conflict explanations of social stratification.

Max Weber: Class, Status, and Power

Max Weber viewed Marx's ideas of social class as being too simplistic. Weber theorized that there were three dimensions of social inequality, class, status, and power. These dimensions are continuous in quality such that a person's social prestige might be relatively higher or lower than another's. Weber also theorized that a single individual's rankings on the three dimensions might be quite different. Thus, a multidimensional aspect of social inequality was important to him. The term used today to reflect this idea is *socioeconomic status* referring to a composite social ranking based on various dimensions of social inequality.

STRATIFICATION AND TECHNOLOGY IN GLOBAL PERSPECTIVE

The Lenskis sociocultural evolutionary model of historical change concerning social stratification combines both structural-functional and social-conflict perspectives. In technologically simple societies age and sex tend to be the only basis of social stratification. As technology advances and surpluses in valued resources occur, social inequality increases and social strata emerge. They further propose that as technology continues to develop in industrial societies social inequality tends to diminish. The Kuznets curve, shown in Figure 9-1 (p. 258), illustrates the pattern discussed by the Lenskis. The patterns of social inequality shown in **Global Map** 9-1 are also in accord with the Kuznets curve.

Social Stratification: Facts and Values

A quote from a Kurt Vonnegut novel describes a fictional America in the later 21st century represented by absolutely no social inequality. It highlights the significant social meaning social inequality actually has for us in our everyday lives.

Theoretical explanations contain both fact and position, or a statement of values. A comparison between the structural-functional and social-conflict paradigms illustrates how the same facts can be perceived and understood differently. It is a complex, but meaningful endeavor.

PART IV: KEY CONCEPTS

Define each of the following concepts in the space provided or on separate paper. Check the accuracy of your answers by referring to the key concepts section at the end of the chapter in the text as well as by referring to italicized definitions located throughout the chapter.

blue-collar occupations
burakumin
caste system
class system
Davis-Moore thesis
ideology
Kuznets curve
meritocracy
primogeniture
samurai
shoguns
socioeconomic status
social inequality
social mobility
social stratification
status inconsistency
structural social mobility
white-collar occupations

PART V: STUDY QUESTIONS

True-False

1. T F Social inequality is found in all societies.
2. T F Ascription is fundamental to social stratification systems based on castes.
3. T F Endogamous marriages tend to be more representative of caste systems than class systems.
4. T F The working class is the largest segment of the population in Great Britain.
5. T F In feudal Japan, shoguns were small agrarian villages where most commoners lived and worked.
6. T F The Davis-Moore thesis is a component of the social-conflict perspective of social stratification
7. T F Structural-functionalists argue that social stratification encourages a matching of talents and abilities to appropriate positions in society.
8. T F Max Weber developed a unidimensional model of social stratification which was very dominant in the early part of this century.
9. T F The Lenskis argue that hunting and gathering societies have greater social inequality than agrarian or horticultural societies.
10. T F The Kuznets curve projects greater social inequality as industrial societies advance through technological change.

Multiple-Choice

1. A system by which entire categories of people within a society are ranked in a hierarchy is called:

    (a) social inequality   (c) meritocracy
    (b) social stratification   (d) social mobility

2. Which of the following principles is not a basic factor in explaining the existence of social stratification?

    (a) Social stratification is universal and variable.
    (b) Social stratification persists over generations.
    (c) Social stratification is supported by patterns of belief.
    (d) Social stratification is a characteristic of society, not simply of individuals.
    (e) All are basic factors in explaining social stratification.

3. Apartheid became law in South Africa in:

    (a) 1948   (d) 1875
    (b) 1916   (e) it was never law
    (c) 1971

4. Which of the characteristics that follow is true of class systems?

    (a) they are more clearly defined than castes
    (b) they have variable status consistency
    (c) they have occupations based on ascription
    (d) all of the above
    (e) none of the above

5. In the text, contemporary Great Britain is identified as a(n):

    (a) neomonarchy   (d) caste system
    (b) estate system   (e) open estate system
    (c) class society

6. The social stratification system in Great Britain today still has vestiges of its feudal caste-like system of the past. Which of the following is true of Britain's feudal stratification system?

    (a) it was an estate system
    (b) it was based on the law of primogeniture
    (c) it consisted of nobility, clergy, and commoners
    (d) all of the above
    (e) a and c only

7. The former Soviet Union (now the Commonwealth of Independent States) is:
   (a) decidedly not classless
   (b) socially stratified
   (c) a society with greater extremes between the wealthy and the poor than American society
   (d) more caste-like than American society

8. Which society was identified as having experienced the most upward social mobility during this century?

   (a) Japan
   (b) United States
   (c) Great Britain
   (d) Soviet Union

9. Ideas that support the interests of some category of a population is the definition for:

   (a) meritocracy
   (b) social stratification
   (c) ideology
   (d) status inconsistency

10. According to Gerhard and Jean Lenski, social stratification is at its peak in:
    (a) hunting and gathering societies
    (b) postindustrial societies
    (c) horticultural, pastoral, and agrarian societies
    (d) industrial societies

Fill-In

1. _____ refers to a system by which categories of people in a society are ranked in a hierarchy.
2. A _____ is a system of social stratification based on ascription.
3. A system of social stratification in which individual achievement is of great importance is called a _____ system.
4. In feudal Great Britain, the law of _____ mandated that only the eldest son inherit property of parents.
5. _____ refers to ideas that reflect and support the interests of some portion of society.
6. The idea that social stratification promotes a matching of talents and abilities to appropriate positions is from the _____ paradigm.
7. A system of social stratification in which personal merit is related to the rewards one receives is termed _____.
8. The idea that social stratification systems reflect the interests of the more powerful members of society is from the _____ paradigm.
9. The three dimensions of Weber's model of social stratification are termed _____, _____, and _____.

10. The Lenskis argue that the level of _____ representative of a society is a very significant factor in determining the nature of social stratification in that society.

Definition and Short-Answer

1. What are the four basic principles which help explain the existence of social stratification?
2. Briefly describe the social stratification system of Great Britain today.
3. According to information provided in the text, why hasn't the Marxian revolution occurred?
4. What are the basic qualities of a caste system?
5. What is meant by the concept "structural social mobility?"
6. What are the components of Weber's multidimensional model of social stratification?
7. What are the three criteria of the Davis-Moore thesis?
8. How do structural-functionalists and social-conflict theorists differ in terms helping us understand social stratification?
9. Discuss the Lenskis sociocultural evolution perspective and how it relates to a global and historical understanding of social stratification.

PART VI: ANSWERS TO STUDY QUESTIONS

True-False

1.	T (p. 240)	6.	F (p. 250)
2.	T (p. 241)	7.	T (p. 250)
3.	T (p. 241)	8.	F (p. 256)
4.	T (p. 244)	9.	F (p. 257)
5.	F (p. 246)	10.	F (p. 258)

Multiple-Choice

1.	b (p. 240)	6.	d (pp. 244-45)
2.	e (pp. 240-41)	7.	b (p. 247)
3.	a (p. 242)	8.	d (p. 247)
4.	b (p. 244)	9.	c (p. 248)
5.	c (p. 244)	10.	c (p. 257)

Fill-In

1. social stratification (p. 240)
2. caste (p. 241)
3. class (p. 243)

4.	primogeniture (p. 244)
5.	ideology (p. 248)
6.	structural-functional (p. 250)
7.	meritocracy (p. 250)
8.	social-conflict (p. 252)
9.	class, status, power (p. 256)
10.	technology (p. 257)

PART VII: ANALYSIS AND COMMENT

Cross-cultural Comparison

"South Africa: Race As Caste"

Key Points: Questions:

Critical Thinking

"Ideology: When Is Inequality Unjust?"

Key Points: Questions:

"Salaries: Are the Rich Worth What They Earn?"

Key Points: Questions:

Social Class In America

10

PART I: CHAPTER OUTLINE

I. Dimensions of Social Inequality
    A. Income and Wealth
    B. Power
    C. Occupational Prestige
    D. Schooling
II. Ascription and Social Stratification
    A. Ancestry
    B. Race and Ethnicity
    C. Gender
    D. Religion
III. Social Classes in the United States
    A. The Upper Class
    B. The Middle Class
    C. The Working Class
    D. The Lower Class
IV. The Difference Class Makes
    A. Class and Health
    B. Class and Values
    C. Class and Politics
    D. Class, Family, and Gender
V. Social Mobility
    A. Social Mobility: Myth and Reality
    B. The "Middle-Class Slide"
    C. The U.S. Structure in Global Perspective
VI. Poverty in the United States
    A. The extent of U.S. Poverty
    B. Who are the Poor
        1. Age
        2. Race and Ethnicity
        3. Gender and Family Patterns
        4. Area of Residence
    C. Explaining Poverty
    D. Homelessness
    E. Class and Welfare: Politics and Values

VII. Summary
VIII. Key Concepts
IX. Suggested Readings

PART II: LEARNING OBJECTIVES

1. To understand the extent of social inequality in the United States.
2. To understand the concept of socioeconomic status and its dimensions.
3. To explain the role of economic resources, power, occupational prestige, and formal education in the American class system.
4. To identify and trace the significance of various ascribed statuses for the construction and maintenance of social stratification in the United States.
5. To describe the general characteristics of the upper, middle, working, and lower classes in American society.
6. To explain the ways in which health, values, family life, and gender are related to the social class system in American society.
7. To distinguish between relative and absolute poverty.
8. To explain the causes of absolute poverty.
9. To describe the demographics of poverty in the United States.
10. To understand the debate over who has responsibility for poverty.
11. To understand how poverty is affected by politics and culture in American society.

PART III: CHAPTER REVIEW

The chapter begins with the story of John Coleman, a man who wanted to find out for himself what it would be like to be homeless. He entered New York City in January and learned two lessons very quickly, becoming poor changes you in the eyes of others, and in your own eyes. Poverty is more than a lack of money, it involves a downward spiral toward a lack of self-worth.

DIMENSIONS OF SOCIAL INEQUALITY

Americans tend to underestimate the extent of social inequality in our society. Four reasons are identified for why this happens. First, American society has no history of feudalism and our country is founded on principles of equality. Second, our focus on individual autonomy and achieved statuses diminishes our recognition of the importance of ascribed statuses. Third, the insulation of many Americans into primary groups prevents us from experiencing the extremes of wealth and poverty. Finally, relative to other societies, Americans perceive themselves to be well-off. Various dimensions of social inequality are discussed, focusing on the SES (*socioeconomic status*) variable.

129

Income and Wealth

An important dimension of economic inequality is *income*, or the occupational wages or salaries and earnings from investments. The median American family income in 1990 was $33,500. Figure 10-1 (p. 265) presents the distribution of income among American families. It suggests great inequality which has been relatively stable over the past 50 years, actually increasing slightly during the 1980s.

Wealth, the total amount of money and valuable goods any person or family controls, is distributed more unequally than income. Figure 10-2 (p. 265) illustrates this distribution. In 1991, the typical wealth for a U.S. family was in the range of the median family income (about $35,000).

Power

Wealth is an important source of power in our society. An important question being raised is, Do the rich in our society dominate political and economic decisions in this country?

Occupational Prestige

In American society, social prestige is accorded to individuals on the basis of several factors. Primary among these is one's occupation. Table 10-1 (pp. 266-67) presents the rank ordering of prestige scores for various occupational categories based on a random sample of American adults. High income and advanced education and training requirements are positively correlated with higher prestige occupations. The occupations labeled white-collar tend to have higher prestige than those labeled blue-collar, though exceptions are noted. Women tend to be concentrated in *pink-collar jobs* (service and clerical), which tend to be low in prestige.

Schooling

The formal education a person receives significantly influences occupational opportunities and income. Education may be the right of everyone although great variation exists in terms of how much formal education different groups of people in our society receive. Table 10-2 (p. 268) indicates this fact. While 76% of adult Americans have a high school education, only 20% have a college degree.

Ascription and Social Stratification

While individual talent and effort are important, several ascribed statuses influence our position in the American social stratification system.

Ancestry

Perhaps nothing affects our social standing more than "the accident of birth." The family into which we are born significantly determines our future in terms of placement in the socioeconomic system. We commonly refer to ancestry as our *social background*.

Race and Ethnicity

Whites have significantly higher SES than blacks on average. African-American family income, for example, is only 60% of that for whites. The **Social Diversity** box (p. 269) focuses on differences between black and white affluence, suggesting that even controlling for SES, differences persist between blacks and whites.

Ethnic background also relates to social stratification. For example, the income of Hispanic families was about 65 percent of the comparable figure for all whites in 1990.

Gender

On average, women have lower incomes, educational levels, and occupational prestige than men.

Religion

Religion influences social standing as well. Many upwardly mobile families actually convert to a "higher prestige" religion. Examples are discussed.

SOCIAL CLASSES IN THE UNITED STATES

Dividing our society up into distinct social classes is quite problematic. Many different criteria can be used to place an individual or family into a particular social class. Therefore, precise placement is not possible. Nevertheless, patterns of social structure do exist in our society. Four general social classes are identified.

The Upper Class

Approximately 3-4% of Americans fall into this class. Even among this group there is stratification. A difference is typically made between the upper-upper class, or "old money" rich and the lower-upper class, or "new money" rich. The former group (blue-bloods) represent about 1% of our population and obtain their standing through ancestry and inheritance. The latter group obtains wealth more typically through earnings. Both groups have tremendous power in society, controlling most of our nation's productive property. The caste-like quality of the upper-upper class is discussed in the **Critical Thinking** box (p. 272) on the *Social Register*.

131

The Middle Class

Roughly 40-45% of Americans fall into this category. Given its size alone, the middle class has a significant influence on patterns of American culture. Rather than exclusiveness and familiarity characterizing this group, an important quality in the middle class is a diversity of family backgrounds. The upper third of this category is referred to as the *upper-middle*, being characterized by prestigious white-collar occupations, relatively high educations, nice homes, annual family incomes ranging from $50,000 to $100,000, and an accumulation of property and wealth during their lifetime.

The Working Class

This category comprises about one-third of our population. This group has lower incomes and have virtually no accumulated wealth. They are characterized by *blue-collar* families. They are vulnerable to unemployment and illness to a greater extent than families in the middle and upper classes. They have lower levels of personal satisfaction also.

The Lower Class

The remaining 20% of our population is identified as the lower class. Roughly 13% of American (33 million people) are officially classified as being poor. The "marginal poor," while not falling below the official poverty line are not much better off and also live very insecure, unstable lives. Most poor people are white, but people of African and Hispanic descent are disproportionately represented among the poor. Most poor adults work; however, they are heavily concentrated in low prestige, minimal income jobs. Typically they have very low educational attainment. The poor tend to be very segregated from the rest of society, particularly in terms of housing. The socialization process for children tends to reinforce a sense of marginality.

THE DIFFERENCE CLASS MAKES

Class and Health

People with higher incomes are more than two times likely to describe themselves as healthy than poor people are. Social class is also positively correlated with life expectancy. Crucial links between health and social class are the cost of nutritional food, safe environments, and the cost of medical care. The poor simply cannot afford these things. Mental health patterns also vary with social class. Poorer people seem exposed more to stressful events leading to emotional distress.

Class and Values

The values and attitudes people support are closely associated with the types of lifestyles they live. Members of the upper-upper class value their sense of family history and hold attitudes regarding behavior consistent with maintaining this as an important element in their lives. People in the lower-upper and middle classes, who often desire to emulate the rich, are sensitive to their patterns of consumption. The working class has less security than the middle and upper classes and are more characterized as emphasizing conformity to conventional beliefs and practices. Members of different social classes also seem to vary in their orientation to time, with the upper class maintaining the past, the middle class being very future orientated, and the poor having a stronger orientation to the present.

Class and Politics

Political orientations vary by social class, though in a more complicated manner. Generally, however, conservative views on economic issues and liberal views on social issues are found among those of higher social standing.

Class, Family, and Gender

Who one marries, how many children are in the family, styles of childrearing, and spousal relationships are all influenced by social class.

SOCIAL MOBILITY

America is characterized by relatively high levels of social mobility. Social mobility, whether the result of personal achievement or societal change in the form of structural social mobility, is experienced as a transition. Social mobility can be upward or downward, and can be intragenerational or intergenerational. *Intragenerational social mobility* refers to a change in social position occurring during a person's lifetime. *Intergenerational social mobility* is defined as the upward or downward social mobility of children relative to their parents.

Social Mobility: Myth and Reality

Central to our sense of social mobility is that people have the opportunity to realize their own individual potential. Social mobility has been characteristic of American society during this century; however much has been the result of structural processes. Within a single generation social mobility is usually incremental rather than dramatic. Further, relative to other industrialized societies, the United States has not had exceptional social mobility rates.

The "Middle Class Slide"

Historically, our society and its economy has been characterized by growth and expansion. The depression years represent one exception. In the last generation though, optimism has been decreasing as structural social mobility has slowed. Average earnings for jobs is actually on the decline, with 40% of all new jobs created during the 1980s falling in the low income category (paying less than $15,000 annually). Figure 10-3 (p. 279) shows the median income pattern for U.S. families between 1950-1990 (in constant 1990 dollars).

The U.S. Class Structure in Global Perspective

Many of the industrial jobs which were the basis of our expanding economy have in recent decades been transferred overseas. Current patterns of change in our economy have undermined many people's expectations about improving their standard of living. This is so, even with over one-half of our families having more than one breadwinner. We are working harder and longer to just hold our positions. Twice as many families during the 1980s showed no improvement in their social standing, or lost ground as compared to the number that improved their positions. We are experiencing what some call the "*deindustrialization of America.*" The box (pp. 280-81) discusses how various segments of our population were affected by these economic changes during the 1980s.

POVERTY IN THE UNITED STATES

Two types of poverty are identified. *Relative poverty* is defined as being deprived of social resources relative to those with more. By definition this type of poverty is universal and inevitable. A more serious form of poverty is termed *absolute poverty*, defined as a deprivation of social resources that is life-threatening. Roughly one-fifth of the world's population lives in such conditions.

The Extent of American Poverty

The U.S. government began officially counting the poor in 1964 as part of its "war on poverty." The *poverty threshold* is the annual income level below which a person or family is defined as poor and, therefore, entitled to certain benefits. The poverty rate in the United States has generally decreased since 1960. However, during the 1980s there has been a slight increase. Figure 10-4 (p. 282) shows the official poverty rate over the years since 1960. At present, about 33 million, or 13.5% of our population are classified as being poor. An additional 12 million people are identified as "marginally poor" (living within 25% of the poverty level). It is suggested that poverty means hunger in America and that federal government spending priorities could be easily changed to eradicate poverty and hunger. Currently about 10% of the federal budget is allocated for antipoverty programs. For an urban family of four the poverty threshold in 1990 was $13,359.

Who are the American Poor?

Age

Children are more likely to be poor than any other age group in our nation. About 20% of the children in America are poor. Some 40% of the people living in poverty are under the age of eighteen.

Race and Ethnicity

About two-thirds of all people living in poverty are white, but a disproportionate percentage of blacks and hispanics are represented among the poor. While only 10% of whites are poor, 32% of blacks and 28% of hispanics are living in poverty. Rates are especially high for black and hispanic children.

Gender and Family Patterns

Poverty rates for women and men are considerably different. Of all poor people, about two-thirds are female. Over one-half of all poor families are headed by women. The widening gap in poverty rates between women and men has been labeled the *femininization of poverty*, referring to females representing an increasing proportion of the poor. The **Social Diversity** box (p. 284) takes a closer look at his pattern. A more complicated picture of the changing profile of the poor is presented. While the proportion of all poor families headed by women has increased, the proportion of all female-headed families living in poverty has declined.

Area of Residence

Though it may be hard to believe, poverty is more common in rural areas than in the cities. Data is presented and discussed.

Explaining Poverty

Sociologists agree that poverty is a product of social structure; however, two distinct views about who is responsible for poverty are debated. A recent national survey, the results of which are summarized in Figure 10-5 (p. 283), suggests that Americans are divided in terms of attaching responsibility. One view holds that the poor are primarily responsible for their own poverty. About 25% of American adults tend to agree with this position.

Edward Banfield is a proponent of the first view, He believes a subculture of poverty, with a "present-time" orientation, dominates the lives of the poor. He sees this to be particularly true in urban areas. This view is an extension of the *culture of poverty* theory developed by Oscar Lewis. Lewis argued in the early 1960s that resignation to their condition as being one of fate perpetuated the condition of the poor.

The idea that society is primarily responsible for poverty is held by about one-third of American adults. William Ryan argues that the culture of poverty perspective leads people to "blame the victim." He suggests poverty results from the unequal distribution of resources in society.

Empirical evidence exists to support both views. For example, while over one-half of the heads of poor families do not work, about one-fifth work full-time, but because of low wages cannot climb out of poverty. Further, inadequacies in child care programs make it difficult for many single-parent women to work. Our author agrees that, on balance, the poor are represented by categories of people who lack the same opportunities as others.

Homelessness

During the 1980s the public has become more aware of the plight of the homeless. Though no precise count of the homeless exists, estimates range from 500,000 to several million. The stereotype of the homeless population has been brought into question recently. It is a diverse population. One characteristic shared by the homeless though is poverty. Both individual and societal processes are involved in creating the homelessness problem.

Class and Welfare in America: Politics and Values

Our cultural values significantly affect our perception of the distribution of wealth and poverty in America. Our values support individual responsibility. For many, the idea of welfare programs undermine initiative. This attitude leads to the "hidden injury of class," a phenomenon which lowers the self-image of the poor person. All this is very interesting, particularly given the fact that "welfare for the rich" is such a major part of our value system.

PART IV: KEY CONCEPTS

Define each of the following concepts in the space provided or on separate paper. Check the accuracy of your answers by referring to the key concepts section at the end of the chapter in the text as well as by referring to italicized definitions located throughout the chapter.

absolute poverty
culture of poverty
femininization of poverty
income
intergenerational social mobility
intragenerational social mobility
lower-class
marginal poor
middle-class

middle-class slide
pink-collar jobs
prestige
relative poverty
social mobility
socioeconomic status
upper-class
wealth

PART V: STUDY QUESTIONS

True-False

1. T F The income gap between the rich and the poor was greater during the beginning of the 1990s than at any other time since World War II.
2. T F The richest 1% of Americans control 85% of our nation's wealth.
3. T F The most important source of social prestige in the our stratification system is one's occupation.
4. T F Less than 25% of American adults have a college degree.
5. T F Families, rather than individuals, are listed in the Social Register, and membership is based on ascription.
6. T F The working-class is the largest social class in our stratification system.
7. T F Parents in working-class families are characterized by an emphasis on conformity to conventional beliefs and practices.
8. T F In marriage, middle-class people maintain a more rigid division of responsibilities between husband and wife, while working-class marriages are somewhat more egalitarian.
9. T F Compared to other modern industrialized societies the United States has been characterized by an average amount of social mobility
10. T F The poverty rate has significantly risen in the United States since 1960.
11. T F According to a recent national poll, the vast majority of American adults believe the poor are responsible for their own poverty.
12. T F Approximately one-half of the heads of poor families did not work during 1990.

Multiple-Choice

1. Americans tend to underestimate the amount of inequality in our society. Which of the following is not a reason for this underestimation:

   (a) because American society had no feudal past
   (b) because Americans are insulated from the extremes of wealth and poverty
   (c) because Americans emphasize their statuses conferred at birth from families
   (d) because American society is very wealthy in comparison to much of the world

137

2. Statistics show that income and wealth of Americans vary considerably. Which of the following statistics is accurate:

    (a) the median American family income in 1990 was $43,341
    (b) the top 5% of American families receive 60% of the total income in the United States
    (c) wealth in the United States is more unequally distributed than income
    (d) the poorest 20% of American families receive about 10% of all income
    (e) the richest 5% of American families own over 75% of the entire nation's wealth

3. Education is distributed unequally in American society as evidenced by the fact that:

    (a) only about 20% of American adults are college graduates
    (b) only 56.6% of American adults are high school graduates
    (c) only 10% of American adults have some college
    (d) all of the above
    (e) none of the above

4. The middle class is represented by approximately what percentage of our society's population?

    (a) 20-25   (d) 55-60
    (b) 30-35   (e) 70-75
    (c) 40-45

5. Which of the values/attitudes below is typically found among the lower class:

    (a) orientation to present time
    (b) sensitivity to consumption patterns
    (c) tolerance of controversial behavior
    (d) sense of family history

6. A change in the social position of children relative to that of their parents is called:

    (a) individual social mobility
    (b) structural social mobility
    (c) intragenerational social mobility
    (d) intergenerational social mobility

7. Which of the following statements is most accurate:

   (a) most poor people are black or hispanics
   (b) most Americans believe that the poor should just take care of themselves
   (c) upward structural social mobility has been increasing during the early 1990s in the United States at a faster rate than at any other time in our history
   (d) social mobility within a single generation in the United States tends to be incremental
   (e) (a) and (b) are correct

8. The "middle-class slide" relates to:

   (a) the slowed economic expansion of our economy
   (b) the trend toward more high-tech jobs in our society
   (c) the trend of a higher proportion of jobs in the U.S. being high-paying and requiring high educational levels
   (d) the trend toward a smaller and smaller percentage of our population being classified as upper class

9. What percentage of our population is officially classified as being poor?

   (a) 5   (d) 26
   (b) 13   (e) 31
   (c) 19

10. Poverty statistics in the United States reveals that:

   (a) the elderly are more likely than any other age group to be poor
   (b) almost 70% of all blacks are poor
   (c) urban dwellers are more likely to be poor than rural dwellers
   (d) about 63% of the poor are female

Fill-In

1. While _____ is defined as occupational wages or salaries and earnings from investments, _____ refers to the total amount of money and valuable goods that any person or family controls.
2. Roughly _____% of the adults in the U.S. have a college degree.
3. About one in _____ black families is considered affluent.
4. While the relationship between social class and politics is complex, generally, members of high social standing tend to have _____ views on economic issues and _____ views on social issues.
5. _____ social mobility refers to a change in social position occurring during a person's lifetime.
6. _____% of the poor in America are under the age of 18.
7. _____% of all poor people in the U.S. are white.

8. Oscar Lewis describes the _____ as characterized by resignation to being poor as a matter of fate.

9. William Ryan suggests the characteristics associated with a "culture of poverty" are not the _____ of poverty but rather the _____.

10. Sennet and Cobb referred to the lowering of self-image due to poverty as the _____ of class.

Definition and Short-Answer

1. What are four reasons why Americans tend to underestimate the extent of social inequality in our society?

2. How are wealth and income distributed (by quintiles) throughout the population in the United States? To what degree has this distribution changed over the last forty to fifty years?

3. What are the basic components of socioeconomic status in the United States? How are these measured?

4. To what extent do ascribed statuses affect a person's place in our social stratification system? Provide examples.

5. Using the factors of health, values, and politics discuss the difference social class makes in the lives of people within our society.

6. What is structural social mobility? Provide two examples.

7. What is meant by the concept "middle-class slide?"

8. What are the basic demographic characteristics of the poor in American society?

9. What is the "culture of poverty?"

10. What is the "femininization of poverty?" To what extent does it characterize the poor population in the United States?

PART VI: ANSWERS TO STUDY QUESTIONS

True-False

1.	T (p. 265)	7.	T (p. 276)
2.	F (p. 265)	8.	F (p. 276)
3.	T (p. 267)	9.	T (p. 278)
4.	T (p. 268)	10.	T (p. 282)
5.	T (p. 272)	11.	F (p. 283)
6.	F (p. 273)	12.	T (p. 286)

Multiple-Choice

1.	c (p. 264)	6.	d (p. 277)
2.	c (pp. 264-65)	7.	d (pp. 277-83)
3.	a (p. 268)	8.	a (p. 278)
4.	c (p. 273)	9.	b (p. 281)
5.	a (p. 275)	10.	d (pp. 282-83)

Fill-In

1. income/wealth (pp. 264-65)
2. 20 (p. 268)
3. 6 (p. 269)
4. conservative/liberal (p. 276)
5. intragenerational (p. 277)
6. 40 (p. 282)
7. 66 (p. 282)
8. culture of poverty (p. 285)
9. cause/consequence (p. 285)
10. hidden injury (p. 288)

PART VII: ANALYSIS AND COMMENT

Social Diversity

"Two Colors of Affluence: Do Blacks and Whites Differ?"

Key Points: Questions:

"Why Poverty is a Women's Issue"

Key Points: Questions:

Critical Thinking

"Caste and Class in America: The Social Register and Who's Who"

Key Points: Questions:

The 1980s: A Decade of Change

"Economic Transformation: Trends in Income Inequality"

Key Points: Questions

141

Global Inequality

11

PART I: CHAPTER OUTLINE

I.   The Importance of Global Perspective
II.   The Three Worlds
    A.   The First World
    B.   The Second World
    C.   The Third World
III.   Third-World Poverty
    A.   The Severity of Poverty
        1.   Relative Versus Absolute Poverty
    B.   The Extent of Poverty
    C.   Third-World Women: Work and Poverty
    D.   Correlates of Third-World Poverty
IV.   Global Inequality: Theoretical Analysis
    A.   Modernization Theory
        1.   Historical Perspective
        2.   The Importance of Culture
        3.   Rostow's Stages of Modernization
        4.   The Role of Rich Nations
    B.   Dependency Theory
        1.   Historical Perspective
        2.   The Importance of Colonialism
        3.   Wallerstein's Capitalist World Economy
        4.   The Role of Rich Nations
V.   The Future of Global Inequality
VI.   Summary
VII.   Key Concepts
VIII.   Suggested Readings

PART II: LEARNING OBJECTIVES

1. To define the three worlds: First, Second, and Third.
2. To be able to identify nations representative of each world and the characteristics they share.
3. To understand both the severity and extensiveness of poverty in the Third World.
4. To recognize the extent to which women are over represented among the poor of the world, and the factors leading to this condition.
5. To identify and understand the correlates of Third World poverty.
6. To identify and understand the two major theories used in explaining global inequality.
7. To identify the stages of modernization.
8. To recognize the problems facing women as a result of modernization in the Third World.
9. To identify the keys to combating global inequality over the next century.

PART III: CHAPTER REVIEW

The extremes of poverty are emphasized in the account of a visit by American students to the Cairo dump. Here, members of a religious minority, the Coptic Christians, live. They are called the Zebaleen and their counterparts live in every country of the world.

THE IMPORTANCE OF GLOBAL PERSPECTIVE

As we must recognize our place in our society to understand ourselves, so to understand our society we must explore how it fits into the larger global order. The interdependence of the world's nations is focused on in this chapter.

THE THREE WORLDS

Americans are very well-off relative to people in most other nations. Even our poor have a higher standard of living than most people living in the Third World. The societies of the world are being classified into three broad categories based on their level of technological development and their political and economic system. The **Global Map** 11-1 (p. 294) illustrates. It is stressed however that great differences exist between societies being placed within each broad category.

The First World

The term *First World* refers to industrialized societies that have predominately capitalist economies. The term First World is used to designate those nations where the industrial revolution occurred first. Roughly 25% of the land surface of the globe, and 15% of the world's population is identified as being part of the First World. Because their economies are all market-driven economic alliances with other First-World nations are made.

The Second World

The *Second World* is composed of industrial societies that are currently transforming their socialist economies. Industrialization occurred later in these nations, and they have less powerful industrial capacities. Relatively more people are involved in agricultural production as well. The Soviet Union dominated the Second World economy. **Global Map 11-1 (p. 294)** shows these nations, sometimes referred to as the "eastern bloc." A differentiation is made to indicate nations affected by the monumentous changes sweeping Eastern Europe during 1989 through 1991. The Second World comprises about 15% of the world's land surface, and holds 10% of the world's population.

The Third World

The *Third World* encompasses primarily agrarian societies that are poor. Most people live in rural areas. Economically these societies are less productive than the rest of the world. These societies comprise about 60% of the earth's land area and 75% of the world's population. While sharing poverty, these societies are not guided by a common economic system. It is argued that we, in modern industrial societies, have difficulty understanding the extent to which poverty encompasses the daily lives of the vast majority of people living in the Third World.

THIRD WORLD POVERTY

Two important distinctions are being made by our author: that poverty in the Third World is more severe and more extensive than in the United States.

The Severity of Poverty

The data presented in Table 11-1 (p. 297) suggest why poverty is more *severe* in the Third World. This table compares the GNP and per-person income between countries from around the world for the year 1991. Further, a *quality of life index* measure is suggested for each nation. Significant differences are indicated. It is pointed out that even beyond these general patterns of global inequality, every society has its own *internal* stratification. Figure 11-1 (p. 298) shows the relative share of global income and population by world region.

Relative Versus Absolute Poverty

Every society experiences relative poverty. In wealthy nations poverty is often viewed as a *relative* matter. In the Third World *absolute* poverty is much more critical. The people there typically lack the resources necessary to survive.

The Extent of Poverty

Poverty in the Third World is more *extensive* also. Most people in the Third World live in conditions far worse than the bottom 15% of our population. These statistics boil down to one devastating fact, people are dying from a basic lack of nutrition. The magnitude of this tragedy is almost impossible to imagine with 40,000 people dying each day from starvation. **Global Map** 11-2 (p. 300) puts nutritional differences between nations in perspective. Other statistics are offered in this section to stress the extensiveness of this great problem. The **Cross-Cultural Comparison** box (p. 302) focuses on the severity and extensiveness of poverty in India where one-third of the world's starving people can be found.

Third-World Women: Work and Poverty

As in the United States, hardships of poverty fall harder on women than on men. Women are overrepresented in the poorest of the poor. Much of the work women engage in is "invisible," being outside the paid labor force. Traditions of male dominance in kinship systems further subordinate women.

Correlates of Third World Poverty

Several factors related to the severity and extent of poverty in the Third World are discussed. These include:

(1) Technology
(2) Population growth
(3) Cultural patterns
(4) Social stratification
(5) Global power relationships

In terms of global power relationships, three key concepts are introduced. First, is the historical factor of *colonialism*, or the process by which some nations enrich themselves through political and economic control of other nations. As a result of this, it is argued, many nations were exploited and remain under-developed. A second concept is *neocolonialism*, referring to a new form of economic exploitation that does not involve formal political control. The argument here is focused on *multinational corporations*, or large corporations whose operations span many different nations.

GLOBAL INEQUALITY: THEORETICAL ANALYSIS

The two dominant explanations for the unequal distribution of the world's wealth and power are *modernization theory* and *dependency theory*. Both overlap to some extent, yet emphasize different factors.

Modernization theory

Modernization theory maintains that global inequality reflects differing levels of technological development among societies.

Historical Perspective

A point made by these theorists is that until a few centuries ago all people in the world were poor. The development of cities during the middle ages and the trade and exploration which emerged, coupled with influence of the industrial revolution in the 18th and 19th centuries launched certain societies ahead in living standards. Therefore, *affluence*, not deprivation is what requires explanation.

The Importance of Culture

This theory suggests that new technology is likely to be exploited only in certain *cultural environments. Traditionalism* is the greatest barrier to economic development. This is consistent with Weber's theory of the influence of ideas on societal development. The Protestant Reformation in Europe toward the end of the middle ages transformed society with its focus on individualism and material affluence.

Rostow's Stages of Modernization

Modernization theorists argue that all societies are converging on one general form, the industrial model. According to W. W. Rostow, four general stages are followed by all societies. These include:

(1) the traditional stage, which is strongly tied to kinship, family, and religion;
(2) the take-off stage during which time a limited market economy emerges. Progressive influences like foreign aid and advanced technologies are critical for Third-World nations to move through this stage;
(3) the drive to technological maturity stage, represented by India, Mexico, and the People's Republic of China, experience rapid economic development along with urbanization and specialization. Education becomes critical during this stage. The role of women begins to change and their status increases. However, as the **Critical Thinking** box (p. 306) suggests, many experience great stress as a result of these changes;
(4) the high mass consumption stage.

The Role of Rich Nations

Rather than seeing the First World as part of the cause for Third-World poverty, modernization theorists see it as part of the solution. They see this to be so in the following respects:

(1)   assisting in population control through exportation of birth control technologies and the promotion of their use,

(2)   increasing food production by introducing "high-tech" farming methods (collectively referred to as the "Green Revolution"),

(3)   introducing industrial technology to increase productivity, and

(4)   instituting programs of foreign aid, particularly in the form of investment capital.

The modernization theory has helped provide perspectives for us in understanding how industrialization affects other dimensions of social life. These theorists point out that several societies have demonstrated significant economic developments with the help of the First World. However, others argue that modernization theory is just an attempt to defend and spread capitalism, and in many ways has fallen short in its own standards of success. Further, this approach tends to ignore historical facts that interfere with development. Other limitations involve a failure to make connections between rich and poor societies to see how Third World development affects rich countries. Finally, the fact that this approach holds the First World as the standard by which to judge all development is ethnocentric. Blaming the Third World for their own poverty takes attention away from the negative effects of the First World.

Dependency Theory

Dependency theory maintains that global poverty historically stems from the exploitation of poor societies by rich societies.

Historical Perspective

Dependency theorists argue that the Third World was better off in the past than it is today. They believe the economic positions of the rich and poor societies are interdependent.

The Importance of Colonialism

The colonialization of the Third World by European societies gave countries like Great Britain and Spain great power and wealth. Colonialism is not longer a force in the world; however this political liberation has not meant economic autonomy. A neocolonialism has emerged. The **Social Diversity** box (p. 310) discusses the controversy surrounding the is of the European conquest of the Americas, and the celebration in 1992 of the 500th anniversary of Christopher Columbus's "discovery of America."

147

Wallerstein's Capitalist World Economy

This model attempts to explain modern world inequality. A major point in this perspective is that the world economy, a global system, is beyond the control of traditional nations, and is dominated by capitalism. The First World is at the core of this world economy. This system perpetuates poverty in the Third World by creating and maintaining the dependency of these nations. This dependency is caused primarily by three factors:

(1)   narrow, export-oriented economies,
(2)   lack of industrial capacity, and
(3)   foreign debt.

The Role of Rich Nations

Dependency theorists argue that rich societies create new wealth through technological innovation. This leads to overdevelopment of some societies and underdevelopment of others. Rich nations then exploit poor nations in order to obtain profits. Further, they believe capitalists encourage Third World nations to believe poverty is a natural consequence of population increase.

Dependency theory has demonstrated interdependence of all nations of the world. Critics argue however that there are weaknesses to this perspective. First, dependency theorists seem to assume all wealth obtained by the First World is from the Third World. Second, those Third-World nations with the closest ties to the First World are not the poorest. Third, while blaming world capitalism, they ignore factors within the Third World which lead to poverty. Fourth, they underestimate the influence of the Second World nations on the Third World. Finally, dependency theory does not produce clear policy-making alternatives.

THE FUTURE OF GLOBAL INEQUALITY

Table 11-2 (p. 314) summarizes the viewpoints of modernization and dependency theories in terms of how each provides perspective for understanding historical patterns, primary causes, and the role of rich nations in affecting global inequality. Those Third-World nations which have surged ahead economically seem to have two qualities in common: (1) they are relatively small, and (2) they have traditions emphasizing individual achievement and economic success.

Both theories are currently going through transformations given upheavals in the Second World bringing socialism under fire and the tendency for Third World nations recently seeing advantages to having more government control of their economies.

These approaches however have uncovered two keys to success during the next century in combating global poverty. The first, offered by modernization theory, is understanding poverty as being in part a problem of technology. The second, derived from dependency theory, is to see poverty as a political issue.

PART IV: KEY CONCEPTS

Define each of the following concepts in the space provided or on separate paper. Check the accuracy of your answers by referring to the key concepts section at the end of the chapter in the text as well as by referring to italicized definitions located throughout the chapter.

absolute poverty
colonialism
dependency theory
First World
modernization theory
multinational corporations
neocolonialism
relative poverty
Second World
Third World
traditionalism
world economy

PART V: STUDY QUESTIONS

True-False

1. T F The term First World is applied to societies, in part, because these societies were the first to become industrialized.
2. T F Approximately 80% of the world's land surface is governed by nations which are part of the Third World.
3. T F The Second World is composed of industrialized societies that are currently transforming their socialist economies.
4. T F The Third World is guided by a common economic system to a greater extent than are the First and Second Worlds.
5. T F Modernization theory suggests the greatest barriers to economic development is traditionalism.
6. T F Modernization theory draws criticism for suggesting that the causes of global poverty lie almost entirely in poor societies themselves.
7. T F Wallerstein's capitalist world economy model is used to illustrate and support dependency theory.
8. T F According to dependency theory, capitalist culture encourages people to think of poverty in the Third World as natural or inevitable.
9. T F Third-World nations that have surged ahead have two factors in common, including being relatively large and having a strong traditional base.
10. T F The keys to combating global inequality during the next century lie in seeing it as partly a problem of technology and also a political issue.

Multiple-Choice

1. The name of the group living in the Cairo dump is the:

    (a) Rohoolen   (d) Zebaleen
    (b) Svendoven   (e) Shileen
    (c) Veeshan

2. What percentage of the world's population lives in the Third World?

    (a) 50   (d) 85
    (b) 60   (e) 95
    (c) 77

3. The average per-person annual income in the United States is?

    (a) $7,000   (d) $20,910
    (b) $11,300   (e) $31,020
    (c) $15,400

4. The First World, representing 15% of the world's population controls
    _____ percent of the world's income:

    (a) 20   (d) 66
    (b) 35   (e) 80
    (c) 50

5. Which of the following is not discussed as a correlate of poverty in the Third
    World?

    (a) cultural patterns   (d) social stratification
    (b) population growth   (e) all are discussed
    (c) technology

6. Neocolonialism is:

    (a) primarily an overt political force
    (b) a form of economic exploitation that does not involve formal political
         control
    (c) the economic power of the Third World being used to control consumption
         patterns in the First World
    (d) the exploitation of the First World by the Third World
    (e) none of the above

7. According to Rostow's modernization model, which stage is Thailand currently in?

   (a) traditional
   (b) take-off
   (c) drive to technological maturity
   (d) high mass consumption
   (e) residual-dependency

8. Which of the following is not a criticism of modernization theory:

   (a) it tends to minimize the connection between rich and poor societies
   (b) it tends to blame the Third World for its own poverty
   (c) it ignores historical facts that thwart development in the Third World today
   (d) it has fallen short of its own standards of success
   (e) all are criticisms of this theory

9. Which of the following is not mentioned in Wallerstein's capitalist world economy model as a reason for the perpetuation of the dependency of the Third World nations?

   (a) narrow, export-oriented economies
   (b) lack of industrial capacity
   (c) foreign debt
   (d) all are mentioned
   (e) none are mentioned

10. Which of the following is not a criticism of dependency theory?

    (a) it assumes that the wealth of the First World is based solely on appropriating resources from poor societies
    (b) it tends to blame the Third World for its own poverty
    (c) it does not lend itself to clear policy making
    (d) it simplistically assumes that world capitalism alone has produced global inequality
    (e) all of these are criticisms of this theory

Fill-In

1. The _____ refers to industrialized societies that have predominately capitalist economies.
2. The _____ World is composed of industrialized societies that are currently transforming their socialist economies.
3. According to our author, poverty in the Third World is more _____ and more _____ than it is in the United States.

4. The United States had a GNP in 1990 of over _____ dollars.
5. _____ is a new form of economic exploitation that does not involve formal political control.
6. _____ suggests global inequality reflects differing levels of technological development among societies.
7. According to Rostow's stages of modernization, all societies are gradually converging to one general form: the _____ model.
8. _____ maintains that global poverty historically stems from the exploitation of poor societies by rich societies.
9. Third World nations that have surged ahead economically have two factors in common. One is they are relatively _____. Another is they have cultural traditions emphasizing _____ and _____.
10. Two keys to combating global inequality during the next century will be seeing it partly a problem of _____ and that it is also a _____ issue.

Definition and Short-Answer

1. Define the terms First, Second, and Third Worlds.
2. How do the economies in each of the three worlds differ from one another?
3. What factors create the condition of women being overrepresented in poverty around the world?
4. What are the correlates of Third-World poverty?
5. What is neocolonialism? Provide an illustration
6. What are the four stages of modernization in Rostow's model of societal change and development?
7. What are the problems faced by women in Third-World nations as a result of modernization?
8. According to modernization theory, in what respects is the First World part of the solution to Third world poverty.
9. Differentiate between how modernization theory and dependency theory view the primary causes of global inequality.

PART VI: ANSWERS TO STUDY QUESTIONS

True-False

1. T (p. 292)
2. F (p. 294)
3. T (p. 294)
4. F (p. 296)
5. T (p. 304)

6. T (p. 307)
7. T (p. 309)
8. T (p. 312)
9. F (p. 315)
10. T (p. 315)

Multiple-Choice

1.	d (p. 291)	6.	b (p. 303)
2.	c (p. 296)	7.	b (p. 305)
3.	d (p. 297)	8.	e (pp. 307-08)
4.	d (p. 298)	9.	d (p. 309-11)
5.	e (pp. 301-03)	10.	b (pp. 312-14)

Fill-In

1. First World (p. 292)
2. Second World (p. 294)
3. severe/extensive (p. 296/298)
4. 5 trillion (p. 297)
5. neocolonialism (p. 303)
6. modernization theory (p. 303)
7. industrial (p. 305)
8. dependency theory (p. 308)
9. small/individual achievement/economic success (p. 315)
10. technology/political (p. 315)

PART VII: ANALYSIS AND COMMENT

Cross-Cultural Comparison

"India: A Different Kind of Poverty"

Key Points: Questions:

Critical Thinking

"Modernization and Women: What are the Drawbacks?"

Key Points: Questions:

Social Diversity

"When Worlds Collide: The Christopher Columbus Controversy"

Key Points: Questions:

Race And Ethnicity 12

PART I: CHAPTER OUTLINE

I.   The Social Significance of Race and Ethnicity
      A.   Race
      B.   Ethnicity
      C.   Minorities
II.   Prejudice
      A.   Stereotypes
      B.   Racism
            1.   Individual Versus Institutional Racism
      C.   Theories of Prejudice
            1.   Scapegoat Theory of Prejudice
            2.   Authoritarian Personality Theory
            3.   Cultural Theory of Prejudice
            4.   Conflict Theory of Prejudice
III. Discrimination
      A.   Institutional Discrimination
      B.   Prejudice and Discrimination: The Vicious Circle
IV.   Majority and Minority: Patterns of Interaction
      A.   Pluralism
      B.   Assimilation
      C.   Segregation
      D.   Genocide
V.   Race and Ethnicity in the United States
      A.   Native Americans
      B.   White Anglo-Saxon Protestants
      C.   African Americans
      D.   Asian Americans
            1.   Chinese Americans
            2.   Japanese Americans
      E.   Hispanic Americans
            1.   Mexican Americans
            2.   Puerto Ricans
            3.   Cuban Americans
      F.   White Ethnic Americans

VI.   American Minorities: A Hundred-Year Perspective
VII. Summary
VIII. Key Concepts
IX.   Suggested Readings

PART II: LEARNING OBJECTIVES

1.   To understand the biological basis for definitions of race.
2.   To distinguish between the biological concept of race and the cultural concept of ethnicity.
3.   To identify the two major characteristics of any minority group.
4.   To describe the two forms of prejudice: stereotyping and racism.
5.   To identify and explain the four theories of prejudice.
6.   To distinguish between prejudice and discrimination.
7.   To provide examples of institutional discrimination.
8.   To explain how prejudice and discrimination combine to create a vicious circle of persistent beliefs and practices.
9.   To compare and contrast the patterns of interaction between minorities and the majority.
10. To describe the history and relative status of each of the racial and ethnic groups identified in the text.

PART III: CHAPTER SUMMARY

A story about the conflict and violence in Yugoslavia between the Croatians and the Serbs is recounted to illustrate the power of ethnicity to divide humanity and to promote hatred.

Ethnicity and race are important sources of group unity; however, their presence also causes conflict. This chapter investigates the meanings and consequences of race and ethnicity.

THE SOCIAL SIGNIFICANCE OF RACE AND ETHNICITY

Race

A *race* is a category composed of men and women who share biologically transmitted traits that are defined as socially significant. Common distinguishing characteristics include skin color, hair texture, shape of facial features, and body type. Over thousands of generations, the physical environments that humans lived in created physical variability. In addition, migration and intermarriage spread genetic characteristics throughout the world. during the 19th century biologists developed a three-part scheme of racial classification, including *caucasian, negroid, and mongoloid*. Research confirms however that no pure races exist. Cultural definitions of race are very important however.

155

Ethnicity

Ethnicity is a cultural heritage shared by a category of people. While race is a biological concept, ethnicity is a cultural one. However, the two overlap. Ethnic characteristics are sometimes incorrectly believed to be racial by members of a society, but while ethnicity is subject to modification over time, racial identity persists over generations.

Minorities

A racial or ethnic *minority* is a category of people, distinguished by physical or cultural traits, who are socially disadvantaged. Table 12-1 (p. 324) presents 1990 data on the approximate sizes of different racial and ethnic groups in the United States. Minority groups have two distinctive characteristics, they maintain a distinctive identity characterized by endogamy, and are subordinated through the social stratification system. While usually being a relatively small segment of a society, there are exceptions, for example blacks in South Africa. The box on **A Decade of Change** (pp. 322-23) discusses the increasing proportion of *people of color* in the United States. The **Cross-Cultural Comparison** box (p. 325) looks at racial and ethnic inequality under the law in Malaysia.

PREJUDICE

Prejudice is a rigid and irrational generalization about an entire category of people. It can be positive or negative in nature. It is also a matter of degree.

Stereotypes

Stereotypes are sets of prejudices concerning some category of people. They involve inaccurate descriptions of a category of people even when evidence would contradict the description. Because it involves strong, emotional attitudes, it is difficult to change.

Racism

A powerful form of prejudice is *racism*, or the belief that one racial category is innately superior or inferior to another. Racism has a long and terrifying history which is briefly described in the text.

Individual Versus Institutional Racism

Individual racism involves acts such as whites who prevent a black family from moving into their neighborhood. An even more serious problem though is *institutional racism*, or racism which guides the very operation of institutions such as schools, the workplace, and the police.

Theories of Prejudice

Scapegoat Theory of Prejudice

Scapegoat theory suggests that frustration leads to prejudice on the part of certain people. It also suggests prejudice is likely to be more common among people who themselves are disadvantaged. A *scapegoat* is a person or category of people unfairly blamed for the troubles of others.

Authoritarian Personality Theory

The *authoritarian personality* view, first suggested by T. W. Adorno at the end of World War II, holds that extreme prejudice is a personality trait linked to persons who conform rigidly to cultural norms and values. Such people typically have little education and were raised by harsh, inconsistent parents.

Cultural Theory of Prejudice

This view suggests that some prejudice takes the form of widespread cultural values. Emory Bogardus developed the concept of social distance to measure the attitudes of Americans toward different racial and ethnic groups. His findings conclude that prejudice is operative throughout society and not limited to "abnormal" people.

Conflict Theory of Prejudice

This approach argues that prejudice results from social conflict among categories of people. Prejudice is used as an ideology to legitimate the oppression of certain groups or categories of people. A different argument is also presented in this context which focuses on the climate of *race consciousness* being created by minorities themselves as a political strategy to gain power.

DISCRIMINATION

Discrimination refers to treating various categories of people unequally. While prejudice concerns attitudes and beliefs, discrimination involves behavior. The interrelationship between prejudice and discrimination is addressed by Robert Merton, whose analysis is reviewed in Figure 12-1 (p. 328). Four types of people are revealed: active bigots, timid bigots, all-weather liberals, and fair-weather liberals.

Institutional Discrimination

Institutional discrimination refers to patterns of discrimination that are woven into the fabric of society. Historically, legal discrimination has confronted many minority groups in our society and others. The 1954 Supreme Court Brown v. The Board of Education

157

of Topeka decision reversing the "separate but equal" principle is an example. However, even with changes in the law and constitutional amendments, inequality between racial and ethnic groups continues. We may stand by the ideal of equality, but reaching this condition has not been achieved.

Prejudice and Discrimination: The Vicious Cycle

It is argued that these characteristics in our society persist because they are mutually reinforcing. The Thomas theorem, discussed in chapter 6, relates to this situation. The stages of the *vicious cycle* of prejudice and discrimination are outlined in Figure 12-2 (p. 329).

MAJORITY AND MINORITY: PATTERNS OF INTERACTION

Four models can be used to describe patterns of interaction between minorities and the majority.

Pluralism

Pluralism is a state in which racial and ethnic minorities are distinct but have social parity. Distinct social identity provides pride in people. America takes pride in its racial and ethnic diversity; however, three barriers exist in our society which results in only a limited pluralism. First, only a small proportion of Americans maintain distinct racial or ethnic identity. Second, American's tolerance for social diversity is limited. And third, racial and ethnic distinctiveness is sometimes forced on people.

Assimilation

Assimilation is the process by which minorities gradually adopt patterns of the dominant culture. The notion of the "melting pot" is linked to the process of assimilation. However, this characterization of American society is a misleading idealism. Instead of a new cultural pattern emerging, minorities more often adopt the traits of the dominant culture.

Herbert Gans argues that first generation immigrants retain their traditional culture to much greater degrees than subsequent generations.

The process of assimilation involves changes in ethnicity, but not race. Racial traits may diminish over the generations through *miscegenation*, or the biological process of interbreeding among racial categories.

Segregation

Segregation is the physical and social separation of categories of people. It is generally an involuntary separation of the minority groups, although voluntary segregation occurs occasionally, such as in the case of the Amish. Racial segregation has a long history in

America. *De jure* segregation, or "by law" has ended, however *de facto*, or "by fact" segregation continues. Residential segregation is discussed as a particularly crucial problem in our society. Many blacks live in what researchers call "*hyper-segregation*" conditions in inner city ghetto.

Most suburbs remain predominant, if not virtually all, white. The inner cities, which are becoming more segregated as time goes on, are often characterized by internal colonialism, with many businesses and residential buildings owned by whites.

Individuals can make significant differences though, as the case of Rosa Parks illustrates.

Genocide

Genocide is the systematic killing of one category of people by another. While being contrary to virtually every moral standard, genocide has existed throughout history. Historical examples from around the world are discussed.

RACE AND ETHNICITY IN THE UNITED STATES

Native Americans

The term *Native Americans* refers to many distinct people who migrated from Asia to the Americas thousands of years ago. They were the original inhabitants of the Americas. Examples of Native Americans include the Cherokee, Sioux, and Inca. Several million Native Americans lived in the Americas when the Europeans began to arrive in the 1500s. The term Indian is traced back to Christopher Columbus who thought he was in India when he arrived in the Caribbean, and so he called the indigenous peoples "Indians." The relationship between European colonists and the Native Americans was violent and costly for the Native Americans who were subjected to disease and destruction introduced by the Europeans. The post-Revolutionary War government of the United States embarked on a pluralist strategy with the Indians but failed to achieve it in the face of their unfair payment for Indian land and discriminatory practices in relocating Indians. In the late 1800s assimilation with the Indians was sought. Yet, this also failed as Indians were made wards of the government on reservations. Today the remaining Native American territories are desired for their vast natural resources. Indians themselves are divided over how to utilize their lands. Citizenship was granted to Indians in 1924 yet their social standing is hampered by poverty and lack of education. Those who have been assimilated into the dominant culture still find prejudice and discrimination. Table 12-2 (p. 334) reviews the social standing of Native Americans along the dimensions of income, poverty rates, and educational attainment. To reassert their rights to control their own land, Indians have organized the Pan-Indian American Indian Movement.

White Anglo-Saxon Protestants

White Anglo-Saxon Protestants, or WASPS, have traditionally enjoyed the status of the dominant ethnic and racial category in American society. Their ancestry is English, although the Scots and Welsh figure into the ancestry of some. They were the early, skilled, achievement-oriented settlers of American society. Their adherence to the Protestant work ethic motivated them to be productive. With the arrival of non-WASP immigrants to this society in the 19th century, socially powerful and wealthy WASPS tended to isolate themselves and form organizations to further their own causes. The influence of WASPs has continued to the present day. WASPs enjoy high income, high-prestige occupations and memberships in the culturally dominant Protestant churches.

African Americans

African Americans accompanied Spanish explorers to the New World in the 15th century and officially arrived in the United States in 1619. Twenty Africans were brought to Jamestown, Virginia and worked as slaves or indentured servants. Soon after, laws recognizing slavery were passed making slavery very profitable for white farm and plantation owners. Estimates put the number of Africans who were forcibly transported to the western hemisphere at 10 million. About half died in transit. Approximately 400,000 came to the United States. Social control exerted by whites barred slaves from receiving an education or becoming independent through other means. A small number of blacks in the North and South were legally free and worked as farmers, skilled workers, or small-business owners. The thirteenth Amendment to the Constitution outlawed slavery in 1865. This did not end racial segregation, however. Jim Crow laws perpetuated the racial division of blacks and whites. Many whites attributed an innate inferior status to blacks in order to rationalize the majority's treatment of blacks in the face of the principles of equality and freedom proclaimed in the Declaration of Independence. Gunnar Myrdal, a sociologist, later coined this contradiction the "*American dilemma.*" In the Dred Scott case of 1857, the Supreme Court answered the issue of whether blacks were citizens by saying no.

Important changes for blacks have occurred in the 20th century. Migration to northern cities brought greater work opportunties. A national civil rights movement won crucial battles that resulted in ending legal support for racially segregated schools and civil rights acts that improved the opportunities for blacks in employment and use of public accommodations. Problems persist, though, in the social standing of blacks. The relative standing of blacks in America in 1990 is summarized in Table 12-3 (p. 337). Their median income is significantly lower than whites and others. Blacks are more likely to be poor. Blacks continue to be overrepresented in the low-paying jobs and unemployment has remained twice as high as for whites. Important gains have been made in education over the last generation. They have made occupational gains but these have spawned additional problems such as the realization that education does not promote upward mobility for blacks in the same way it does for whites. Recently, blacks have made strides on their acquisition of political power by increased registration of black voters and increased numbers of black elected officials.

The **Critical Thinking** box (pp. 338-39) addresses the issue of affirmative action and whether it is a problem of a solution.

Asian Americans

Asian Americans have great cultural diversity while sharing certain racial characteristics. Asian Americans constitute 40 percent of all the immigrants to the United States. Asian Americans of Chinese and Japanese ancestry began immigrating to the West over a century ago. Filipinos, Koreans, and Vietnamese have immigrated to this country in recent years.

Chinese Americans

Chinese Americans have experienced interactions with the dominant culture that have at times been discriminatory and at times supportive of their ambitions. Prior to the economic depression of the 1870s their labor was highly valued in the expansion of the West. After 1870 the Chinese were barred from some occupations as a result of competition with whites for jobs. Violence and threats of violence were directed toward them. A legal end to immigration by Chinese created a sex-ratio imbalance among the Chinese population. Some Chinese moved to eastern cities and established urban Chinatowns protected by clans and kinship networks. In the 1940s, Chinese immigration was expanded and Chinese Americans moved out of Chinatowns and assimilated into the dominant culture. The 1950s brought upward social mobility. Outstanding educational and scientific achievements have been made by Chinese Americans in recent decades. Racial hostility has persisted while racial discrimination has lessened dramatically.

Japanese Americans

Japanese immigrants began to arrive in the United States in the 1860s. They worked in the Hawaiian Islands for low wages. The Japanese, perhaps due to their small numbers, escaped the prejudice and discrimination directed at the Chinese in the 1870s. Japanese immigrants later demanded high pay and experienced a curb on male Japanese immigration as a result. Japanese women were allowed to immigrate to adjust the sex-ratio imbalance. Immigration laws in the 1920s practically ended Japanese immigration. Overt prejudice and discrimination were directed toward Japanese. Two important differences between the Japanese and Chinese enhanced the position of the Japanese in the United States. First, the Japanese knew more about American culture and were ready to assimilate. Second, the Japanese began to farm in rural areas as opposed to living and working exclusively in urban enclaves. However the purchase of farmland by noncitizens was legally outlawed in 1913. Since the Japanese of foreign birth were not granted citizenship until 1953, efforts to purchase farmland earlier was accomplished in the names of their American-born children. The Japanese also leased farmland. With World War

161

II and the Japanese destruction of Pearl Harbor, the Japanese were treated with overt discrimination. With short notice, Japanese families were relocated inland to prison camps on the assumption that they might be disloyal to the U.S. The policy which led to the internment of the Japanese has been severely criticized in subsequent years. One profound consequence of it was to economically devastate the majority of the Japanese in the U.S. Even against this hardship, the Japanese recovered, entered a wide range of new occupations, and have been socially mobile within recent decades. Table 12-4 (p. 341) reviews the relative social standing of Chinese and Japanese Americans.

Hispanic Americans

Hispanic Americans are typically the descendants of a combination of Spanish, African, and Native American peoples. A few Hispanics have pure Spanish ancestry. Hispanic Americans represent three main cultures: Mexican American, Puerto Rican, and Cuban. Hispanic Americans represent roughly 10 percent of our population and is this percentage growing rapidly due to high immigration and birth rates. The relative social standing of these three groups is presented in Table 12-5 (p. 343).

Mexican Americans

There are about 12 million Mexican Americans in the United States. Illegal entry into this country puts the actual figure higher. Prejudice and discrimination have marked the relationship of Mexican Americans and whites for several decades. Mexican Americans hold low-paying jobs for the most part and one-fourth of Mexican Americans are poor. A lack of education also inhibits a rise in their relative standing, although some increase in this sphere has been seen since 1980.

Puerto Ricans

Puerto Ricans became citizens of the United States in 1917 and many sought economic advantage by moving to cities like New York in the 1940s and later. Currently there are about three million Puerto Ricans living in the United States. They have not found the advantages they originally envisioned in the U.S. however. Strong ethnic identity is maintained because over three-quarters of them continue to speak Spanish in their homes, and they are able to move between the mainland and Puerto Rico easily. This has insulated them somewhat. Puerto Ricans have a lower social standing than other Hispanics as evidenced by more female-headed households, a fairly low median family income, and a high level of poverty.

Cuban Americans

Cubans immigrated to the United States after the 1959 socialist revolution. Currently about one million Cubans reside in the U.S. They are highly educated, have a higher median family income, and have less poverty than the other Hispanics. They have made significant contributions to the communities in which they live in large numbers, especially Miami and New York City. A recent immigration of 125,000 Cuban refuges has added a poorer and less educated component to the Cuban American population in the United States.

White Ethnic Americans

Many white Americans have traditionally been proud of their ethnic heritage. Those who are non-WASPs have been identified as *white ethnics*. Examples include German, Irish, Italian, and Jews. These immigrants, arriving mainly after 1840, faced hostility from the WASPs who had settled already. Overt discrimination was focused on the white ethnics during the height of immigration in the U.S.: 1880-1930. Immigration quotas restricted their immigration between 1921 and 1968 as a result of opposition by nativist elements. The white ethnics resisted the discrimination by forming ethnic enclaves. For many, economic prosperity and cultural assimilation followed. For others, relative social deprivation exists today. White ethnics and blacks sometimes find themselves on opposite sides of issues due to competition over valued resources in society.

AMERICAN MINORITIES: A HUNDRED-YEAR PERSPECTIVE

America's great cultural diversity is the result of immigration. The pattern of immigration to the U.S. by decade between 1821 and 1990 is outlined in Figure 12-3 (p. 343). Immigration rates today, roughly 400,000 annually, at about the same level as was representative of the great immigration era of a century ago. The countries from which the people are primarily coming is changing. They face prejudice and discrimination as did immigrants before them; however, they also share the hope of opportunity, and the hope that ethnic diversity will someday be viewed as a matter of difference rather than inferiority.

PART IV: KEY CONCEPTS

Define each of the following concepts in the space provided or on separate paper. Check the accuracy of your answers by referring to the key concepts section at the end of the chapter in the text as well as by referring to italicized definitions located throughout the chapter.

affirmative action
American dilemma
assimilation
authoritarian personality
Brown vs. the Board of Education of Topeka
de facto
de jure
discrimination

ethnicity
genocide
hypersegregation
internal colonialism
institutional discrimination
minority
miscegenation
Native American
pluralism
prejudice
race
racism
scapegoat theory
segregation
stereotype
WASP
white ethnics

PART V: STUDY QUESTIONS

True-False

1. T F According to the author of our text, for sociological purposes the concepts of race and ethnicity can be used interchangeably.
2. T F A racial or ethnic minority is a category of people, distinguished by physical or cultural traits, who are socially disadvantaged.
3. T F The scapegoat theory links prejudice to frustration and suggests that prejudice is likely to be pronounced among people who themselves are disadvantaged.
4. T F In Merton's typology of patterns of prejudice and discrimination an unprejudiced-nondisriminator is labeled an "all-weather liberal."
5. T F According to the author, as a cultural process, assimilation involves changes in ethnicity but not in race.
6. T F Native Americans were not granted citizenship in the United States until 1924.
7. T F The Dred Scott Supreme Court decision declared that blacks were to have full rights and privileges as citizens of the United States.
8. T F Though a "silent minority," Chinese Americans have higher poverty rates and lower average family incomes than blacks and hispanics.
9. T F Cuban Americans have the lowest average family income and highest poverty rates of all Hispanic Americans.
10. T F The highest rates of immigration to the United States occurred during the 1920s and 1930s.

Multiple-Choice

1. The two ethnic groups discussed at the beginning of the chapter who are in conflict with each other are the:

    (a) Jews and Arabs
    (b) Serbs and Croats
    (c) Russians and Afghans
    (d) Zorconians and Izods

2. According to the text, Jews are:

    (a) both a race and an ethnic group
    (b) a race
    (c) an ethnic group
    (d) neither a race nor an ethnic group

3. Minority groups have two major characteristics:

    (a) race and ethnicity
    (b) religion and ethnicity
    (c) physical traits and political orientation
    (d) sexual orientation and race
    (e) distinctive identity and subordination

4. A form of prejudice that views certain categories of people as innately inferior is called:

    (a) stereotyping
    (b) racism
    (c) discrimination
    (d) scapegoating

5. One explanation of the origin of prejudice is found in the concept of the authoritarian personality. Such a personality exhibits:

    (a) an attitude of authority over others believed to be inferior
    (b) frustration over personal troubles directed toward someone less powerful
    (c) rigid conformity to cultural norms and values
    (d) social distance from others deemed inferior

6. Robert Merton's study of the relationship between prejudice and discrimination revealed one behavioral type that discriminates against persons even though s/he is not prejudiced. This person would be called a(n):

    (a) active bigot
    (b) all-weather liberal
    (c) timid bigot
    (d) fair-weather liberal

7. According to the work of W.I. Thomas, a "vicious cycle is formed by which variables?

   (a) miscegenation and authoritarianism
   (b) race and ethnicity
   (c) pluralism and assimilation
   (d) segregation and integration
   (e) prejudice and discrimination

8. Pluralism has only limited application in American society Because:

   (a) most Americans only want to maintain their distinctive identities to a point
   (b) society does not always allow distinctive categories to maintain separate ways of life
   (c) distinctive identities are sometimes forced on minority groups
   (d) all of the above

9. The society that comes closest to true pluralism is:

   (a) Switzerland   (c) the United States
   (b) England   (d) Sweden

10. The Hispanics who have the highest incomes, highest-prestige jobs, and highest levels of education are the:

    (a) Mexican Americans   (c) Puerto Ricans
    (b) Cuban Americans   (d) Haitians

Fill-In

1. The term _____ refers to a category composed of men and women who share biologically transmitted traits deemed socially significant.
2. The three part scheme of racial classification developed by biologists during the 19th century included _____, _____, and _____.
3. While race is a _____ concept, ethnicity is a _____ concept.
4. Two major characteristics of minorities are that they have a _____ identity and are _____ by the social stratification system.
5. A _____ is a set of prejudices concerning some category of people.
6. _____ refers to patterns of discrimination that are woven into the fabric of society.
7. _____ is the process by which minorities gradually adopt patterns of the dominant culture.

8. Myrdal argued that the denial of basic rights and freedoms to entire categories of Americans led to the _____.

9. People of European ancestry, non-WASPs, are referred to by a term coined in the 1960s called _____.

10. The annual number of immigrants during the 1980s was approximately _____.

Definition and Short-Answer

1. Identify the four explanations of why prejudice exists.
2. Differentiate between the concepts prejudice and discrimination.
3. What are the four types of people identified by Merton's typology of patterns of prejudice and discrimination? Provide an illustration for each.
4. What is institutional discrimination? Provide an example.
5. Discuss the racial and ethnic diversity of Malaysia and how that society deals with the variety of groups comprising their nation.
6. What are the four stages in the vicious cycle of prejudice and discrimination.
7. What are the four models representing the patterns of interaction between minority groups and the majority group?
8. In what two important ways did Japanese immigration and assimilation into our society differ from the Chinese?
9. How do Native Americans, African Americans, Hispanic Americans, and Asian Americans compare to whites in terms of relative social standing using the variables of educational achievement, family income, and poverty rates.
10. What was the Dred Scott ruling by the Supreme Court? What was the Court's ruling Brown v. Board of Education of Topeka case?

PART VI: ANSWERS TO STUDY QUESTIONS

True-False

1.	F (p. 321)	6.	T (p. 334)
2.	T (p. 321)	7.	F (p. 335)
3.	T (p. 326)	8.	F (p. 340)
4.	T (p. 328)	9.	F (p. 343)
5.	T (p. 331)	10.	F (p. 345)

Multiple-Choice

1.	b (p. 319)	6.	d (p. 328)
2.	c (p. 321)	7.	e (p. 329)
3.	e (p. 322)	8.	d (p. 330)
4.	b (p. 324)	9.	a (p. 330)
5.	c (p. 327)	10.	b (p. 343)

Fill-In

1. race (p. 320)
2. caucasian, negroid, mongoloid (p. 321)
3. biological/cultural (p. 321)
4. distinctive/subordination (p. 322)
5. stereotype (p. 324)
6. institutional discrimination (p. 329)
7. assimilation (p. 331)
8. American dilemma (p. 335)
9. white ethnics (p. 344)
10. 400,000 (p. 345)

PART VII: ANALYSIS AND COMMENT

A Decade of Change

"The Coming of Minority-Majority"

Key Points:

Questions:

Cross-Cultural Comparison

"Unequal Under the Law: Race and Ethnicity in Malaysia"

Key Points:

Questions:

168

Critical Thinking

"Affirmative Action: Problem or Solution?"

    Key Points:

    Questions:

Gender And Sex $\boxed{13}$

PART I: CHAPTER OUTLINE

I. Sex and Gender
    A.   Sex: A Biological Distinction
    B   Sexual Orientation
    C.   Gender: A Cultural Distinction
        1.   An Unusual Case Study
        2.   The Israeli Kibbutzim
        3.   Cross-Cultural Research
    D.   Patriarchy and Sexism
        1.   Is Patriarchy Inevitable?

II. Gender and Socialization
    A.   Gender and the Family
    B.   Gender and the Peer Group
    C.   Gender and Schooling
    D.   Gender and the Mass Media
    E.   Gender and Adult Socialization

III. Gender and Social Stratification
    A.   Working Men and Women
        1.   Gender and Occupations
    B.   Housework: Women's "Second Shift"
    C.   Gender, Income, and Wealth
    D.   Gender and Education
    E.   Gender and Politics
    F.   Minority Women
    G.   Are Women a Minority?
    H.   Violence Against Women
        1.   Sexual Harassment
        2.   Pornography

IV. Theoretical Analysis of Gender
    A.   Structural-Functional Analysis
        1.   Talcott Parsons: Gender and Complementarity
    B.   Social-Conflict Analysis
        1.   Friedrich Engels: Gender and Class

V.   Feminism
      A.   Basic Feminist Ideas
      B.   Variations Within Feminism
            1.   Liberal Feminism
            2.   Socialist Feminism
            3.   Radical Feminism
      C.   Resistance to Feminism
VI.   Gender in the Twenty-First Century
VII. Summary
VIII. Key Concepts
IX.   Suggested Readings

PART II: LEARNING OBJECTIVES

1.   To know the distinction between sex and gender.
2.   To explain the biological distinction of sex and sexual orientation.
3.   To explain the cultural component in gender and sexual orientation.
4.   To know the various types of social organization based upon the relationship between males and females.
5.   To know the arguments in the debate over whether patriarchy is inevitable.
6.   To describe the link between patriarchy and sexism.
7.   To describe the role that gender plays in socialization in the family, the peer group, schooling, the mass media, and adult interaction.
8.   To explain how gender stratification occurs in the workworld, housework, economics, education, and politics.
9.   To identify the key arguments in the debate over whether women constitute a minority.
10.   To compare and contrast the two sociological analyses of gender: structural-functional analysis and social-conflict analysis.
11.   To define and explain the central ideas of feminism, variations of feminism, and social resistance to feminism.

PART III: CHAPTER REVIEW

This chapter begins with a brief account of a legal case in Botswana concerning the status of women in that African nation. The suit brought by Unity Dow against her government concerned the *patrilineal* kinship model followed Botswana, and the significance it has in terms of determining citizenship.

SEX AND GENDER

While women have made important gains relative to men during the last century and a half, in many ways the position of men remains privileged. The issue raised concerns the extent to which society and/or innate qualities construct these differences.

Sex: A Biological Distinction

Sex is defined as the division of humanity into biological categories of male and female. It is determined at the moment of conception. Each fertilized egg contains 23 chromosome pairs. One of these pairs determines sex. The female always contributes the X chromosome, and the male contributes either an X or a Y chromosome. If the male contributes an X, the embryo will develop into a female. If the male contributes a Y, the embryo will develop into a male. Sex differentiation occurs during the sixth week after conception. In the male embryo, the hormone testosterone is produced which stimulates the development of male genitals.

At birth, both males and females are distinguished by *primary sex characteristics*, the genitals, used to reproduce the human species. During adolescence, continued biological differentiation results in *secondary sex characteristics*, physical traits, other than genitals, that distinguish males and females. Examples of these are reviewed. However, these are general differences, with a wide range existing for both sexes.

Two variations from male and female sexes are discussed. *Hermaphrodite*, a term derived from Greek mythology, refers to humans with some combination of male and female internal and external genitalia. Our culture tends to be intolerant and even hateful of such people. However, their status in society varies cross-culturally. Another category is that of *transsexuals*, or people who feel they are one sex when biologically they are the other. Some of these people have surgery to alter their sex because of feeling "trapped" in the wrong body.

Sexual Orientation

Sexual orientation refers to the manner in which people experience sexual arousal and achieve sexual pleasure. The meaning of different sexual orientations varies cross-culturally, but all societies endorse heterosexuality, by which a person is attracted to the opposite sex. However, *homosexuality*, or attraction to members of one's own sex, is not uncommon. Homosexuals, or gays, in the U.S. continue to be subjected to prejudice and discrimination, though tolerance is improving. The term *lesbian* is used to refer to female homosexuals. In 1974 the American Psychiatric Association removed homosexuality from its list of mental disorders.

Homophobia, or fear of gay people is still quite evident in our society. This has perhaps increased in recent years since the identification of the AIDS virus and its link to homosexuals.

The pioneering work of Alfred Kinsey during the middle of this century showed that exclusive homosexuality represented about 4 percent of our male population and 2 percent of our female population. Though, 25 percent of our population had experienced at least one homosexual encounter. People who have combined homosexual and heterosexual orientations are called *bisexuals*.

Sexual orientation is determined by a combination of factors, including biological facts present at birth, hormonal influences, and social experiences. Further, sexual orientation is probably not established exactly the same for every person.

Gender: A Cultural Distinction

Gender refers to society's division of humanity, bases on sex, into two distinctive categories. Typically they are differentiated into masculine and feminine traits. Involved here are all culturally learned differences between males and females, and the social inequality which results. Various statistics are reviewed in the text to illustrate.

Biologically, males and females reveal limited differences. Society dramatically affects the impact of these differences. The significance played by culture in the development of gender is illustrated by various types of research.

An Unusual Case Study

A case study of twin boys, one of whom had his penis severed during surgery at seven months of age, clearly reveals the significance of socialization. He was raised a girl, having further surgery to change his sex. The twins learned different *gender identity*, or the ways males and females, guided by culture, learn to think of themselves.

The Israeli Kibbutzim

The significance of culture is revealed using studies which focus on egalitarian gender role patterns in Israeli kibbutzim. However, close examination of the kibbutzim suggests that biology may undermine efforts to achieve complete gender equality.

Cross-Cultural Research

Other cross-cultural evidence, for example the research by anthropologist Margaret Mead in New Guinea, again uncovers the variety of ways in which masculine and feminine traits are defined and experienced by males and females. Research by George Murdock involving over 200 preindustrialized societies reveals some general patterns about gender roles cross-culturally

Patriarchy and Sexism

While conceptions of gender vary cross-culturally and historically, there is an apparent universal pattern of *patriarchy*, a form of social organization in which males dominant females. *Matriarchy*, defined as a form of social organization in which females dominate males is not known to have ever existed. The relative power of males over females does however vary significantly. Patriarchy is based on *sexism*, or the belief that one sex is innately superior to the other. Some researchers argue that sexism is very similar in form to racism. Table 13-1 (p. 355) highlights the common characteristics or racism and sexism. *Institutionalized sexism*, or sexism built into the various institutions of our society, is evident. It is further argued that society itself, as well as men pay a price for sexism. It is not just women who are being rigidly defined.

Is Patriarchy Inevitable?

This discussion illustrates that patriarchy in societies with simple technology tends to reflect biological sex differences. In industrialized societies, technology minimizes the significance of any biological differences. Cross-cultural evidence on gender roles (focusing on housework) is presented in Global Map 13-1 (p. 357).

Generally, the opinion of sociologists is that gender is principally a social construction and is subject to change.

GENDER AND SOCIALIZATION

Males and females are encouraged through the socialization process to incorporate gender into their personal identities. Table 13-2 (p. 356) identifies the traditional gender identity characteristics along the dimensions of masculinity and femininity. Studies show that even with the cultural norms which script behavior, women and men don't exclusively exhibit gender appropriate attributes. Some score high on masculine characteristics, some high on feminine, some high on both, and some low on both. The pattern suggests however that scripts may be more imposing on males than on females.

Gender roles are attitudes and activities that a culture links to each sex. They are the active expression of gender identity. Considerable social pressure is experienced by individuals to conform to gender role expectations.

Gender and the Family

Jesse Bernard, introduced in the **Profile** box (p. 358), suggests that girls and boys are born into different worlds, the "pink" and the "blue." She further argues that sociology, dominated by males, has not adequately studied females.

Research reveals many interesting differences in the patterns of interaction between parents and their female and male children.

Gender and the Peer Group

Janet Lever's research on peer group influences on gender suggests that the cultural lessons being taught boys and girls are very different. Boys are more likely to play in team sports with complex rules and clear objectives. Girls are more likely to be engaging in activities in smaller groups involving fewer formal rules and more spontaneity, and rarely leading to a "victory." The **Sociology of Everyday Life** box (p. 359) reviews one boy,s sense of being socialized into masculinity.

Carol Gilligan has conducted research on moral reasoning and has demonstrated differences between boys and girls. Girls seem to understand morality in terms of responsibility and maintaining close relationships. Boys, on the other hand, reason according to rules and principles.

Gender and Schooling

Research has shown that historically, males are the focus of attention in literature to a considerably greater extent than females. Further, females depicted are more typically portrayed as "objects." In the last decade this pattern has begun to change.

At the college level, females and males still tend to select different majors and extracurricular activities. This may be in part the result of a "second curriculum", or informal messages in our schools which direct females and males into different interests.

Gender and the Mass Media

The mass media has portrayed males as the dominant category of American culture. Women have tended to be shown as less competent than men, and often as sex objects. Children's programs also reinforce gender stereotypes. While changes are occurring, they are doing so very slowly. This is particularly true in advertising which has clung to traditional cultural views of women.

Erving Goffman's research on how men and women are presented in photos for advertisements is discussed and reveals many subtle examples of sexism.

Gender and Adult Socialization

Pamela Fishman's research on marital relations, specifically communication patterns between wives and husbands, reveals interesting examples of male dominance. Husband-initiated conversations are sustained longer, with wives attempting to "keep it going," and wives asking more questions.

GENDER AND SOCIAL STRATIFICATION

Gender stratification refers to the unequal distribution of wealth, power, and privileges between the sexes. The general conclusion is that women around the world have fewer of their society's valued resources than men.

Working Men and Women

In the U.S. most adult men and women are in the labor force. Figure 13-1 (p. 362) presents statistics on labor force participation rates for women and men since 1950. The participation rate for women is increasing significantly. Several different categories of women, married, single, married with children, and divorced are discussed. In 1991 66.4 percent of people in the U.S. over the age of fifteen were working for income (76.2 percent of men and 57.4 percent of females). Seventy-six percent of the women were working full-time.

Gender and Occupations

However impressive the inclusion of women in the work force may be, women are still positioned in the lower-paying, traditionally female occupations. Almost one-half of working women fall into one of two broad occupational categories - clerical or service. Table 13-3 (p. 363) reviews the jobs with the highest concentration of women. Men dominate virtually all other job categories. Even within a given occupational category (i.e., teaching), the higher prestige jobs and higher paying jobs are usually held by males.

Housework: Women's "Second Shift"

Housework is a domain of activity that almost exclusively falls on women to complete. The significance of housework is discussed as a cultural contradiction; essential, yet carrying minimal reward and prestige. The burden of this type of work is further increased by the monotony of the tasks involved. The increasing role of women in the labor force has not affected men's involvement in housework. The areas where responsibility is shared only seems to include the disciplining of children and finances.

Gender, Income, and Wealth

Income tends to reinforce women's disadvantaged position in society. Women working full-time earn only 72 percent of what their male counterparts earn. Research shows that two-thirds of this difference to be attributed to the type of work in which males and females are employed, and family related factors. Still, one-third is attributable to discrimination. The issue of "comparable worth" is discussed. Table 13-4 (p. 365) presents statistics on earning differences between women and men for several different types of occupations. The **Critical Thinking** box (p. 366-67) discusses a controversial proposal (referred to as the "mommy-track") intended to benefit corporate women.

Gender and Education

Higher education was traditionally the domain of males. However, this pattern has been changing in recent decades. Over one-half of all college students today are females, and females earn half of all M.A. degrees conferred. Further, females are pursuing programs traditionally dominated by males. However, significant differences still exist, particularly in the percentage of Ph.Ds granted, and the in the areas of law and medicine.

Gender and Politics

American political history reveals a significant pattern of male dominance. Key events in the history of women in American politics are placed in chronological order in Table 13-5 (p. 368).

While the political power of women has increased dramatically during the last century, at the highest levels of government women's roles are still minimal compared to men.

Minority Women

Income statistics indicate that minority women are doubly disadvantaged, earning less than men of their own minority group. The femininization of poverty is evident by the fact that over 50 percent of households headed by black or hispanic women are living in poverty.

Are Women a Minority?

Our author argues that as a category women must be viewed as a minority group because of being socially disadvantaged, and identifiable by physical traits. However, subjectively, most women do not perceive themselves as such because of living within families which are distributed across the social class structure of society, and due to being socialized to accept their position.

Violence Against Women

Because violence is commonplace in our society, and closely linked to gender, it is often found where men and women interact most intensively (i.e., dating and the family). Sexual violence, it is argued, is mostly about *power*.

Sexual Harassment

Sexual harassment is defined as comments, gestures, or physical contact of a sexual nature that is deliberate, repeated, and unwelcome. The Anita Hill/Clarence Thomas case is discussed as an illustration of alleged sexual harassment. Sexual harassment is discussed as being inherently ambiguous in many instances, though often creating a *hostile environment*.

Pornography

The definition of pornography is very ambiguous as well. Current law requires different jurisdictions to decide for themselves what violates "community standards" of decency and lacks any redeeming social value. The point is made that there seems to be a pattern in our society of now seeing pornography as a *political* issue as well as a *moral* one. Like sexual harassment, pornography raises complex and conflicting concerns.

THEORETICAL ANALYSIS OF GENDER

Structural Functional Analysis

Theorists using this perspective understand gender role patterns over history and cross-culturally to be the result of the functional contributions these patterns make to the survival of the society within its social and physical environments. Industrial technology has allowed greater variation in gender roles, however gender roles still reflect long-standing institutionalized attitudes.

Talcott Parsons: Gender and Complementarity

Talcot Parsons theorized that gender plays a part in maintaining society in industrial times by providing men and women with a set of complementary roles (*instrumental* and *expressive*). Through socialization males and females adopt these roles. The primary societal responsibility of women, in this view, is child-rearing. Thus, they are socialized to display expressive qualities. Men are responsible for achievement in the labor force and therefore are socialized to exhibit instrumental traits.

Criticisms of this approach include the lack of recognition that many women have traditionally worked outside the home, the over-emphasis on only one kind of family, and the neglect of the personal strains associated with such a family orientation.

Social-Conflict Analysis

Social-conflict analysis of gender stratification focuses on the inequality of men and women. This theoretical view holds that women are a minority group and men benefit by the unequal relationship which is perpetuated by sexism and sexist ideology.

Friedrich Engels: Gender and Class

Friedrich Engels identified the historical formation of social classes to the origins of gender inequality. The basis of social class and private property marked the point at which males gained dominance over women in Engel's view. William Goode's research suggests that men are less likely to see gender as a source of inequality given their advantageous position relative to women. The complexities of male and female relationships which interfere with objective understanding of the inequality present are discussed using Goode's insights.

One criticism of this approach is that it neglects the cooperation of females and males in the institution of the family. Another criticism is that capitalism is not the origin of gender stratification since socialist societies are patriarchal as well.

FEMINISM

Feminism is defined as the advocacy of social equality for the sexes leading to opposition to patriarchy and sexism. Its first wave in this country occurred in the 19th century, culminating with the right to vote for women. The second wave began in the 1960s and continues today.

Basic Feminist Ideas

Feminism shares at least two qualities with the sociological perspective. First, the questioning of our basic assumptions about social patterns. And second, an awareness of the relationship between personal experiences and society. However, feminism is decidedly political and critical, seeing the division of the sexes as necessarily harmful to individuals and society. Further, feminists are concerned with the implications of the gender division for social stratification patterns and sexuality issues. Five ideas considered central to feminism are explained, these include:

(1) The importance of change
(2) Expanding human choice
(3) Eliminating gender stratification
(4) Ending sexual violence
(5) Promoting sexual autonomy

Variations within Feminism

Three distinct forms of feminism are identified. These include: (1) *liberal feminism*, which accepts the basic organization of society, but seeks the same rights and opportunities for women and men, (2) *socialist feminism*, which supports the reforms of liberal feminists but believes they can be gained only though the elimination of the capitalist economy and socialist revolution, and (3) *radical feminism*, which advocates the elimination of patriarchy altogether by organizing a gender-free society.

Resistance to Feminism

Feminism has been resisted by both men and women. Reasons for this opposition include a preference for traditional gender and family definitions, a concern that our self-identity will be subject to change, and a fear or ignorance of what feminism is in actuality. A final issue concerns opinions about how change should occur.

The ERA; first proposed in Congress in 1923, has had considerable support, however the failure to formally enact the ERA suggests resistance is still strong.

GENDER IN THE TWENTY-FIRST CENTURY

While sociologists differ in their projections (speculations) about the future of gender roles in American society, certain general observations are being made in the text.

First, the trend over the last century or so in our society has been toward greater equality between the sexes. Second, while strong opposition to the feminist movement remains, deliberate policies toward reducing patriarchy are advancing the status of women in America. Finally, our author suggests that while radical change in America's view of gender is not likely in the short term, movement toward greater equality in rights and opportunities for females will continue to gain strength.

PART IV: KEY CONCEPTS

Define each of the following concepts in the space provided or on separate paper. Check the accuracy of your answers by referring to the key concepts section at the end of the chapter in the text as well as by referring to italicized definitions located throughout the chapter.

expressive qualities
female infanticide
feminism
gender
gender identity
gender roles
gender stratification
hermaphrodite
heterosexuality
homosexual
instrumental qualities
kibbutzim
patriarchy
primary sex characteristics
secondary sex characteristics
sex
sexual orientation
transsexuals

PART V: STUDY QUESTIONS

True-False

1. T F   Hermaphrodites are scorned and viewed negatively in all known cultures.
2. T F   The research by Kinsey suggests sexual orientations may not be mutually exclusive.

3. T F The conclusions made by Margaret Mead in her research on the three New Guinea societies is consistent with the sociobiological argument that "persistent biological distinctions may undermine gender equality."

4. T F In global perspective, the vast majority of activities are consistently defined as feminine or masculine.

5. T F Gender roles are the active expression of gender identity.

6. T F Given the fact that males are more aggressive and more difficult to control than females, male infanticide is more common worldwide than is female infanticide.

7. T F Carol Gilligan's research on patterns of moral reasoning suggests that boys learn to reason according to rules and abstract principles more so than girls.

8. T F Women with children have a higher proportion of their number working in the labor force than women with no children at home.

9. T F Minority women earn more than white women.

10. T F The ERA was first proposed in Congress in 1923.

Multiple-Choice

1. _____ refers to the division of humanity into the biological categories of female and male.

    (a) sex   (c) sexuality
    (b) gender   (d) sexual orientation

2. Which of the following is correct?

    (a) women always contribute the Y chromosome during conception
    (b) the male always contributes the Y chromosome during conception
    (c) more males are born than females
    (d) gender refers to the biological categories of male and female
    (e) none of the above

3. The female embryo will develop if:

    (a) the father contributes an X chromosome and the mother contributes an X chromosome
    (b) the father contributes an X chromosome and the mother contributes a Y chromosome
    (c) the mother contributes an X chromosome and the father contributes a Y chromosome
    (d) the mother contributes a Y chromosome and the father contributes a Y chromosome

4.   A hormone imbalance before birth that results in the birth of a child with some male and female internal and external genitals is termed a(n):

(a)   transsexual   (c)   hermaphrodite
(b)   bisexual   (d)   aphrodisiac

5.   The social inequality of men and women has been shown to be culturally based rather than exclusively biological by which of the following studies?

(a)   medical case studies
(b)   Israeli kibbutzim
(c)   New Guinea studies by Margaret Mead
(d)   all of the above
(e)   none of the above

6.   Among the Mundugumor, Margaret Mead found:

(a)   both females and males to be very passive
(b)   females to be very aggressive and males to be passive
(c)   both males and females to be aggressive and hostile
(d)   sex roles to be very similar to what they are in the U.S.

7.   A form of social organization in which females are dominated by males is termed:

(a)   matriarchy   (c)   patriarchy
(b)   oligarchy   (d)   egalitarian

8.   A sociologist who has urged other sociologists to include both males and females in their theory and research is:

(a)   Talcott Parsons   (c)   Max Weber
(b)   Jesse Bernard   (d)   C. Wright Mills

9.   Women in the labor force are:

(a)   usually single
(b)   usually married without children
(c)   usually married with children
(d)   usually married with grown children

10. Talcott Parsons argues that there exists two complimentary role sets which link males and females together within social institutions. He calls these:

   (a)   rational and irrational
   (b)   effective and affective
   (c)   fundamental and secondary
   (d)   residual and basic
   (e)   instrumental and expressive

Fill-In

1. _____ are physical traits other than genitals that distinguish males and females.
2. The irrational fear of gay people is known as _____.
3. _____ refers to the ways females and males, guided by culture, incorporate traits into their personalities.
4. _____ are attitudes and activities that a culture links to each sex.
5. In 1991, 76.4 percent of men and _____ percent of women over the age of 16 were in the labor force.
6. On average in the U.S., for every dollar earned by a man, a woman earns _____ cents.
7. Roughly _____ of the earnings disparity between women and men are accounted for by type of work and family responsibilities.
8. In 1991, _____ percent of all college students were female.
9. _____ is defined as the advocacy for social equality of the sexes, in to opposition to patriarchy and sexism.
10. The three types of feminism are _____, _____, and _____.

Definition and Short-Answer

1. Briefly review the Unity Dow case in Botswana. To what extent and in what ways do you believe women are treated as second-class citizens in the United States?
2. What does Alfred Kinsey mean by the statement that "in many cases, sexual orientations are not mutually exclusive"?
3. Compare the research by Margaret Mead in New Guinea with the research done at the Israeli kibbutzim in terms of the cultural variability concerning gender.
4. What generalizations about the linkage between sex and gender can be made based on the cross-cultural research of George Murdock?
5. Review table 10-1. Based on your analysis of the variables identified, to what extent do you feel sexism and racism are equivalent? Briefly explain your answer. In what ways are sexism and racism different?
6. According to our author, is patriarchy inevitable? Why? What roles have technological advances and industrialization played in terms of changing the relative status of women and men in our society.

7. Discuss the issue of sexual harassment against women in our society. What needs to be done help solve this problem?

8. In what ways is pornography an underlying factor for violence against women in our society? Explain.

9. Table 10-2 presents lists of traits linked to the traditional gender identities of femininity and masculinity. Develop a questionnaire using the traits identified to survey females and males in order to determine the extent to which these traits differentiate between the sexes.

10. What are Erving Goffman's points about how the mass media portrays females and males? Provide three illustrations in support of this view.

11. Carol Gilligan suggests that moral reasoning is different for females and males. Briefly explain her points. How could a researcher measure for such a difference in moral reasoning?

12. What is the meaning of the phrase "housework as a second shift for women"? What evidence exists of this in our society today?

13. Identify five important demographic facts about gender stratification within the occupational domain of our society.

14. What is meant by the policy of the "mommy-track"? What is your opinion about such a policy?

15. Are women a minority group? What are the arguments for and against this idea?

16. Compare and contrast the analyses of gender stratification as provided by structural-functionalists and social-conflict theorists.

17. What are the three types of feminism? Briefly differentiate between them in terms of the arguments being made about gender roles in our society.

18. What are the five basic ideas of feminism? Briefly explain.

PART VI: ANSWERS TO STUDY QUESTIONS

True-False

1.	F (p. 351)	6.	F (p. 358)
2.	T (p. 351)	7.	T (p. 359)
3.	F (p. 354)	8.	T (p. 362)
4.	F (p. 354)	9.	F (p. 368)
5.	T (p. 356)	10.	T (p. 374)

Multiple-Choice

1.	a (p. 350)	6.	c (p. 353)
2.	c (p. 350)	7.	c (p. 354)
3.	a (p. 350)	8.	b (p. 358)
4.	c (pp. 350-51)	9.	c (p. 362)
5.	d (pp. 352-54)	10.	e (p. 372)

Fill-In

1. secondary sex characteristics (p. 350)
2. homophobia (p. 351)
3. gender identity (p. 352)
4. gender roles (p. 356)
5. 57.4 (p. 362)
6. 72 (p. 364)
7. two-thirds (p. 365)
8. 54 (p. 356)
9. feminism (p. 374)
10. liberal, socialist, radical (pp. 375-76)

PART VII: ANALYSIS AND COMMENT

Window on the World

"Global Map 13-1: Housework in Global Perspective"

Key Points:

Questions:

Profile

"Jesse Bernard"

Key Points:

Questions:

Sociology of Everyday Life

"Masculinity as Contest"

    Key Points:

    Questions:

Critical Thinking

"Corporate Women: The "Mommy Track" controversy"

    Key Points:

    Questions:

Aging And The Elderly 14

PART I: CHAPTER OUTLINE

I.   The Graying of the United States
II.   Growing Old: Biology and Culture
       A.   Biological Changes
       B.   Psychological Changes
       C.   Aging and Culture
       D.   Aging and Social Stratification
III.   Transitions and Problems of Aging
       A.   Social Isolation
       B.   Retirement
       C.   Aging and Poverty
       D.   Abuse of the Elderly
IV.   Theoretical Analysis of Aging
       A.   Structural-Functional Analysis: Aging and Disengagement
       B.   Symbolic-Interaction Analysis: Aging and Activity
       C.   Social-Conflict Analysis: Aging and Inequality
V.   Ageism
       A.   The Elderly: A Minority?
VI.   Death and Dying
       A.   Historical Patterns of Death
       B.   The Modern Separation of Life and Death
       C.   Bereavement
VII.   Summary
VIII. Key Concepts
IX.   Suggested Readings

PART II: LEARNING OBJECTIVES

1. To define and explain the development of the graying of America.
2. To describe the interrelationship and respective roles of biology and culture in growing old.
3. To explain the role of the elderly in cross-cultural and historical perspectives.
4. To describe the relationship between adjusting to old age and personality type.
5. To describe the problems and transitions involved in growing old.
6. To describe, compare and contrast the three sociological explanations of aging.
7. To explain ageism and its impact on the elderly.
8. To identify the key arguments in the debate over whether the elderly constitute a minority group.
9. To describe the changing character of death throughout history and into modern times.
10. To describe the process of bereavement.

PART III: CHAPTER REVIEW

This chapter begins with a discussion about the best-selling book *Final Exit*. It is a book about dying, more specifically, a "how-to book" on suicide. The author of the book, Derek Humphrey, is the founder and executive director of the *Hemlock Society*, an organization which offers support and practical assistance to those who which to die.

THE GRAYING OF THE UNITED STATES

It is pointed out that a powerful revolution is occurring in our society. It is referred to as the graying of America. The aged population is growing twice as fast as the general population. Figure 14-1 (p. 382) portrays the extent to which the age structure of American society is changing. The two major causes identified for this pattern are the aging of the baby boom generation and the increasing life expectancy in our society.

These changes are affecting our society in many significant ways. The demands placed on social resources, particularly the federal budget, is becoming critical. Social security and health-care costs for our society are dramatically increasing as our population ages. Other social changes of great importance include the changes in interaction patterns between different age groups as the proportion of the aged increases, and the increased responsibility of adult children for their aged parents. The **Critical Thinking** box (pp. 384-85) discusses this later point in some detail, referring to these adult children as the "sandwich generation."

GROWING OLD: BIOLOGY AND CULTURE

Gerontology is the study of aging and the elderly. This field provides great insight for us in understanding aging. Biological changes which are part of the aging process are indeed significant. However, so are the changes in social definitions that structure a person's everyday experiences.

Biological Changes

Biology by itself does not necessarily create social distinctions. However, we are a youth oriented-society. Changes that accompany old age are typically viewed more negatively than positively. Our general view seems to be that people reach a point when they "stop growing up and start growing down."

Cultural stereotypes of problems which complicate aging exaggerate differences between young and old. Gerontological research suggests differences do exist. For example, older people show declines in vitality and strength, suffer more chronic illnesses, are at a greater risk of many illnesses and diseases, and experience a decline in sensory abilities. However, patterns of change vary greatly between individuals and social groups. For example, the correlation between high social class and a sense of good or excellent health is very strong.

Alzheimer's disease is discussed as a critical problem facing the aged today, affecting some 3 million (10 percent) of the population over the age of 65.

Psychological Changes

Most elderly people do not suffer from mental or psychological problems. To more adequately assess mental functioning, psychologists have more precisely defined the concept of intelligence. Research suggests that measures of intelligence focusing on sensorimotor coordination do show decline in aged persons. Intelligence tests focusing on knowledge show no decline. Verbal and numerical skills even show rising ability with age. Psychological research has also shown that personality changes little as we grow old.

Aging and Culture

The significance of age comes from social constructs. Age is a relative term. Life expectancy shows significant cross-cultural variation (see **Global Map 14-1** P. 388), and it affects the cultural perception of age. Technological advances in medicine and health are important, but the critical role played by social relationships is perhaps even more significant. The **Cross-Cultural Comparison** box (pp. 390-91) provides an illustration from Abkhasia in the Commonwealth of Independent States.

Aging and Social Stratification

Age stratification is defined as the unequal distribution of wealth, power, and privileges among people of different ages. This varies cross-culturally, and the old seem to generally have more power in societies in which they can accumulate wealth. Pastoral, horticultural, and agrarian societies have the technological capabilities to produce surpluses to enable accumulation to occur. Such societies tend toward *gerontocracy*, a form of social organization in which the elderly have the most wealth, power, and privileges. Industrialization tends to create a decline in the relative power and prestige of the aged as the prime source of wealth shifts away from the land and geographical mobility

189

undermines the strength of families. The rapid change in technology also diminishes the expertise of the elderly. Many elderly are pushed toward nonproductive roles as the productivity of industrial society increases. Japan is discussed as an example of a culture in which the productive role and status of the elderly in the family and labor force has remained intact, providing the aged with greater prestige.

TRANSITIONS AND PROBLEMS OF AGING

It is argued that old age, as a stage in the human life cycle, presents the greatest of personal challenges. Recognizing one's own mortality and maintaining self-esteem during a period of physical decline are central to this challenge. Bernice Neugarten identified four different personality types and their differing adjustments to old age. From most successful to least successful they are: *integrated*, *defended*, *passive-dependent*, *disintegrated* and *disorganized*. A major point being made is that negative stereotypes of old age are misleading, and the experience of old age varies greatly from individual to individual.

Social Isolation

Central among the adjustments an individual must make during old age is the accommodation to increased social isolation. Negative stereotypes, retirement, and physical problems diminish social interaction. The most profound social isolation however occurs with the death of a significant other, particularly a spouse.

Table 14-1 (p. 392) outlines the living arrangements of the elderly. Critical differences between males and females are discussed. It is further pointed out that many elderly people live close to adult relatives. Contact with their children is more frequent than most of us might think, with only 10 percent reporting no visit with any of their children in the last month. Families are a meaningful cushion in lessening social isolation.

Retirement

Historically, particularly for men, occupational identity has been critical for a sense of self. Retirement is discussed as being a recent phenomenon. Before the Social Security Act of 1935 the vast majority of men had to continue their participation in the labor force out of economic necessity. Retirement has been promoted because of advanced technology reducing the need for labor and placing such importance on up-to-date skills. Congress phased out mandatory retirement policies in 1987; however most people still retire at age 65.

Aging and Poverty

Aging is typically associated with a decline in income. While poverty rates rise somewhat for people over the age of 65, relative to the entire population their poverty rate is below the average. Social Security, pensions, occupational and interest income are all important sources of income for the elderly. In the box (p. 394) economic policies and programs for the elderly are discussed.

Figure 14-2 (p. 393) shows the proportion of different age groups in America living in poverty. Gaps between racial and ethnic groups, and between men and women continue. Differences in earnings between women and men are outlined in Table 14-2 (p. 395). The income gap for elderly women is greater than for younger women.

Abuse of the Elderly

The government estimates that 3 percent of the aged in our society are victimized by some type of maltreatment each year. Perhaps one in ten suffers abuse at some time during old age. Much of the abuse is attributed to the stress resulting from the elderly person's child caring for them.

THEORETICAL ANALYSIS OF AGING

Structural-Functional Analysis: Aging and Disengagement

Disengagement theory refers to an analysis linking the disengagement by elderly people from positions of social responsibility to the orderly operation of society. This theory is based on Talcott Parson's structural-functional analysis. An orderly transfer of various statuses and roles from the old to the young provides benefits for both society and individuals. A problem with this view is that many older people do not want to relinquish their statuses and roles and are quite capably functioning within them.

Symbolic-Interaction Analysis: Aging and Activity

Activity theory is an analysis linking personal satisfaction in old age to a high level of activity. Disengagement is viewed as diminishing satisfaction and meaning in life. While disengaging from certain statuses and roles, the elderly shift to new ones based on their own distinctive needs, interests, talents and capabilities. The diversity of the aged population is emphasized. This approach may however underestimate the degree of health restrictions present among the aged.

Social-Conflict Analysis: Aging and Inequality

Using this approach one sees different age categories across the life cycle competing for scarce resources. The status of the elderly relative to younger people is viewed as being disadvantaged. This is the result of the emphasis in capitalist societies on valuing people for what they do rather than for who they are. While focusing our attention on the age stratification which does exist in society, this approach tends to ignore the improvement in social standing of the elderly in recent decades.

AGEISM

Ageism refers to prejudice and discrimination against the elderly. Over time it becomes institutionalized in society. This can often take very subtle forms. Ageism causes unwarranted generalizations about the aged which creates stereotypes that perpetuate inequalities between the aged and the young. Some research suggests that such negative stereotyping has diminished in recent years, particularly in the mass media. Examples are discussed.

The Elderly: A Minority?

Sociologists vary in their opinion concerning the classification of the aged as a minority group. Certain general characteristics of the aged population seem consistent with such a status, however the social disadvantages faced by the elderly are less substantial than those experienced by other categories of people labeled as minorities. Their situation is labeled as an open status, not permanent or exclusive. Our author concludes that while being a distinctive segment of the American population the aged should not carry the status of minority group.

DEATH AND DYING

The Bible tells us of two certainties: the fact of birth and the inevitability of death. The character of death is discussed in this section as being variable over history.

Historical Patterns of Death

Throughout much of human history death was a part of everyday life. Disease and natural catastrophes were widespread. In preindustrial societies, less productive people (infants and the aged) were sometimes put to death (infanticide/geronticide) for the sake of preserving the group. As societies began to gain some measure of control over death through technological advances, attitudes about death changed. It was no longer an everyday experience in the lives of people. The **Critical Thinking** box (p. 401) discusses some ethical and economic issues being raised given the longer life expectancy and larger aged population in our society.

The Modern Separation of Life and Death

Death is now looked at as something unnatural. Death is becoming, in a sense, separate from life. Death and dying are now physically removed from the rest of life. Dying now typically occurs away from the family, in a hospital. Fear and anxiety dominate our feelings about death.

This sense of dying may not be quite so representative of the aged who are sick, who may see it as being more a release from suffering. Many ethical issues are being raised concerning the extent to which a life should be prolonged by artificial means.

Bereavement

Elizabeth Kubler-Ross's stages of death are briefly discussed, and it is argued that the bereavement process parallels these stages of dying. One program, *Hospice*, is discussed as an attempt to provide support for dying people and their families. Bereavement may last a long period of time and cause social isolation and disorientation.

PART IV: KEY CONCEPTS

Define each of the following concepts in the space provided or on separate paper. Check the accuracy of your answers by referring to the key concepts section at the end of the chapter in the text as well as by referring to italicized definitions located throughout the chapter.

activity theory
ageism
age stratification
defended personality
disengagement theory
disintegrated and disorganized personality
integrated personality
gerontocracy
gerontology
Hemlock Society
Hospice
open status
passive-dependent personality

PART V: STUDY QUESTIONS

True-False

1. T F   Given the recent rise in the birth rate in the U.S. the median age in our society is decreasing.
2. T F   The elderly account for almost two-thirds of all medical expenditures in the U.S.
3. T F   The sensory abilities of people tend to diminish in old age.
4. T F   Most psychological research shows that personality characteristics of a person change considerably as they grow old.
5. T F   A gerontocracy is a form of social organization in which elderly people have the most wealth, power, and privileges.
6. T F   Most elderly women live alone.
7. T F   Most American workers retire at age 65 or earlier.
8. T F   Children are more likely to be poor in American society than are the aged.

9. T F   Females working full-time past the age of 65 earn more than their male counterparts.

10. T F   Our author argues that the elderly clearly represent a minority group in our society.

Multiple-Choice

1. Currently, the aged represent _____ percent of our population.

    (a) 6.4   (c) 17.5
    (b) 12.7   (d) 20.6

2. Between 1990-2020, the number of elderly Americans, aged 65 and over, will increase by _____ percent; during that time, the number of people under the age of 50 will rise by only ____ percent.

    (a) 75/2   (c) 50/50
    (b) 30/10   (d) 25/40

3. The share of the federal budget directed toward the aged is:

    (a) 10   (d) 50
    (b) 21   (e) less than 5
    (c) 33

4. The Abkhasian society exhibits exceptional longevity due to:

    (a) a healthy diet
    (b) regular exercise
    (c) positive self-image of the elderly in society
    (d) all of the above

5. Which of the following is not a personality type identified by Neugarten in her study of adjustment to old age?

    (a) disintegrated and disorganized
    (b) residual-active
    (c) passive-dependent
    (d) integrated
    (e) defended

194

6. Most elderly males:

    (a)   live alone
    (b)   live in nursing homes
    (c)   live with extended family members
    (d)   live with their spouse

7. Approximately what percentage of the aged population in the U.S. lives in poverty?

    (a)   less than 5   (d)   33
    (b)   18   (e)   12
    (c)   25

8. Activity theory is a sociological theory of aging that is based upon:

    (a)   structural-functional analysis
    (b)   social-conflict analysis
    (c)   symbolic-interaction analysis
    (d)   social-exchange analysis

9. Some sociologists argue that the elderly constitute a minority group while others disagree. Which of the following reasons is an argument against the elderly being a minority group?

    (a)   the status of being elderly is an open status
    (b)   the elderly think of themselves in terms of sex, race, and ethnicity
    (c)   the social disadvantages of the elderly are not as great as for other categories of people
    (d)   all of the above

10. In modern American society death has become:

    (a)   more common to everyday experience
    (b)   less of an ethical issue
    (c)   an event that occurs often in the home of the dying person
    (d)   easier to accept
    (e)   defined as an unnatural event

Fill-In

1. Today's younger adults may well become a _____ generation, spending as much time caring for their aging parents as for their own children.
2. _____ is the study of aging and the elderly.

3. Most of Neugarten's aged subjects had what she labeled a _____ personality.
4. Approximately _____ percent of elderly women in the U.S. live with a spouse.
5. _____ theory is an analysis linking disengagement by elderly people from positions of social responsibility to the orderly operation of society.
6. _____ refers to prejudice and discrimination against the elderly.
7. Our author believes the aged should not be identified as a minority group, but rather be considered a _____ segment of the American population.
8. In 1900, about _____ of all deaths in the U.S. occurred before the age of five. By the late 1991, almost _____ percent of Americans died after the age of 55.
9. While our ancestors accepted death as part of life, we now approach the prospect of dying with _____ and _____.
10. It is estimated that health care costs for the aged in the year 2000 will reach _____ annually.

Definition and Short-Answer

1. What is the Hemlock Society? What are your thoughts and feelings about this organization and its purposes? What are some of the broader concerns relating to this issue?
2. Define gerontology.
3. Define age stratification. How does it vary between hunting and gathering, horticultural, agrarian, and industrial societies?
4. What are the four types of personalities identified by Neugarten? In what ways are they different in terms of helping a person adjust to old age?
5. Differentiate between activity theory and disengagement theory in terms of how each helps us understand the changing status of the aged in society.
6. Why is elder abuse so common in the U.S.?
7. Discuss the relative economic condition of the aged in our society today?
8. According to social-conflict theorists, why is the status of the aged diminished in capitalist societies?
9. What are the arguments in the debate concerning whether the aged are a minority group?
10. What are Daniel Callahan's points concerning how much old age can America afford?

PART VI: ANSWERS TO STUDY QUESTIONS

True-False

1.	F (p. 382)	6.	F (p. 391)
2.	F (p. 383)	7.	T (p. 393)
3.	T (p. 385)	8.	T (p. 393)
4.	F (p. 386)	9.	F (p. 395)
5.	T (p. 387)	10.	F (p. 398)

Multiple-Choice

1.	b (p. 382)	6.	d (p. 380)
2.	a (p. 382)	7.	e (p. 393)
3.	c (p. 383)	8.	c (p. 396)
4.	d (pp. 390-91)	9.	e (p. 398)
5.	b (pp. 389-90)	10.	e (p. 400)

Fill-In

1. sandwich (pp. 383-85)
2. gerontology (p. 383)
3. integrated (p. 390)
4. 50 (p. 380)
5. disengagement (p. 396)
6. ageism (p. 397)
7. distinctive (p. 398)
8. one-third/85 (p. 400)
9. fear/anxiety (p. 400)
10. 200 billion (p. 401)

PART VII: ANALYSIS AND COMMENT

Critical Thinking

"The Sandwich Generation: Who Should Care for Aging Parents?"

Key Points: Questions:

"Setting Limits: How Much Old Age Can We Afford?"

Key Points: Questions:

Cross-Cultural Analysis

"Growing (Very) Old in Abkhasia"

Key Points: Questions:

A Decade of Change

"The Elderly: A Financial Windfall"

Key Points: Questions:

Family

15

PART I: CHAPTER OUTLINE

I.   The Family: Basic Concepts
II.   The Family in Cross-Cultural Perspective
    A.   Marriage Patterns
    B.   Residential Patterns
    C.   Patterns of Descent
    D.   Patterns of Authority
III. Theoretical Analysis of the Family
    A.   Functions of the Family
        1.   Socialization
        2.   Regulation of Sexual Activity
        3.   Social Placement
        4.   Material and Economic Security
    B.   Social Inequality and the Family
        1.   The Family, Class, and Race
        2.   The Family and Patriarchy
    C.   Other Theoretical Analyses
        1.   The Social Construction of Family Life
        2.   Social-Exchange Analysis
IV.   Stages of Family Life
    A.   Courtship
    B.   Settling In: Ideal and Real Marriages
    C.   Childrearing
    D.   The Family in Later Life
V.   Varieties of Family Life
    A.   Social Class
    B.   Ethnicity and Race
        1.   Hispanic-American Families
        2.   African-American Families
    C.   Gender
VI.   Transition and Problems in Family Life
    A. Divorce
        1.   Who Divorces?
        2.   Problems of Divorce

        B.   Remarriage
        C.   Family Violence
                1.   Violence Against Women
                2.   Violence Against Children
VII.   Alternative Family Forms
        A.   One-Parent Families
        B.   Cohabitation
        C.   Gay Male and Lesbian Couples
        D.   Singlehood
VIII.   New Reproductive Technology and the Family
        A.   In Vitro Fertilization
        B.   Ethical Issues
IX.   The Family in the Twenty-First Century

PART II: LEARNING OBJECTIVES

1.   To define the basic concepts of kinship, family, family of orientation, family of procreation, and marriage.
2.   To cross-culturally compare and contrast marriage patterns, residential patterns, patterns of descent, and patterns of authority.
3.   To describe the four functions of the family from the structural-functional perspective.
4.   To explain the link between family and social inequality using the social-conflict perspective.
5.   To identify the contributions that symbolic-interaction analysis and social-exchange analysis have made to the sociological knowledge of the family.
6.   To describe the life course of the average American family.
7.   To explain the impact of social class, race, ethnicity, and gender socialization on the family.
8.   To describe the problems and transitions that seriously affect family life: divorce, remarriage, spousal and child abuse.
9.   To describe the composition and prevalence of alternative family forms: one-parent families, cohabitation, gay males and lesbian couples, and singlehood.
10.   To explain the impact, both technologically and ethically, of new reproductive techniques on the family.
11.   To identify four sociological conclusions about the family as we enter the twenty-first century.

PART III: CHAPTER REVIEW

The controversial issue of *surrogacy* is discussed at the beginning of this chapter. In 1991 twins were born to Arlette Schweitzer. What is significant about this is that they are her grandchildren. Surrogacy is only one of many issues which confronts our tradition notion of the family.

THE FAMILY: BASIC CONCEPTS

Kinship refers to social relationships based on blood, marriage, or adoption. The functional significance of this institution tends to decline with industrialization. The *family* is defined as a relatively permanent social group of two or more people, who are related by blood, marriage, or adoption and who usually live together. Two different types of families are differentiated. A *family of orientation* is the family into which a person is born and receives early socialization, while a *family of procreation* is a family within which people have or adopt children of their own. In most societies, families begin with *marriage*, or a socially approved relationship involving economic cooperation and allowing sexual activity and childbearing, that is expected to be relatively enduring. The significance of marriage for childbearing is evident in the labels *illegitimacy* and *matrimony*. Controversy exists today in terms of how the family, both structurally and functionally, is to be understood, and how it is to be defined officially. For instance, *families of affinity*, or groups whose members are drawn together and who think of themselves as a family, are becoming more common.

THE FAMILY IN CROSS-CULTURAL PERSPECTIVE

While all societies recognize families there are great cross-cultural variations in the structures and functions of this institution. Industrial societies recognize the *nuclear family*, a social unit composed of one or, more commonly, two parents and children. This is sometimes referred to as the *conjugal family*. In preindustrial societies the *extended family*, a social unit including parents, children, and other kin, is more common. This type of family is also referred to as a *consanguine family*, meaning based upon blood ties.

What does the future hold for the family? The **Cross-Cultural Comparison** box (pp. 408-09) looks at Sweden, a very progressive society, and addresses the issue of how strong their family is today.

Marriage Patterns

Norms identify categories of people suitable for marriage for particular individuals. *Endogamy*, refers to a normative pattern of marriage between people of the same social group or category. It is differentiated from the norm of *exogamy*, or marriage between people of different social groups or categories. All societies enforce varying degrees of each type. *Monogamy* means marriage that joins one female and one male. Serial monogamy refers to a number of monogamous marriages over one's lifetime. *Polygamy* is defined as marriage that unites three or more people. Polygamy takes one of two forms. One type is called *polygyny*, by far the most common, referring to a marriage that joins one male with more than one female. The second type is called *polyandry*, referring to marriage that joins one female with more than one male. **Global Map 15-1** (p. 410) looks at marital form in global perspective.

Residential Patterns

Where people live after they are married also varies cross-culturally. *Neolocality*, a residential pattern in which a married couple lives apart from the parents of both spouses, is the most common form in industrial societies. In preindustrial societies residing with one set of parents is more typical. *Patrilocality* is a residential pattern in which a married couple lives with or near the husband's family. *Matrilocality* is a residential pattern in which a married couple lives with or near the wife's family. This latter pattern is rare.

Patterns of Descent

Descent refers to the system by which kinship is traced over generations. Industrial societies follow the **bilateral descent** system of tracing kinship through both males and females. Preindustrial societies typically follow one of two patterns of unilineal descent. The more common, *patrilineal descent,* is a system tracing kinship through males. *Matrilineal descent* refers to a system of descent tracing kinship through females. Patrilineal systems are typically pastoral or agrarian societies, while matrilineal systems are common in horticultural societies.

Patterns of Authority

The universal presence of patriarchy is reflected in the predominance of polygyny, patrilocality, and patrilineal descent. No known society is clearly matriarchal.

THEORETICAL ANALYSIS OF THE FAMILY

Functions of the Family

The structural-functionalists focus on several important social functions served by the family.

Socialization

The family serves as the primary agent in the socialization process during the entire life course of an individual.

Regulation of Sexual Activity

Some restrictions on sexual behavior is characteristic of every culture. Every society has some type of *incest taboo*, a cultural norm forbidding sexual relations and marriage between certain kin. However, the specific kinship members who are subject to the taboo varies greatly cross-culturally. The significance of the incest taboo is most basically social rather than biological. It minimizes sexual competition, creates alliances between families through exogamous marriages, and establishes specific linkages of rights and obligations between people.

Social Placement

Many ascribed statuses are determined at birth through the family. Transmission of social standing through the family is universal.

Material and Economic Security

Families are to provide for the physical and financial support of its members. Self-worth and security are established within the intense and enduring relationships characteristic of the family.

Structural-functionalists tend to underemphasize problems in families, and underestimate the great diversity of family forms.

Social Inequality and the Family

The focus of the social-conflict approach to the study of the family is how this institution perpetuates patterns of social inequality.

The Family, Class, and Race

Social class divisions are preserved by the inheritance of wealth. Racial and ethnic inequalities are maintained through endogamy.

The Family and Patriarchy

Further, patriarchal values and patterns have established and maintained the subordinate status of women. The fact that women still bear most of the responsibility for childrearing, even given their increased participation in the paid labor force is a critical issue.

Other Theoretical Analyses

The structural-functional and social-conflict paradigms provide a macro-level perspective from which to understand the institution of the family.

The Social Construction of Family Life

Symbolic-interaction analysis is used to study how specific realities are constructed within specific families. Varying experiences and perceptions of different family members are stressed.

Social-Exchange Analysis

Social-exchange theory draws attention to the power of negotiation within families. People are seen as exchanging socially valued resources with each other. As gender roles are converging,so is what ales and females have to exchange.

While providing a meaningful counterbalance to the macro-level approaches, the micro-level is limited in its ability to allow us to see the cultural forces impacting upon the family.

STAGES OF FAMILY LIFE

Family life is viewed as dynamic, consisting of changing patterns over its life cycle.

Courtship

Preindustrial societies typically are characterized by *arranged marriages* where the kinship group determines marriage partners. Marriages are viewed as alliances between different kinship groups for economic and political purposes.

In industrial societies personal choice in mate selection dominates, with tremendous emphasis on *romantic love*. This is particularly true in the U.S. Romantic love is a less stable foundation for marriage than are social and economic considerations. Figure 15-1 (p. 415) shows how the average age at first marriage for women and men has changed over the last century. Economic patterns in society affects the average age at first marriage.

Homogamy is very common. This is defined as marriage between people with the same social characteristics.

Settling In: Ideal and Real Marriages

The institutions of marriage and family tends to be idealized by most people, with real life experiences never quite meeting expectations. The realities of marriage and its responsibilities and routines are often very different from courtship relationships. Changing patterns of sexual experiences and norms have affected courtship and marriage as well. Table 15-1 (p. 417) presents data on the frequency of sexual activity among married couples. Research on extramarital sex suggests that this phenomenon is a reality in a fairly significant percentage of marriages.

Childrearing

Childrearing creates major transitions for families. Childrearing presents significant changes for family relationships, some very problematic for marriage. Table 15-2 (p. 418) presents statistics concerning American adults' ideas about the ideal number of children for a family. Most people desire two or three children. Several factors have brought about a decline in the birth rate in America. Children are no longer economic assets for families as they were in the past. Birth control technology has also affected birth rates. Further, with most women in the labor force, this creates difficulties in having larger families.

As vital as parenthood is, we do very little officially to prepare people for its responsibilities. With most women in the labor force and also having to maintain their traditional domestic responsibilities, many other challenges and problems have been created. For instance, there are many *latchkey kids* - children of working parents who are left to care for themselves for portions of the day.

The Family in Later Life

With life expectancy increasing, the number of years a couple live together without children during what is known as the "empty-nest" years is increasing. Many new challenges are faced by couples during these years. The departure of children and the maintenance of relationships with them, the increased value of companionship in marriage, retirement, and death of one's spouse are major events in later life.

VARIETIES OF FAMILY LIFE

Social Class

Social class has a major impact on the family, including determining a family's standard of living, economic security, and likelihood of unemployment. Further, research by Lillian Rubin suggests that differences in the lifestyles of working-class and middle-class families affect relationships within a family and typical concerns of its members. Research also illustrates how social class also affects the relationship of spouses, with middle-class couples being more open and expressive with each other. Differences in socialization patterns between classes is also discussed.

Ethnicity and Race

Hispanic American Families

The traditional extended family system remains strong among this segment of our population. Conventional gender role patterns are also maintained. *Machismo*, masculine strength, daring, and sexual prowess, along with the resulting double-standard are also strong. Assimilation is gradually changing traditional patterns.

African-American Families

A critical fact concerning this segment of our population is the reality of their economic disadvantage. African-American families earn only 60 percent of the average for all American families. Given these conditions maintaining family stability is very difficult.

The Moynihan Report of 1965 generated a controversy of opinion over the extent to which black Americans were responsible for their high poverty rates. Moynihan emphasized the "pathological" black family as a cause of a cycle of poverty. Critics of this view, such as William Ryan, argue instead that black Americans suffer economic disadvantages. Ryan sees the unstable family structure as a consequence, not a cause of poverty.

Figure 15-2 (p. 422) shows the differences in family structure between whites, African-Americans, Asians, and Hispanic-Americans.

Gender

Cultural views regarding gender in American society significantly affect the family. Jesse Bernard suggests every marriage is actually two separate ones, "his" and "hers." Cultural values tend to promote the idea that marriage is more beneficial for women than for men. Marriage apparently provides many advantages for men.

Research has identified four different types of marriages related to different levels of depression in men and women. These include: (1) the traditional marriage in which the husband is the sole breadwinner and the wife is responsible for all housekeeping and childrearing, (2) a marriage where both spouses are in the labor force, the wife out of economic necessity, where once again the wife is responsible for all household chores and childrearing, (3) a marriage similar to (2), however here the wife works for the psychological benefits of employment, and (4) an egalitarian marriage where both are happy to be working outside the home and both share household and childrearing responsibilities. Figure 15-3 (p. 424) shows how depression levels vary for women and men by marital type.

TRANSITION AND PROBLEMS IN FAMILY LIFE

Divorce

The divorce rate in the U.S. during this century has fluctuated dramatically with changing conditions in society. Figure 15-4 (p. 425) illustrates these patterns. America has one of the highest marriage rates in the world. However, while the marriage rate has remained stable over the century, the divorce rate has risen significantly. A number of broad societal changes have influenced the increase on divorce rates. These factors include: spending less time together as families, the greater labor force participation rate for women, and the romantic love basis for marriage. Further, with more families having dual-earner marriages at their heart, childrearing becomes more burdensome. Divorces are also more likely due to greater geographic mobility and more liberal divorce laws.

Who Divorces?

Divorce is more common among young couples (especially teen and young marriages resulting from an unexpected pregnancy), the lower classes, couples with alcohol problems, couples with dissimilar social backgrounds, the geographically mobile, and in marriages in which women have successful careers. Further, people who have divorced once are more likely to divorce again than people in their first marriages.

Problems of Divorce

Paul Bohannan has suggested divorce involves different adjustments for men and women. These include *emotional*, *legal*, *psychic*, *community*, *economic*, and *parental*. Divorce is also discussed in terms of the effects on children.

Remarriage

About 80 percent of people who divorce in the U.S. remarry. Remarriage rates are higher for men than for women. The chances of the remarriage being successful are less than first marriages. Ann Goetting links the same transitions to remarriage as Bohannan does to divorce (emotional, legal, etc.).

Remarriage often creates a *blended family* consisting of a biological parent and stepparent, along with children of their respective first marriages and any children of the blended marriage. This provides a context in which stress and conflict is often greater than in other families.

Family Violence

Many families are characterized by *family violence*, or emotional, physical, or sexual abuse of one family member by another. The family has been characterized as one of the most violent institutions in our society.

Violence Against Women

Violence transcends the boundaries of social class. Common stereotypes of abusers are brought into question using empirical data. Low reporting rates of family violence deflates the statistics. One-sixth of all couples have relationships characterized by at least some violence each year. The argument is made that the seriousness of abuse is greater for wives than for husbands.

Marital rape is a form of family violence that has gotten much attention in recent years in the mass media. The historical factor of wives as property has negatively influenced our understanding of this problem.

Traditionally, women have had few options and the violent marriage acts as a trap for many women. The traditional view of domestic violence as a private concern of families has also hindered programs and policies in terms of their effectiveness in dealing with this problem.

Violence Against Children

About two million children are victims of abuse each year, though this is only a rough estimate. Abuse is argued to be both physical and emotional. These children often feel guilt, self-blame, and psychological problems as a result of the abuse. Most abusers are men. Their abusive behaviors are often learned during their own childhoods.

ALTERNATIVE FAMILY FORMS

One-Parent Families

Over the last twenty years there has been a dramatic increase in the percentage of single-parent families. Figure 15-5 (p. 430) indicates the change in the proportion of single-parent families in 1970 and 1991. Women are four times more likely than men to head a single-parent family. Distributions for whites, African-Americans, and Hispanic Americans are discussed. Single-parent families are not by themselves detrimental to children's development; however, economic hardships often occur in female-headed, single-parent families.

Cohabitation

Cohabitation is the sharing of a household by an unmarried couple. There has been a five-fold increase in cohabitation over the last twenty years. This particular household structure is very common among college students. Most cohabitating couples do not marry, and only a small percentage have children. Commitment tends not to be as strong as in marriage.

Gay and Lesbian Couples

In 1989 Denmark became the first country to legalize homosexual marriages. However, even there, legal adoption is still not allowed for such couples. A few legal benefits of marriage for gays exist in some metropolitan areas in the U.S. Many gay couples form long-term relationships. Some of these couples are raising children. Their interpersonal relationships parallel heterosexual relationships in terms of communication, finances, and domestic division of labor. Many feel they must keep their relationships a secret to avoid prejudice and discrimination. This situation can place considerable strain on relationships.

Singlehood

Singlehood is increasing in the U.S. as portrayed in Figure 15-6 (p. 432). About one in four households contains a single adult. Singlehood is still primarily a transitory stage, although financially independent women now comprise a fast-growing component that choose singlehood rather than being resigned to it. As women reach their 30s and 40s unmarried, the availability of men relative to themselves decreases significantly.

NEW REPRODUCTIVE TECHNOLOGY AND THE FAMILY

The impact of new reproductive technology on the family in recent years has been significant, with many benefits having been realized. However, the new technology has brought with it many difficult ethical problems.

In Vitro Fertilization

This process involves the union of the male sperm and the female ovum in glass rather than in the woman's body. The benefits are twofold. First, about 20 percent of couples who otherwise could not conceive are able to using this technique. Second, the genetic screening of sperm and eggs reduces the incidence of birth defects.

Ethical Issues

Several ethical issues have been created with the new reproductive technology. One concerns the fact that the benefits are expensive and only available to those who can afford them. A second issue involves the control medical experts have over who the technology is made available to. Another problem concerns surrogate motherhood. Moral and cultural legal standards to guide this option remain ambiguous at this time. The **Critical Thinking** box (p. 433) discusses views of the Catholic Church on these new technologies.

THE FAMILY IN THE TWENTY-FIRST CENTURY

Family life has dramatically changed in recent decades. Four general conclusions are proposed looking ahead to the next century. First, marriage "till death do us part" appears unrealistic for most people. Second, family life will be highly variable,being represented by many family forms. Third, more children will be raised in single-families. And fourth, new reproductive technology will shape families in the next century. Marriage and family are likely to remain the foundation of our society.

PART IV: KEY CONCEPTS

Define each of the following concepts in the space provided or on separate paper. Check the accuracy of your answers by referring to the key concepts section at the end of the chapter in the text as well as by referring to italicized definitions located throughout the chapter.

bilateral descent
blended family

cohabitation
consanguine family
descent
endogamy
exogamy
extended family
family
family of orientation
family of procreation
family violence
homogamy
incest taboo
kinship
marriage
matrilineal descent
matrilocality
monogamy
neolocality
nuclear family
patrilineal descent
patrilocality
polyandry
polygamy
polygyny
serial monogamy

PART V: STUDY QUESTIONS

True-False

1. T F The family into which one is born is referred to as the family of procreation.
2. T F Norms of endogamy are found in every society.
3. T F Matrilocality occurs most frequently in cultures where families define daughters as more valued economic assets than sons.
4. T F Every known culture has some type of incest taboo.
5. T F While the actual number is smaller, the "ideal" number of children to have for most married American adults is three or more.
6. T F Lillian Rubin's research focuses on the interaction between social class and marital relationship.
7. T F The divorce rate in the U.S. is lower than is true for most other modern industrialized societies.
8. T F According to the text, most child abusers are men.

9. T F   The percentage of households with single adults has actually been decreasing over the last two decades.
10. T F   Test-tube babies are, technically speaking, the result of the process of in vitro fertilization.

Multiple-Choice

1. The consanguine family is also known as the:

    (a) conjugal family   (d) family of orientation
    (b) nuclear family   (e) family of procreation
    (c) extended family

2. The predominant family form in American society has always been the:

    (a) nuclear family   (c) exogamous
    (b) consanguine   (d) extended

3. Exogamy and endogamy are cultural norms relating to:

    (a) marriage patterns   (d) residence patterns
    (b) descent regulations   (e) authority patterns
    (c) beliefs about romantic love

4. A marriage form that unites one woman with two or more men is termed:

    (a) monogamy   (c) polyandry
    (b) polygyny   (d) endogamy

5. Which of the following is not a descent pattern?

    (a) matrilineal
    (b) patrilineal
    (c) bilateral
    (d) neolocal
    (e) all are descent patterns

6. Preindustrial societies that are agrarian or pastoral in nature typically exhibit:

    (a) neolocality   (c) patrilineal descent
    (b) bilateral descent   (d) matrilineal descent

7. The type of sociological analysis of the family that holds that the family serves to perpetuate patriarchy is:

   (a) social-exchange analysis
   (b) social-conflict analysis
   (c) structural-functional analysis
   (d) symbolic-interaction analysis

8. Sociologists have noted that romantic love as a basis for marriage:

   (a) is reinforced by cultural values
   (b) acts as a strong incentive to leave one's original family of orientation to form a new family of procreation
   (c) is not as stable a basis for marriage as social and economic bases
   (d) all of the above

9. Which of the following is not an accurate statement?

   (a) over 40 percent of black families are headed by women
   (b) black household income is only about 57% of white family income on average
   (c) the U.S. has one of the highest marriage rates in the world
   (d) about 79% of families with children have two parents at home
   (e) egalitarian marriages tend to be happier for women, but very frustrating and unfulfilling for men

10. Daniel Moynihan published a controversial interpretation of the American black family in the 1960s. Which of the following is a criticism of Moynihan's analysis?

    (a) Moynihan neglected to analyze the most commonly occurring black family headed by two parents
    (b) Moynihan implied that the female-headed, single-parent family was the cause of poverty among blacks
    (c) Moynihan claimed that female-headed black families were pathological
    (d) all of the above

11. Remarriage often creates families composed of both biological parents and stepparents and children. These are called:

   (a) second families   (c) focal families
   (b) blended families   (d) families of orientation

Fill-In

1. The family into which one is born and receives early socialization is termed the _____ of _____. A family within which people have their own children is termed the _____ of _____.
2. The _____ family is based on blood ties.
3. _____ is the normative pattern referring to marriage between people of the same social group or category.
4. _____ is a marriage that joins one female with more than one male.
5. Cultural norms that forbid sexual relations or marriage between specified kin are called _____ _____.
6. In the year after a divorce, _____ experience a decrease in their standard of living while _____ experience an increase.
7. The term for one woman biologically bearing another woman's child is _____ _____.
8. The _____ has recently condemned all of the new reproductive technologies as reducing human life to an object of research.
9. Family life in the twenty-first century is likely to be _____ rather than monolithic in sociologists' view.
10. Sociologists predict that there will be a noticeable _____ in the importance of males in child rearing as a result of many different family forms.

Definition and Short-Answer

1. What are the four basic functions of the family according to structural-functionalists?
2. Define and describe the three patterns of descent outlined in the text.
3. What were the basic conclusions of the Moynihan Report of 1965? What are some criticisms of this report?
4. Why has the divorce rate increased in recent decades in the U.S.?
5. What are the four stages of the family life cycle which are outlined in the text? Describe the major events which occur during each stage.
6. Six adjustments to divorce are identified by Paul Bohannan. Identify and describe each.
7. Four types of marriages are described which are related to depression in men and women. what are these?
8. In what ways are middle-class and working-class marriages different according to research cited in the text?
9. What are the four conclusions being made about marriage and family into the twenty-first century?

PART VI: ANSWERS TO STUDY QUESTIONS

True-False

1.	F (p. 406)	6.	T (p. 420)
2.	T (p. 407)	7.	F (p. 425)
3.	T (p. 409)	8.	T (p. 429)
4.	T (p. 411)	9.	F (p. 432)
5.	F (p. 418)	10.	T (p. 432)

Multiple-Choice

1.	c (p. 406)	7.	b (p. 413)
2.	a (p. 406)	8.	d (p. 415)
3.	a (p. 407)	9.	e (pp. 421-22)
4.	c (p. 407)	10.	d (p. 422)
5.	d (pp. 410-11)	11.	b (p. 427)
6.	c (p. 411)		

Fill-In

1. family/procreation   family/orientation (p. 406)
2. consanguine (p. 406)
3. endogamy (p. 407)
4. polyandry (p. 407)
5. incest taboos (p. 411)
6. women/men (p. 426)
7. surrogate motherhood (p. 433)
8. Catholic Church (p. 434)
9. variable (p. 434)
10. decrease (p. 434)

PART VII: ANALYSIS AND COMMENT

Cross-Cultural Comparison

"Sweden: The Weakest Families on Earth?"

Key Points: Questions:

Critical Thinking

"Are New Reproductive Technologies Immoral?
 The Catholic Churches View"

    Key Points: Questions:

Education

16

PART I: CHAPTER OUTLINE

I.   Education: A Global Survey
    A.   Schooling in Japan
    B.   Schooling in Great Britain
    C.   Schooling in the Commonwealth of Independent States
    D.   Schooling in the United States
II.   The Functions of Schooling
    A.   Socialization
    B.   Cultural Innovation
    C.   Social Integration
    D.   Social Placement
    E.   Latent Functions of Schooling
III. Schooling and Social Inequality
    A.   Social Control
    B.   Testing and Social Inequality
    C.   Tracking and Social Inequality
    D.   Inequality Among Schools
        1.   Public and Private Schools
        2.   Inequality in Public Schooling
    E.   Unequal Access to Higher Education
    F.   Credentialism
    G.   Privilege and Personal Merit
IV.   Problems in American Education
    A.   School Discipline
    B.   Bureaucracy and Student Passivity
    C.   College: The Silent Classroom
    D.   Dropping Out
    E.   Academic Standards and Educational Quality
V.   Recent Issues in U.S. Education
    A.   Magnet Schools
    B.   Schooling the Disabled
    C.   Adult Education
    D.   Schooling for Profit
    E.   Schooling, Computers, and the Future

VI. Summary
VII. Key Concepts
VIII. Suggested Readings

PART II: LEARNING OBJECTIVES

1. To describe the role of education throughout history.
2. To compare and contrast schooling in Great Britain, Japan, the Soviet Union, and the United States.
3. To identify and describe the functions of schooling.
4. To explain how education supports social inequality through social control, testing, and tracking.
5. To distinguish between the quality of education between different public schools, and between public and private schools.
6. To describe the problems associated with unequal access to higher education and credentialism.
7. To identify and analyze the problems facing American education today: school discipline, student passivity, and the decline of academic standards.
8. To describe and explain the reason for development of alternative types of schooling, such as magnet schools, schooling for the disabled, adult education, and the use of computers in schools.

PART III: CHAPTER REVIEW

We are introduced to the Masuo family of Yokohama, Japan. Education in Japan is very competitive, and rigorous application of oneself to its demands is critical through primary and secondary levels to even hope to achieve high enough scores on national tests to get into a national university. Many children go to the Juku, or "cram school," several days a week after their regular day at school.

Education refers to the various ways in which knowledge-including factual information and skills as well as cultural norms and values, is transmitted to members of society. An important kind of education in industrial societies is *schooling*, or formal instruction under direction of specially trained teachers.

EDUCATION: A GLOBAL SURVEY

While today the Japanese and Americans live in advanced industrialized societies which rely heavily on a formal education system, the history of education reveals that preindustrial societies relied on the family to teach the young the necessary skills to survive. With the introduction of agrarian societies education was centered in the relationship between the craftperson and the apprentice. The church provided schooling during the Middle Ages. In European societies of the West, school was an opportunity for the rich only. Mass education was first adopted as a principle in the U.S. *Mandatory education laws*, or legal requirements that children receive a minimum of formal education, began to be enacted in the 1850s. The median number of years of schooling was 8.1 in 1910 and rose to 12.7 by 1991. Table 16-1 (p. 440) summarizes the educational achievement levels of Americans (by decade) from 1910-1991.

While all industrialized societies provide formalized schooling, each does so in its own particular and unique way. **Global Map** 16-1 (p. 441) looks at illiteracy rates around the world.

Schooling in Japan

Mandatory education laws began in 1872. The cultural values of tradition and family are stressed in the early grades. In their early teens, students begin to face the rigorous and competitive exams of the Japanese system. Test scores determine whether a person will go to college, rich and poor alike. Some 90 percent of Japanese students graduate from high school, compared with 76 percent in the U.S. However, only 30 percent go on to college compared to 60 percent in the U.S. Japanese mothers of school age children participate in the labor force at considerably lower rates than American mothers in order to devote themselves to the educational success of their children. The results of their system seem impressive, particularly in the areas of math and science.

Schooling in Great Britain

Schooling in Great Britain has long been associated with the elite. Traditional social distinctions still exist, with many children from wealthy families attending public schools, the equivalent of our private boarding schools. Expansion of the university system during the 1960s and 1970s has allowed all children to compete for Britain's government funded college system. However, graduates of the elite schools of Oxford and Cambridge have considerable economic and political power in Britain.

Schooling in the Commonwealth of Independent States

The former Soviet Union adopted mandatory education laws in the 1930s. According to official policy all children, boys and girls from all ethnic backgrounds, have equal access to higher education. Their system is highly standardized. Much like Japan they have very competitive examinations to identify and advance their most academically advanced students. The government pays for all educational costs.

Schooling in the United States

As is true of the other educational systems discussed, the American educational system has been shaped by distinctive cultural patterns. Democratic ideals have characterized our system, though the ideal of equal opportunity has not been fully achieved. Still, the U.S. has a higher proportion of its population attending college than any other industrialized society.

Americans value practicality, and this fact has influenced the types of studies emphasized in schools. Earlier in this century, John Dewey was a foremost proponent of *progressive education*. While reflecting this view, George Herbert Mead, a symbolic-interactionist, stressed these same ideas. The **A Decade of Change** box (p. 445) shows recent trends in the types of Bachelor's degrees conferred and how these follow trends in jobs.

THE FUNCTIONS OF SCHOOLING

Structural-functional analysis focuses our attention on the functions which educational systems have for society.

Socialization

As societies become more technologically advanced, social institutions must emerge beyond the family to help socialize members of the society to become functioning adults. Important lessons on cultural values and norms are learned in schools at all levels.

Cultural Innovation

Education is not merely a transmission of culture, it is also a factor in the creation of culture through critical inquiry and research.

Social Integration

Through the teaching of certain cultural values and norms, people become more unified. This is a particularly critical function in culturally diverse societies.

Social Placement

Schooling serves as a screening and selection process. Performance is evaluated on the basis of achievement. It provides an opportunity for upward mobility; however ascribed statuses still influence people in terms of their success in our educational system.

Latent Functions of Schooling

Schools serve as babysitters for younger children, and by occupying the time of teenagers, keeps them from engaging in higher rates of socially disruptive behaviors. Lasting relationships are also established in school.

The structural-functionalists stress the ways in which education supports the operation of the industrial economy. One weakness of this approach however is that it fails to focus on how the quality of education varies greatly for different groups of people.

SCHOOLING AND SOCIAL INEQUALITY

Social-conflict analysis views schooling as a perpetuation of social stratification in the United States.

Social Control

Using social-conflict analysis, social control is viewed as an outcome of schooling because youth are socialized to accept the status quo. The term *hidden curriculum* refers to the content of schooling that is often unrecognized. Compliance, punctuality, and discipline are part of the hidden curriculum.

Testing and Social Inequality

An example of a culturally biased question on an achievement test is reviewed. The argument is that standardized tests favor upper-middle class backgrounds. The validity of such tests is therefore being questioned.

Tracking and Social Inequality

Standardized tests are used for the basis of *tracking*, categorically assigning students to different types of educational programs. Proponents of this approach argue that students with superior innate abilities and high motivation should be placed in learning environments with similar students to maximize their learning experience. Critics argue that it perpetuates inequalities and labels certain people as inferior without giving them a change to prove themselves. Tracking has a clear and strong impact on a student's self-concept, with those in the higher tracks being affected positively and those in the lower negatively.

Inequality Among Schools

Public and Private Schools

In 1990, ninety percent of the sixty-five million American students in primary and secondary levels were in public schools. Most students in private educational institutions and the primary and secondary levels attend parochial schools. An increase in fundamentalism has caused some Protestants to send their children to Christian schools where academic and disciplinary standards are more to their liking. Desegregation policies have also caused some parents to place their children in private, more racially homogeneous schools. A small number of families send their children to prestigious preparatory schools. Higher rates of academic achievement are found among students attending private schools than among students attending public schools.

Inequality in Public Schooling

Funds available for public schools vary considerably across the United States. We have some 15,000 school districts in the United States, with annual per-student spending varying from over 8,000 in some areas to under 3,000 in others.

The 1966 Coleman Report revealed that racially segregated schools, officially illegal since 1954, provided inferior education. This report helped initiate busing policies. Coleman however found only a weak relationship between funding and academic qualities of schools. Families and peer groups, and the attitudes of teachers seemed to be most highly correlated with academic achievement.

Unequal Access to Higher Education

Most parents want their children to attend college, and most high school students what to go to college. The most crucial factor affecting access to higher education is money. The cost is high and rapidly increasing. In many respects however equal access has improved in recent decades, though family income continues to affect chances of attending college. Figure 16-1 (p. 451) shows the correlations between family income levels and college attendance rates. The pattern clearly illustrates the significance of social class in determining who goes to college. Figure 16-2 (p. 453) shows the educational achievement levels for different categories of people. Whites are more likely than minorities to complete high school, and the gap increases with each higher level in the educational system.

Table 16-2 (p. 453) shows the differences in annual earnings and education levels for males and females. At all levels males earn significantly more than females. Further, minorities, who are represented disproportionately in lower income families, are finding it more difficult to obtain a college degree.

Even those who make it to college do not necessarily receive equivalent educations. People from lower income families are more likely to be attending community colleges or public universities. Equal opportunity policies and financial aid has certainly opened the doors of higher education for many people who in past decades would not have been able to attend. A college education certainly expands career opportunities and lifetime earning potential.

Credentialism

Sociologist Randall Collins refers to the U.S. as a credential society, meaning degrees and diplomas are used as a sign of a person's ability to perform a specialized occupational role.

Credentialism is the requirement that a person hold some particular diploma or degree as a condition of employment. It acts as a gatekeeping strategy, say conflict theorists, who argue that often credentials bear little relation to the skills and responsibilities of specific jobs.

221

Credentialism has produced *overeducation*, a situation in which workers have more formal education than the performance of their occupation requires. In many respects educational attainment has outpaced the job market's demand for it.

Privilege and Personal Merit

An important theme of social-conflict analysis is that schooling turns social privilege into personal merit. College is seen as a rite of passage for children of wealthier families. In contrast, the **Social Diversity** box (p. 455) discusses the process of transforming social disadvantage into personal deficiency in the life of one bright but disillusioned boy.

The social-conflict approach focuses on education in terms of social inequality. However, it ignores how different kinds of schooling may actually meet the needs and talents of specific students and different categories of students.

PROBLEMS IN AMERICAN EDUCATION

Attitudes of Americans about education are mixed. This is illustrated in Table 16-3 (p. 455). Violence is viewed as a major problem in many schools. Passivity of students is seen as another significant problem. Further, many argue that school standards have dropped in recent decades.

School Discipline

Seventy-five percent of the National Education Association's members believe discipline is a problem in schools. The key to overcoming this problem appears to be firm disciplinary policies in schools, with support from parents and local law enforcement agencies. A school in Los Angeles is discussed as an example.

Bureaucracy and Student Passivity

There is perceived to be a lack of active student participation in the learning process. It is being referred to as *student passivity*. This seems to hold true in all types of schools. Students seem to view education as a series of hurdles rather than as a privilege. Theodore Sizer argues that our bureaucratic structure in schools, while necessary, causes five serious problems. These include: uniformity tending to ignore cultural variation within local communities, defining success by numerical ratings of performance while overlooking less quantifiable factors, forcing rigid expectations on all students regardless of their particular talents or situations, creating too specialized a division of labor, and giving students little responsibility for their own learning.

Suggested changes in the bureaucratic system include smaller classes, more broadly trained teachers, elimination of rigid class schedules, and basing graduation on what is learned rather than on the amount of time spent in school.

College: The Silent Classroom

What little research has been done in college classroom settings, for example research by David Karp and William Yoels, suggests that patterns of interaction are very predictable and involve little student initiative or creative thinking. Smaller classes seem to generate more student participation, but participation rates in these classes are still low.

Research on reasons why students believe their participation rates are low are reviewed in Table 16-4 (p. 458). Students see passivity as mostly their own fault; however, this may be due to the bureaucratic process of which they are a part.

Academic Standards and Educational Quality

A 1983 report by the National Commission on Excellence in Education entitled "*A Nation At Risk*," found that American education had deteriorated during the previous decade. This report points out lowering SAT scores as a major indicator of this decline. Further, it noted the extent of *functional illiteracy*, or the lack of basic reading and writing skills needed for everyday life. About one in eight American students complete secondary school without learning to read or write. The extent of functional illiteracy is discussed in the **Critical Thinking** box (p. 460). The 1983 report recommends more stringent educational requirements including raising standards, requiring certain courses, keeping students in school until they reach certain levels of achievement, increasing the salaries of teachers, and professional training. Figure 16-3 (p. 461) shows length of the school year for different countries. The U.S. has a relatively short academic year.

RECENT ISSUES IN AMERICAN EDUCATION

Magnet schools

Magnet Schools are schools that attract students through special facilities and programs promoting educational excellence. Purposes of this type of school include improving educational performance and making inner-city schools more attractive to more affluent people.

Schooling the Disabled

Our educational system requires our society to provide basic educational opportunities for everyone. However, in our bureaucratized system many physically and mentally handicapped children receive little if any services. Several obstacles are discussed which makes providing educational service to these children difficult.

One recent trend had been toward *mainstreaming*, the integration of disabled students into the educational program as a whole. Advantages of this policy include enabling these children the broadest range of educational experiences and to have other people learn to interact with the disabled. Costs of such programs and policies is very expensive.

223

Adult Education

Twenty-five million adults are currently enrolled in educational programs. Most are from the middle and upper classes. The motivation for them to return to school is generally work related.

Schooling for Profit

A proposal gaining support in many parts of the country, including the White House, is to turn education over to private companies to be operates as a profit-making business. The debate on this proposal is part of the bigger issue of "*educational choice*." It is a controversial approach.

Schooling, Computers, and the Future

The computer revolution is reshaping education. Not only are computers important to learn about for eventual application at work, but also as a means of changing the very nature of the learning environment at school.

PART IV: KEY CONCEPTS

Define each of the following concepts in the space provided or on separate paper. Check the accuracy of your answer by referring to the key concepts section at the end of the chapter in the text as well as by referring to italicized definitions located throughout the chapter.

"A Nation At Risk"
Coleman Report
credentialism
education
functional illiteracy
hidden curriculum
Juku
magnet schools
mainstreaming
mandatory education laws
overeducation
schooling
student passivity
tracking

PART V: STUDY QUESTIONS

True-False

1. T F The U.S. was among the first nations to embrace the principle of mass education.
2. T F Only about twenty percent of American adults have a college degree.
3. T F More American students graduate high school and then go on to college than do Japanese students.
4. T F John Dewey was the foremost advocate of the idea that schooling should have practical consequences.
5. T F Over the last decade or so, with our concern with social problems confronting our society, the proportion of college students obtaining a degree in the social sciences has been increasing.
6. T F Hidden curriculum refers to categorically assigning students to different types of education programs.
7. T F Roughly seventy-five percent of American primary and secondary school children attend public schools.
8. T F The Coleman Report determined that educational funding was the most important factor in determining educational achievement.
9. T F Male college graduates can expect to earn about 40 percent more in their lifetime than women college graduates.
10. T F The argument is being made that an emphasis on credentialism in our society leads to a condition of undereducation as people seek the status of a career and its earning over the completion of degree program at college.

Multiple-Choice

1. The extra, intensive schooling received by Japanese elementary school children in the afternoon takes place within the:

   (a) huanco   (d) juku
   (b) mitchou   (e) kiturya
   (c) taruko

2. Mandatory education laws were found in every state in America by:

   (a) 1781   (d) 1894
   (b) 1822   (e) 1918
   (c) 1850

3. In 1991 the median number of years of schooling completed in the U.S. was:

(a) 8.1   (d) 16.1
(b) 11.2   (e) 12.7
(c) 10.0

4. Who advocated the idea that schooling should have practical consequences?

(a) James Coleman   (c) John Dewey
(b) Daniel Moynihan   (d) Christopher Jencks

5. Which of the following functions of formal education helps to forge a population into a single, unified society?

(a) socialization   (c) social placement
(b) social integration   (d) cultural innovation

6. Compliance, punctuality, and discipline are an important part of the _____ in formal education.

(a) manifest functions   (c) hidden curriculum
(b) tracking system   (d) residual system

7. Which of the following conclusions about American education was reached by Coleman and his associates?

(a) schools alone cannot overcome social inequality
(b) educational reform can overcome social inequality
(c) social inequality has decreased greatly in American schools during the last 40 years
(d) social inequality has dramatically increased in recent years in public education

8. Karp and Yoels did a study of student passivity in college and concluded that, from the students' point of view, _____ was ranked as the number one source of their passivity.

(a) the large size of classes
(b) the possibility that other students might not respect their point of view
(c) the chance they would appear unintelligent in the eyes of the teacher
(d) the fact that they had not done the reading assignment

9. The National Commission on Excellence in Education (1983) issued a report called "A Nation At Risk," in which it recommended:

   (a) ending student passivity
   (b) increasing credentialism
   (c) more stringent educational requirements
   (d) reducing the length of time students spend in school
   (e) reducing our educational focus on reading, writing, and arithmetic

10. Functional illiteracy refers to:

   (a) an inability to read and write at all
   (b) an inability to read at the appropriate level of schooling one is in
   (c) an inability to write
   (d) an inability to read and write well enough to carry out everyday activities

Fill-In

1. The various ways in which knowledge is transmitted to members of society is called _____.

2. Many wealthy families in England send their children to what the British call _____, the equivalent to American private boarding schools.

3. The term _____ refers to the content of schooling that is often unrecognized.

4. _____ refers to categorically assigning students to different types of educational programs.

5. The Coleman Report prompted the policy of _____.

6. _____ is the requirement that a person hold some particular diploma or degree as a condition of employment.

7. The 1983 report by the National Commission on Excellence in Education was entitled _____.

8. _____ million adult Americans have eighth-grade language skills or less.

9. _____ are schools that attract students through special facilities and programs promoting educational excellence.

10. _____ refers to the integration of disabled students into the educational program as a whole.

Definition and Short-Answer

1. Describe the four basic functions of education as reviewed in the text. What are the latent functions of education?

2. What were the basic methods and findings of the Coleman Report?

3. How do lifetime earnings differ for men and women given different levels of educational achievement?

4.	What are the five serious problems with the bureaucratic nature of our educational system?
5.	What recommendations were made in the report "A Nation At Risk"?
6.	Review the data reported in Table 16-4. What are your reactions to the findings?
7.	Discuss the similarities and differences between schooling in Japan, Great Britain, the commonwealth of Independent States, and the United States.
8.	Discuss the issue of testing an inequality within our educational systems.
9.	What are the major problems confronting schools in the United States today? What is being done about these problems? What do you think we should be doing?

PART VI: ANSWERS TO STUDY QUESTIONS

True-False

1.	T (p. 440)	6.	F (p. 448)
2.	T (p. 440)	7.	F (p. 449)
3.	T (p. 442)	8.	F (p. 450)
4.	T (p. 444)	9.	T (p. 453)
5.	F (p. 445)	10.	F (p. 454)

Multiple-Choice

1.	d (p. 439)	6.	c (p. 448)
2.	e (p. 440)	7.	a (p. 451)
3.	e (p. 440)	8.	d (p. 458)
4.	c (p. 444)	9.	c (p. 459)
5.	b (p. 446)	10.	d (p. 459)

Fill-In

1.	education (p. 439)
2.	public schools (p. 442)
3.	hidden curriculum (p. 448)
4.	tracking (p. 449)
5.	busing (p. 450)
6.	credentialism (p. 454)
7.	"A Nation At Risk" (p. 459)
8.	50 (p. 460)
9.	magnet schools (p. 461)
10.	mainstreaming (p. 462)

PART VII: ANALYSIS AND COMMENT

A Decade of Change

"Following the Jobs: Trends in Bachelor's Degrees"

    Key Points:

    Questions:

Social Diversity

"Cooling Out The Poor: Transforming Disadvantage into Deficiency"

    Key Points:

    Questions:

Critical Thinking

"Functional Illiteracy: Must We Rethink Education?"

    Key Points:

    Questions:

Religion

17

PART I: CHAPTER OUTLINE

I. Religion: Basic Concepts
   A. Religion and Sociology
II. Theoretical Analysis of Religion
   A. The Functions of Religion
      1. Social Cohesion
      2. Social Control
      3. Providing Meaning and Purpose
   B. The Social Construction of the Sacred
   C. Religion and Social Inequality
   D. Liberation Theology
III. Types of Religious Organization
   A. Church and Sect
   B. Cult
IV. Religion in History
   A. Religion in Preindustrial Societies
   B. Religion in Industrial Societies
V. World Religions
   A. Christianity
   B. Islam
   C. Hinduism
   D. Buddhism
   E. Confucianism
   F. Judaism
VI. Religion in the United States
   A. Religious Affiliation
   B. Religiosity
   C. Correlates of Religious Affiliation
      1. Social Class
      2. Ethnicity and Race
      3. Political Attitudes
VII. Religion in a Changing Society
   A. Secularism
   B. Civil Religion

C. Religious Revival in America
  1. Religious Fundamentalism
D. The Electronic Church
E. The Future of Religion
VIII. Summary
IX. Key Concepts
X. Suggested Readings

PART II: LEARNING OBJECTIVES

1. To define the basic concepts of religion, faith, profane, sacred, and ritual.
2. To explain the aspects of religion that sociology addresses.
3. To identify and describe the three functions of religion as developed by Emile Durkheim.
4. To identify and describe the view that religion is socially constructed.
5. To identify and describe the role religion plays in maintaining inequality.
6. To compare and contrast the basic types of religious organizations: church (two types), sect, and cult.
7. To distinguish between preindustrial and industrial societies in terms of religious beliefs and practices.
8. To identify and describe the size, location, and type of belief system of the major world religions: Christianity, Islam, Hinduism, Buddhism, Confucianism, and Judaism.
9. To explain the religious affiliation, religiosity, and the correlations of religious affiliation in the United States.
10. To describe the pattern of secularization and the development of civil religion in American society.
11. To identify and describe religious revival in American society.

PART III: CHAPTER REVIEW

The case of David Van Horn, a contract archeologist, who unearthed some human bones in the prairie town of Indian Wells California, is discussed. At issue, the distinction between the otherworldly and the ordinary, which lies at the heart of religion.

RELIGION: BASIC CONCEPTS

Religion primarily concerns the purpose and meaning of life. These are areas where scientific knowledge is inadequate. Durkheim suggested human beings distinguish between the *profane*, meaning ordinary elements of everyday life, and the *sacred*, or that which is defined as extraordinary, inspiring a sense of awe, reverence, and even fear. This differentiation, according to Durkheim, is the key to religious belief. *Religion* is therefore a system of beliefs and practices based upon recognizing the sacred. Because it transcends everyday experience its truth cannot be tested by science. Religion is a matter of *faith*, or belief anchored in conviction rather than scientific evidence. The sacred is approached through *ritual*, or formal, ceremonial behavior.

231

Religion and Sociology

Sociology is concerned with the analysis of the consequences of religion, not with passing judgments on its validity.

THEORETICAL ANALYSIS OF RELIGION

The Functions of Religion

Durkheim argued society has an existence of its own, beyond the lives of the people who create it. Society and the sacred are inseparable in Durkheim's view. Durkheim believed that the power of society was understood by people through their creation of sacred symbols. In technologically simple societies a *totem* is an object within the natural world that is imbued with sacred qualities. Ritual behavior with the totem provided unity for the community. He saw religion as providing major functions for society.

Social Cohesion

Religion unites members of a society through shared symbolism, values, and norms.

Social Control

Every society promotes some degree of social conformity. Mores, for example, are justified using religious doctrine.

Providing Meaning and Purpose

Religion provides people with a sense of meaning and purpose by addressing the ultimate issues of life.

A weakness in the structural-functional view is that it down-plays the dysfunctions of religion, particularly its role in producing destructive social conflict.

The Social Construction of the Sacred

Peter Berger, operating from the symbolic-interaction view, theorized that religion is a socially constructed reality much as the family and economy are. The sacred can provide a permanence for society as long as society's members ignore the recognition that the sacred is socially constructed.

Religion and Social Inequality

The social-conflict view of religion draws attention to the social ills perpetuated by the existence of religion. Karl Marx theorized that the powerful in society benefit by religion because it defines the present society as morally just.

Religion can also promote social change and encourage greater social equality. Therefore, while providing meaning and insight, this approach does have limitations in helping us to understand religion in society. The **Social Diversity** box (p. 472) addresses the question of the extent to which religion favors males, fitting into the social-conflict view for the study of religion.

Liberation Theology

Liberation theology is a fusion of Christian principles with political activism, often Marxist in character. This view originated in the 1960s, and asserts that not only is the teaching of Christianity necessary for liberation from human sin, but the Church must help people liberate themselves from the poverty of the Third World. Adherents tend to follow three basic principles: human suffering in the Third World is tragic and beyond comprehension by Westerners, global inequality contradicts Christianity, and global poverty is preventable.

TYPES OF RELIGIOUS ORGANIZATION

Church and Sect

A *church* is a formal religious organization that readily seeks accommodation with the larger society. Two types of church organization are the *ecclesia*, a church that is formally allied with the state, and a *denomination*, or a church that recognizes religious pluralism. The Catholic Church of the Roman Empire and the Anglican Church of England are examples of ecclesia. The Methodist, Presbyterian, and Catholic churches in the U.S. are examples of denominations.

A *sect*, distinct from a church, is a type of religious organization that resists accommodation with the larger society. Sects tend to lack the formal organization of a church. They exalt personal experience. Leaders are often those people who manifest *charisma*, or, in a religious context, evidence of God's favor in the behavior of the individual. Proselytizing is important to obtain new members through *conversion*, a personal transformation resulting from new religious beliefs. Sects tend to reject the established society. These terms church and sect are ideal-type concepts with any religious organization having qualities of each to some degree.

Cult

A *cult* is a religious organization with roots outside the dominant religious traditions of society. It represents something almost completely new. They often arise from the diffusion of religious ideas cross-culturally. They tend to be more extreme than sects, requiring members to change their entire lifestyle and self-concepts.

RELIGION IN HISTORY

Religion in Preindustrial Societies

Archaeological research suggests religious ritual has existed for at least 40,000 years. Among hunting and gathering societies religion typically takes the form of *animism*, or the belief that natural objects are conscious forms of life that can affect humanity. In such cultures, a shaman, or religious leader may be recognized, however not as occupying a full-time position as a specialist. With technological development religion moves out of the family and emerges as a distinct social institution, often closely tied to politics.

Religion in Industrial Societies

With industrialization, science begins as a force which diminishes the scope of religious power and thinking. Yet science has not caused religion to be eliminated as it cannot answer certain fundamental questions. The relationship between religion and science has been uneasy. Recent debate focuses on the issue of the origin of humanity. The **Critical Thinking** box (pp. 478-79) addresses the issue of creationism, and the extent to which science threatens religion.

WORLD RELIGIONS

Religion is found virtually everywhere in the world. Many of the thousands of religions are highly localized, but a few may be termed *world religions* because they have millions of followers.

Christianity

Christianity is the world's largest religion with 1.6 billion followers. Christianity is based on *monotheism*, or religious beliefs recognizing a single divine power. When this view first emerged it challenged the Roman Empire's tradition of *polytheism*, or religious beliefs recognizing many gods. Eventually Christianity become the official religion of the Roman empire. Over the centuries there have been several divisions within Christianity, each however shares the belief that Jesus of Nazareth was sent by God to provide salvation. The **Global Maps 17-1 through 17-4** (pp. 480-82) shows us four major world religions in global perspective.

Islam

Islam is the world's second largest religion with almost one billion followers called Muslims. This religion is based on the life of Muhammad, born in Mecca in 570. He is seen as a prophet, not a divine being. Allah is the God of Islam. Islam means "submission and peace." While divisions exist, there are five pillars of Islam: recognition of Allah as the one true God and Mohammed as God's messenger, ritual prayer, giving alms to the poor, regular fasting, and making at least one pilgrimage to Mecca.

Hinduism

Hinduism is probably the oldest religion, coming into existence about 4500 years ago. It has about 700,000 to 800,000 followers. Hinduism and Indian society are closely fused, so unlike Islam Christianity it is not easily diffused. Also, it is not linked to the life of one person. Therefore, beliefs and practices vary greatly. All Hindus generally believe that a force confronts all people with moral responsibility termed dharma. Karma, a belief in the spiritual progress of a person's soul and involving reincarnation, is also a fundamental aspect of this religion. Hinduism is neither monotheistic nor polytheistic.

Buddhism

Buddhism emerged in India about 2500 years ago. Siddharta Gautama was its founder. After years of travel and meditation he reached "bodhi," or enlightenment. Followers began spreading his teachings, the *dhamma*. Buddhists see existence as suffering and reject the idea of wealth as a solution to human problems. Reincarnation is also a belief in this religion. The answer to world problems lies in personal transformation toward a spiritual existence.

Confucianism

Confucianism was the official religion of China from 200 B.C.E. until the beginning of this century. This religion was shaped by K'ung-Fu-Tzu (Confucius) who lived in the 6th and 5th centuries B.C.E. This religion is based on the concept of the jen, humaneness. Lacking a clear concept of the sacred, it is more a disciplined way of life than a religion.

Judaism

Like Confucianism, Judaism is historical in focus. The critical event in Jewish history is the Exodus from Egypt in the 13th century B.C.E. After this event, Judaism became monotheistic. The Covenant, a special relationship with God, is a distinctive element of this religion. The Torah, or first five books of the Bible, is of special importance for Jews. Judaism emphasizes moral behavior in this world as opposed to being concerned with salvation. There are divided interpretations of doctrine, but a keen awareness of their cultural history and historical endurance of prejudice and discrimination (antisemitism) are central to the Jews' understanding of their religious faith.

RELIGION IN THE UNITED STATES

Religious Affiliation

About 90 percent of Americans identify with a specific religion, and some two-thirds have formal affiliation with one. Table 17-1 (p. 485) outlines the religious identifications among Americans. America is described as religiously pluralistic. Figure 17-1 (p. 486) suggests however that certain religious affiliations predominate within certain regions of the country.

Religiosity

Religiosity is the importance of religion in a person's life. This concept can be measured in a number of different ways. Charles Glock has distinguished five distinct dimensions of religiosity: *experiential*, *ritualistic*, *ideological*, *consequential*, and *intellectual*.

The vast majority of Americans (95%) believe in a divine power of some kind. Some two-thirds of Americans believe that God exists, without doubt. In ideological terms Americans seem less religious, with 70 percent believing in an afterlife, 50 percent praying each day, one-third attending church weekly or almost weekly. Religiosity is therefore a difficult concept to measure. Figure 17-2 (p. 488) provides one illustration of the strength of American religious beliefs.

Correlates of Religious Affiliation

Social Class

Jews, and among Protestants, Episcopalians and Presbyterians, have the highest social standing in our society on average. Catholics, and among Protestants, Lutherans and Baptists, are more representative of the lower social strata. Those Protestants which have the higher average social standing typically represent Northern European societies, making immigration to this country easier, with less prejudice and discrimination.

Certain stereotypes, for example, Jews' success being linked to banking involvement, are confronted and rejected.

Ethnicity and Race

Religion is also closely related to ethnicity and race, with certain religions predominating particular geographic regions. Examples of patterns are provided, including a discussion of the historical importance of the church for African-Americans.

Political Attitudes

The relationship here is perhaps more complex. It can be noted, however, that Protestants tend to be conservative due to their historical privileged class position. Catholics and Jews, largely of distinct ethnic backgrounds, are more liberal.

RELIGION IN A CHANGING SOCIETY

Secularization

An important and controversial pattern of social change is *secularization*, or a historical trend away from the supernatural and the sacred. This is common among modern, technologically advanced societies. Advances in science have significantly influenced our relationship with the world of ideas and the world of nature. Yet, religion is still an important part of society and very significant in many people's lives. Two-thirds of Americans maintain identification with a religious affiliation (two times higher than in 1900 and four times higher than in 1850). A decline in some aspects of religion may be accompanied by increases in others. Secularization cannot be viewed as a matter of moral advance or decline.

Civil Religion

Secularization has brought about a decline in certain traditional religious beliefs, but has also affected the advancement of new forms. *Civil religion*, a quasi-religious loyalty binding individuals within a basically secular society, is strong in American society. Patriotic ties are an example. Civil religion involves much ritual behavior, like the celebration of Thanksgiving and the 4th of July. It is not related to a specific religious doctrine.

Religious Revival in America

Membership in established religions may be declining, however membership in other religious organizations is increasing. The human need for security seems to always give rise to some form of religious activity and commitment.

Religious Fundamentalism

Religious fundamentalism, or conservative religious organizations that seek to restore what are viewed as fundamental elements of religion, has been increasing in the U.S. over the last decade or so. Four characteristics identify Christian fundamentalists: the literal interpretation of scripture, less tolerance for religious diversity, a sectlike emphasis on the personal experience of religion, and a sectlike adversity toward the modern world and secularization. About 20 percent of American adults, for example, believe in the literal interpretation of the Bible. Jerry Falwell's "moral majority" is discussed as an example of a fundamentalist movement operating during the 1980s.

The Electronic Church

Fundamentalists have heavily used the mass media, particularly television and radio, to attract and maintain followers. About 5 percent of Americans are regular viewers of televangelists, with 20 percent watching at least once a month. Several scandals, including those involving Jimmy Swaggart and Jim and Tammy Bakker are noted.

The Future Of Religion

The point is being made that secularization is not squeezing out religion from our society. Processes of change appear to be creating more need for religion.

PART IV: KEY CONCEPTS

Define each of the following concepts in the space provided or on separate paper. Check the accuracy of your answers by referring to the key concepts section at the end of the chapter in the text as well as by referring to italicized definitions located throughout the chapter.

animism
anti-semitism
charisma
church
civil religion
consequential religiosity
conversion
covenant
creationism
creation science
cult
denomination
dhamma
dharma
ecclesia
experiential religiosity
ideological religiosity
jen
karma
liberation theology
monotheism
nirvana
polytheism
profane
religion
religious fundamentalism
religiosity
ritual
ritualistic religiosity
sacred
sect
secularism
shaman
Torah
totem

PART V: STUDY QUESTIONS

True-False

1. T F A major component of Durkheim's approach to the study of religion was to determine whether a divine power exists or not.
2. T F Two types, or forms, of churches identified in the text are the ecclesia and the denomination.
3. T F Whereas a cult is formed by a schism from established religious organizations, a sect represents something almost entirely new.
4. T F In hunting and gathering societies, a shaman, or religious leader may be recognized, but shamanism is not a full-time, specialized activity.
5. T F There are more followers of Islam around the world than for any other religion.
6. T F Most Americans believe in a nonreligious evolutionary view that human life evolved from lower forms of life over millions of years.
7. T F Hindus generally believe that a force in the universe confronts everyone with moral responsibility termed dharma.
8. T F According to research cited in the text, religiosity among Catholics is higher than among Protestants.
9. T F Ideological religiosity concerns an individual's degree of belief in religious doctrine; while consequential religiosity has to do with how much religious beliefs influence a person's daily behavior.
10. T F A quasi-religious loyalty binding individuals with a basically secular society is called civil religion.

Multiple-Choice

1. _____, according to Durkheim, is that which is defined as extraordinary, inspiring a sense of awe, reverence, and even fear.

   (a) the sacred   (c) religion
   (b) the profane   (d) jen

2. A totem--an object imbued with sacred qualities--is characteristically found within which of the following societies?

   (a) technologically simple   (c) heathen
   (b) modern advanced   (d) agrarian

3. Which of the following is a function of religion according to Durkheim?

   (a) social cohesion
   (b) social control
   (c) providing meaning and purpose
   (d) all are functions identified by Durkheim
   (e) none are as he saw religion as having negative consequences for society

4. Liberation theology, developed in the later 1960s, advocates a blending of religion with:

   (a) family   (c) economy
   (b) education   (d) politics

5. Which of the following is not a feature of a sect?

   (a) charismatic leaders
   (b) membership through conversion
   (c) animism
   (d) result of a religious schism

6. Which of the following world religions has the most followers?

   (a) Islam   (c) Buddhism
   (b) Christianity   (d) Hinduism

7. The Creation debate found a main stage in the little town of Dayton, Tennessee in 1925 during the _____ trial.

   (a) Brown   (d) Newton
   (b) Bryan   (e) Scopes
   (c) Jennings

8. Which of the following world religions is the oldest, contains beliefs related to dharma, and is neither monotheistic nor polytheistic?

   (a) Islam   (c) Buddhism
   (b) Hinduism   (d) Confucianism

9. Buddha's teachings are known as:

   (a) karma   (c) dharma
   (b) jen   (d) the covenant

10. Which of the following is the largest Protestant denomination?

(a) Baptist   (d) Presbyterian
(b) Methodist   (e) Episcopalian
(c) Lutheran

Fill-In

1. Durkheim labeled the ordinary elements of everyday life the _____.
2. A _____ is an object within the natural world that is imbued with sacred qualities.
3. _____ theology is a fusion of Christian principles with political activism.
4. An _____ is a church that is formally allied with the state.
5. _____ refers to extraordinary personal qualities that can turn audiences into followers.
6. _____ is the belief that natural objects are conscious forms of life that can affect humanity.
7. _____ is the second largest religion in the world, with one billion followers who are called _____.
8. Confucianism is based on the concept of _____, or humaneness.
9. A historical trend away from the supernatural and the sacred is referred to as _____.
10. A _____ religion is a quasi-religious loyalty binding individuals within a basically secular society.

PART VI: ANSWERS TO STUDY QUESTIONS

True-False

1. F (p. 469)   6. F (p. 479)
2. F (pp. 473-74)   7. T (p. 481)
3. F (pp. 474-75)   8. T (p. 487)
4. T (p. 476)   9. T (p. 487)
5. F (p. 477)   10. T (p. 490)

Multiple-Choice

1. a (p. 468)   6. b (p. 477)
2. a (p. 469)   7. e (p. 478)
3. d (pp. 469-70)   8. b (p. 481)
4. d (p. 473)   9. c (p. 483)
5. c (p. 474)   10. a (p. 485)

Fill-In

1. profane (p. 458)
2. totem (p. 469)
3. liberation (p. 473)
4. ecclesia (p. 474)
5. charisma (p. 475)
6. animism (p. 476)
7. Islam/Muslims (p. 478)
8. jen (p. 483)
9. secularization (p. 490)
10. civil (p. 490)

PART VII: ANALYSIS AND COMMENT

Social Diversity

"Religion and Patriarchy: Does God Favor Males?"

Key Points:

Questions:

Critical Thinking

"The Creation Debate: Does Science Threaten Religion?"

Key Points:

Questions:

Politics And Government

18

PART I: CHAPTER OUTLINE

I. Power and Authority
    A.   Traditional Authority
    B.   Rational-Legal Authority
    C.   Charismatic Authority
II. Politics in Global Perspective
    A.   Politics in History
    B.   Contemporary Political Systems
        1.   Monarchy
        2.   Democracy
        3.   Democracy and Freedom: Contrasting Approaches
        4.   Authoritarianism and Totalitarianism
III. Politics in the United States
    A.   Culture, Economics, and Politics
    B.   Political Parties
        1.   Functions of Political Parties
    C.   The Political Spectrum
        1.   Economic Issues
        2.   Social Issues
        3.   Mixed Positions
        4.   Party Identification
    D.   Special-Interest Groups
        1.   The Agenda of Special-Interest Groups
        2.   Political Action Committees
    E.   Politics and the Individual
        1.   Political Socialization
        2.   Voter Apathy
VI. Theoretical Analysis of Power in Society
    A.   The Pluralist Model
        1.   Research Results
    B.   The Power-Elite Model
        1.   Research Results
V. Power Beyond the Rules
    A.   Revolution
    B.   Terrorism

VI.   War and Peace
    A.   The Causes of War
    B.   Militarism and the Arms Race
    C.   Nuclear Weapons and War
    D.   Social Diversity and the Military
    E.   The Pursuit of Peace
VII.   Chapter Summary
VIII. Key Concepts
X.   Suggested Readings

PART II: LEARNING OBJECTIVES

1.   To explain the difference between power and authority.
2.   To distinguish among the three types of authority: traditional, rational-legal, and charismatic.
3.   To describe the concepts of political state and nation state.
4.   To compare and contrast the four principle kinds of political systems.
5.   To describe the relationship between individualism and government in American society.
6.   To identify what a political party is and the functions political parties serve in American society.
7.   To distinguish between economic issues and social issues and their relationship to the political spectrum in American society.
8.   To identify the composition and agenda of special-interest groups in American society.
9.   To describe the ways in which people participate in the political system focusing on political socialization and voting patterns.
10. To compare and contrast the pluralist model of political power and the power-elite model of political power.
11. To describe the types of political power that exceed, or seek to eradicate, established politics.
12. To identify the factors which are involved in creating conditions which increase the likelihood of war.
13. To recognize the historical pattern of militarism in the United States, and around the world.
14. To identify factors which can be used in the pursuit of peace.

PART III: CHAPTER REVIEW

This chapter begins with a poem by Chang Pin, written halfway around the world one thousand years ago. The poem raises a number of timeless questions about why people often feel they have little control over their lives, why people die in service to a few, and how power is distributed in society.

The dynamics of power in and between societies is the focus of this chapter. *Politics* is the institutionalized system by which a society distributes power and makes decisions.

POWER AND AUTHORITY

Max Weber defined *power* as the ability to achieve desired ends despite possible resistance from others. The most basic form is sheer force, physical or psychological coercion. History demonstrates that this type of power is difficult to maintain. *Authority* is defined by Weber as power people perceive as legitimate rather than coercive.

The social context will determine to a large degree how power is perceived. Also, to be accepted it must be consistent with cultural norms. Authority demands obedience to norms from those who command as well as those who obey. Weber identified three general contexts in which power is commonly defined as authority.

Traditional Authority

Traditional authority is defined as power legitimated by respect for long-established cultural patterns. This type of power is very common in preindustrialized societies. It has a sacred character. The power of ancient Chinese emperors and nobility in medieval Europe are examples. As societies industrialize traditional authority declines, yet forms still exist in modern societies. Patriarchy and parental dominance over children are examples.

Rational-Legal Authority

Rational-legal, or bureaucratic authority, is defined as power legitimated by legally enacted rules and regulations. Bureaucratic authority stresses achievement over ascribed characteristics, and underlies most authority in the United States today. This type of authority is closely linked to *government*, or formal organizations that direct the political life of a society.

Charismatic Authority

Charismatic authority is defined as power legitimated through extraordinary personal abilities that inspire devotion and obedience. This type of power doesn't rest on a person's position or office. It is frequently used to move people away from the customary and established order in society. Examples of charismatic leaders from around the world throughout history are discussed.

Societies have typically directed charismatic women to domains of life other than politics, while certainly a few exceptions exist.

Charismatic movements are very dependent on their leader. The long-term persistence of such a movement requires *routinization of charisma*, the transformation of charismatic authority into some combination of traditional and bureaucratic authority. Christianity is an example of this process.

POLITICS IN GLOBAL PERSPECTIVE

Politics in History

In hunting and gathering societies, leaders typically emerge as a result of having some unusual amount of strength, hunting skill or charisma. These leaders exercise only modest power over others, and while having special prestige, they do not have more wealth. In agrarian societies traditional authority develops. As political organization grows it leads to the formation of a *political state*, a formal government claiming the legitimate use of coercion to support its rule. The advance of technology significantly increases the power of the political state.

During the last several centuries political organizations have evolved toward nation-states. At the present time approximately 185 *nation-states* are recognized.

Contemporary Political Systems

Four types of political systems which manage the affairs of contemporary nation-states are reviewed.

Monarchy

A *monarchy* is a type of political system in which power is passed from generation to generation within a single family. It is legitimated primarily through tradition. Absolute monarchies dominated from England to China, and remained widespread until early in the 20th century. Historical examples are discussed.

Democracy

Democracy refers to a political system in which power is exercised by the people as a whole. In large societies it is not possible for everyone to directly be involved in politics. Therefore, a representative democracy, which places authority in the hands of elected officials who are accountable to the people develops. This type of system is most common in the relatively rich industrial societies of the world. They are characterized by rational-legal patterns of authority and function as bureaucracies. The United States, for example, has three million people working for the federal government.

Democracy and Freedom: Contrasting Approaches

While the East and the West have had different political systems for most of this century, both claim to provide freedom for their people. In the West, political freedom means *liberty*, or the freedom to vote for one's preferred leader or otherwise act with minimal interference from government. In the socialist nations of the old Soviet bloc, freedom was understood as "freedom from basic want." The two competing approaches to freedom, including effects of the dramatic political changes in the past Soviet Union

246

and Eastern Europe are discussed in the **Decade of Change** (pp. 504-05). **Global Map** 18-1 looks at political freedom in global perspective. Evidence presented suggests that 40 percent of the world's population can be classified as "politically free."

Authoritarianism and Totalitarianism

Authoritarianism refers to denying the majority participation in government. While to some degree this is true for all political systems, as used here, authoritarianism characterizes political systems that are indifferent to people's lives. Examples include the Person's rule of Argentina in the 1940s and 1950s, the Marcos' rule in the Philippines which ended in the mid-1980s, and Noriega's rule in Panama until 1989.

A more severe political control characterizes *totalitarianism*, or denying the majority participation in a government that extensively regulates people's lives. Such systems have emerged only within this century as technological means have enabled such leaders to rigidly regulate citizen's lives. Such systems bridge the political continuum from the far right, like Nazi Germany, to the far left, like the People's Republic of China. Socialism, an economic system, is not to be confused with totalitarianism, a political system.

A century and a half ago, Alexis de Tocqueville wrote of his concern that as modern governments grew in size they had the potential to become totalitarian. He pointed out that this could be counteracted by citizens if they formed various voluntary associations.

POLITICS IN THE UNITED STATES

As a democracy, the American system is distinctive given certain historical events, economic forces, and cultural traits.

Culture, Economics, and Politics

These factors are forged in a complimentary fashion in American society. Our tradition of valuing individualism is guaranteed in the Bill of Rights, and the self-reliance and competition which emerges supports our capitalist economy. While Americans do not like "too much" government, almost everyone thinks that government is necessary. Table 18-1 (p. 507) shows the growth of the federal government's spending from 1795 through 1988. Federal spending today accounts for almost one quarter of our GNP.

Table 18-2 (p. 508) presents the findings of a national survey concerning the public's attitudes about the role of government in our society. The results show Americans are divided about the proper role of government.

Political Parties

Political parties are organizations operating within a political system that seeks control of the government. The United States Constitution makes no mention of political parties. The two major parties, the Democratic and Republican, were established right after the Civil War.

Functions of Political Parties

Political parties persist in American society because they serve certain important functions. These include: promoting political pluralism, increasing political involvement, selection of political candidates, forging political coalitions, and maintaining political stability.

The Political Spectrum

The *political spectrum* ranges from the extreme liberals on the left to the extreme conservatives on the right. Historically the Republican Party has been more conservative and the Democratic Party more liberal. However, within each Party there are both conservative and liberal wings.

American attitudes differ on two kinds of issues, economic and social. Public opinion on these is discussed.

Economic Issues

The great depression caused Americans to see the reality of the economic insecurity of most of our population. The New Deal programs created by Roosevelt during the 1930s greatly expanded the role of government in economic matters in our society. Today, Democrats tend to support more extensive government involvement in the economy than the Republicans would support.

Social Issues

Social issues span many topics. The Democratic Party is more socially liberal than the Republican Party. Both parties, however, favor government action when it advances their aims. Examples of the ERA and anti-abortion campaigns are discussed.

Mixed Positions

Political attitudes vary by race, with blacks being more liberal. Ethnicity does not seem to be an important factor today in affecting political attitudes. The **Social Diversity** box (p. 511) discusses the fact that while only 5 percent of African-Americans identify themselves as members of the Republican Party, their ideas for the most appropriate strategies for improving the social position of the black community is changing to some degree.

Social class is also identified as a factor related to political attitudes. Fop example, people who identify themselves as in the working class or lower-middle class tend to take liberal stances on economic issues and more conservative stances on social issues. This pattern is reversed for the affluent of our society.

Party Identification

Political party identification in the U.S. is relatively weak compared to European democracies. Table 18-3 (p. 510) reviews the political party identification of Americans.

Special-Interest Groups

A *special-interest group* refers to political alliances of people with an interest in a particular economic or social issue. Most voluntary associations would be examples. Many such groups employ lobbyists who represent their concerns to the government.

The Agenda of Special-Interest Groups

The most powerful special-interest groups focus on economic issues. While declining in numbers, unions in America represent some 20 million workers. Religious organizations are involved in influencing public opinion on many social issues.

Political Action Committees

Political action committees (PACs) are organizations formed by special-interest groups, independent of political parties, to pursue political aims by raising and spending money. Their success is determined by their ability to raise money. They are often very controversial. Examples are discussed.

Politics and the Individual

Political Socialization

The family is a strong influence on one's political attitudes, and this is reinforced by the social composition of the neighborhood in which the family lives. Further, schools are involved in the transmission of dominant political values.

Voter Apathy

Despite socialization influences, formal and informal, many Americans express indifference concerning politics. Voter apathy has recently been found to be worse in the United States than in 23 other industrialized democracies. The likelihood of voting increases with age and varies by race, ethnicity, and sex.

There are many causes for this apathy. Registration rules, physical disabilities, and illiteracy are all important factors. Being satisfied with social conditions as they are can also reduce voter participation.

THEORETICAL ANALYSIS OF POWER IN SOCIETY

The Pluralist Model

This approach is linked to the structural-functional paradigm. The *pluralist model* is an analysis of politics that views power as dispersed among many competing interest groups.

Research on the power structure operating in New Haven, Connecticut by Nelson Polsby during the 1950s supports this view. In review this research in the 1960s, Robert Dahl came to similar conclusions.

The Power-Elite Model

The *power-elite model* is an analysis of politics that views power as concentrated among the rich. The term power-elite was introduced by C. Wright Mills in 1956. He perceived American society, its economy, government, and military, as being dominated by a coalition of families.

Research by Robert and Helen Lynd suggests that this was true in a typical American city they studied (Muncie, Indiana), which in their study was referred to as Middletown.

How these models help us answer certain questions concerning the distribution and operation of power in American society is reviewed in Table 18-4 (p. 517).

POWER BEYOND THE RULES

Revolution

Political revolution is the overthrow of one political system in order to establish another. While reform involves change within a system, revolution means change of the system itself. No political system is immune to revolution. Historical examples are identified to illustrate. Several general patterns characterize revolutions. These include: rising expectations, deprivation and social conflict, nonresponsiveness of the government, radical leadership by intellectual, and establishing a new legitimacy.

Terrorism

Terrorism, or the use of violence or the threat of violence by an individual or group as a political strategy, characterized the decade of the 1980s. Three insights are offered about terrorism. First, it elevates violence to a legitimate political tactic. Second, it is especially compatible with totalitarian governments as a means of sustaining widespread fear and intimidation. Third, extensive civil liberties make democratic societies vulnerable to terrorism. While many societies are targets, one-fourth of all acts of terrorism worldwide are directed against the U.S. What response should be made is problematic to determine as exactly who is responsible is often difficult to determine.

An additional form of terrorism is *state terrorism*, or the use of violence without support of law against individuals or groups by a government or its agents. This type of terrorism has a long history. Examples are discussed.

WAR AND PEACE

War is defined as armed conflict among people of various societies, formally directed by their governments. *Peace* implies the absence of war, although not necessarily all conflict. Figure 18-1 (p. 521) records the number of Americans killed in ten major wars from the American Revolution to date.

The Causes of War

War, according to research, is not the result of some natural human aggressive tendency. It is a product of society. The following factors are identified by Quincy Wright as ones promoting war: perceived threats, social problems, political objectives, moral objectives, and the absence of alternatives.

Militarism and the Arms Race

The cost of militarism runs far greater than actual war. To fund it, governments must divert resources away from social needs. Thirty percent of our federal budget goes to fund our military. The *arms race*, a mutually reinforcing escalation of military might has developed.

Nuclear Weapons and War

The destructive capability of the 50,000 nuclear weapons in existence today is discussed. *Nuclear proliferation* refers to the acquisition of nuclear weapons technology by more and more societies. The current list of nations possessing nuclear capability are identified, as well as those who are close to having such capability. The extent to which nuclear weapons capabilities have advanced since the end of World War II cannot be stressed to much.

Social Diversity and the Military

Issues concerning discrimination against women and gays in the military are discussed. Figure 18-2 (p. 523) shows the extent of gender-based exclusion in the military by branch. The role of women in the military is changing however. In regard to gays, the military formally bars homosexual men and women from military service. The rational for this is discussed.

The Pursuit of Peace

Several approaches are identified as means to reduce the danger nuclear war. These include: maintaining the status quo, high-technology defence, like the strategic defence initiative, diplomacy and disarmament, and resolving underlying conflict.

PART IV: KEY CONCEPTS

Define each of the following concepts in the space provided or on separate paper. Check the accuracy of your answers by referring to the key concepts section at the end of the chapter in the text as well as by referring to italicized definitions located throughout the chapter.

arms race
authoritarianism
authority
charismatic authority
democracy
government
military-industrial complex
monarchy
nuclear proliferation
peace
pluralist model
political action committee
political parties
political revolution
political state
politics
power
power-elite model
rational-legal authority
routinization of charisma
special-interest group
state terrorism
strategic defence initiative
terrorism
totalitarianism
traditional authority
voter apathy
war

PART V: STUDY QUESTIONS

True-False

1. T F Authority is power widely perceived as legitimate rather than coercive.
2. T F In hunting and gathering societies leaders tend to enjoy special prestige and have more wealth, and far more power than everyone else.
3. T F Monarchies remained widespread into the early 20th century.
4. T F Government spending, as a proportion of the GNP, has actually been decreasing over the past twenty years.
5. T F According to data obtained in a national survey, American adults overwhelmingly believe that the government is doing too much in its role in trying to solve our society's problems.
6. T F Most working-class Americans identify themselves as "economically" conservative and "socially" liberal.
7. T F Most American adults claim identification with the Republican Party.
8. T F Political action committees are organizations formed by special-interest groups, independent of political parties, to pursue political aims.
9. T F While voter apathy has been a problem in recent years in the United States, still, a greater percentage of American adults vote than in virtually any other industrial democracy.
10. T F Research by Robert and Helen Lynd in Muncie, Indiana (the Middletown study) supported the power-elite model concerning how power is distributed in the United states.

Multiple-Choice

1. Who defined power as the likelihood that a person can achieve personal ends in spite of possible resistance from others?

   (a) C. Wright Mills   (c) Max Weber
   (b) Alexis de Tocqueville (d) Robert Lynd

2. Which of the following is not one of the general contexts in which power is commonly defined as authority?

   (a) traditional   (c) charismatic
   (b) rational-legal (d) democratic

3. Power that is legitimated by respect for long-established cultural patterns is called:

   (a) traditional   (d) sacred
   (b) political   (e) charismatic
   (c) power-elite

4. The survival of a charismatic movement depends upon _____, according to Max Weber.

   (a) pluralism
   (b) political action
   (c) routinization
   (d) pluralism

5. According to the research cited in the text, the majority of Americans:

   (a) hold mixed political views
   (b) are liberal on both economic and social issues
   (c) are conservative on both economic and social issues
   (d) are conservative on social issues and liberal on economic issues

6. With which general sociological paradigm is the power-elite model associated?

   (a) exchange
   (b) structural-functional
   (c) symbolic-interaction
   (d) social-conflict

7. Which idea below represents the pluralist model of power?

   (a) power is highly concentrated
   (b) voting cannot create significant political changes
   (c) the American power system is an oligarchy
   (d) wealth, social prestige, and political office are rarely combined

8. In which stage of a revolution does the danger of counter-revolution occur?

   (a) rising expectations
   (b) nonresponsiveness of the old government
   (c) establishing a new legitimacy
   (d) radical leadership by intellectuals

9. Quincy Wright has identified which of the following circumstances as conditions which lead humans to go to war?

   (a) perceived threats
   (b) social problems
   (c) moral objectives
   (d) political objectives
   (e) all are identified

10. Which of the following was not identified in the text as a means of reducing the danger of nuclear war?

    (a) maintaining the status quo
    (b) high-tech defense
    (c) diplomacy and disarmament
    (d) resolving underlying conflict
    (e) all were identified as ways of reducing the danger of nuclear war

Fill-In

1. _____ is the institutionalized system by which a society distributes power and makes decisions.
2. Power widely perceived as legitimate rather than coercive is referred to as _____.
3. _____ authority is power legitimated through extraordinary personal abilities that inspire devotion and obedience.
4. A _____ is a formal government claiming the legitimate use of coercion to support its rule.
5. _____ percent of the world's people are "politically free."
6. _____ is political control denying the majority participation in a government that extensively regulates people's lives.
7. _____ percent of Americans label themselves as "middle of the road" politically.
8. Many special-interest groups employ _____ who earn their living by representing the concerns of one group or another to political officials.
9. _____ are organizations formed by special- interest groups, independent of political parties, to pursue political aims by raising and spending money.
10. The _____ model, closely allied with the social-conflict paradigm, is an analysis of politics that views power as concentrated among the rich.

Definition and Short-Answer

1. Differentiate between the concepts of power and authority.
2. Differentiate among Weber's three types of authority.
3. Four types of political systems are reviewed in the text. Identify and describe these systems.
4. It is pointed out in the text that political views of Americans differ on two kinds of issues. What are these issues? What are the general patterns of the attitudes of Americans on these issues?
5. What is voter apathy? What are its causes? To what extent is voter apathy a problem in the U.S. as compared to other industrialized democracies?
6. Differentiate between the pluralist and power-elite models concerning the distribution of power in the United States.
7. What are the five general patterns identified in the text concerning revolutions?
8. What are the five factors identified in the text as promoting war?
9. Several approaches to reducing the chances for nuclear war are addressed in the text. What are these approaches?

PART VI: ANSWERS TO STUDY QUESTIONS

True-False

1.	T (p. 498)	6.	F (p. 509)
2.	T (p. 500)	7.	F (p. 510)
3.	T (p. 501)	8.	T (p. 512)
4.	F (p. 507)	9.	F (p. 514)
5.	F (p. 508)	10.	T (p. 516)

Multiple-Choice

1.	c (p. 497)	6.	d (p. 515)
2.	d (pp. 498-99)	7.	d (p. 515)
3.	a (p. 498)	8.	c (p. 518)
4.	c (p. 499)	9.	e (pp. 520-21)
5.	a (p. 509)	10.	e (pp. 524-25)

Fill-In

1. politics (p. 497)
2. authority (p. 498)
3. charismatic (p. 499)
4. political state (p. 500)
5. 40 (p. 503)
6. totalitarianism (p. 504)
7. 38.5 (p. 508)
8. lobbyists (p. 512)
9. political action committees (p. 512)
10. power-elite (p. 515)

VII: ANALYSIS AND COMMENT

A Decade of Change

"The 1980s: A Decade of Democracy"

Key Points:

Questions:

Social Diversity

"African-Americans Conservatives: Some New Thinking on Old Issues"

    Key Points:

    Questions:

The Economy
And Work

19

PART I: CHAPTER OUTLINE

I.   The Economy: Historical Overview
        A.   The Agricultural Revolution
        B.   The Industrial Revolution
        C.   The Postindustrial Society
        D.   Sectors of the Modern Economy
II.   Comparative Economic Systems
        A.   Capitalism
        B.   Socialism
        C.   Socialism and Communism
        D.   Democratic Socialism in Europe
        E.   Relative Advantages of Capitalism and Socialism
                1.   Productivity
                2.   Distribution of Income
        F.   Changes in Socialist Countries
III.   Work in the Postindustrial Economy
        A.   The Decline of Agricultural Work
        B.   From Factory Work to Service Work
        C.   The Dual Labor Market
        D.   Labor Unions
        E.   Professions
        F.   Self-Employment
        G.   Unemployment
        H.   The Underground Economy
        I.   Social Diversity and the Workplace
        J.   Technology and Work
IV.   Corporations
        A.   Economic Concentration
        B.   Conglomerates and Corporate Linkages
        C.   Corporations and Competition
        D.   Corporations and the Global Economy
V.   The Economy of the Twenty-First Century
VI.   Summary
VII.   Key Concepts
VIII.   Suggested Readings

PART II: LEARNING OBJECTIVES

1. To identify the elements of the economy
2. To explain the history and development of economic activity from the agricultural revolution through the industrial revolution to the postindustrial society.
3. To identify and describe the primary, secondary, and tertiary sectors of the economy.
4. To compare and contrast the economic systems of capitalism and socialism.
5. To identify the differences between democratic socialism and capitalism.
6. To explain the difference between socialism and communism.
7. To identify the advantages and disadvantages of capitalism and socialism on productivity, income, economic, and political factors.
8. To describe the general characteristics and trends of work in American postindustrial society.
9. To compare and contrast corporations and conglomerates and analyze competition in the American economy.
10. To explain the impact of multinational corporations on the world economy.

PART III: CHAPTER REVIEW

This chapter focuses on the economy as a social system which is operating within a complex global market. The degree of the complexity involved just within the issue of "buy American" is suggested by one community's attempt in 1992 to help our ailing economy.

THE ECONOMY: HISTORICAL OVERVIEW

The *economy* is the institutionalized system for production, distribution, and consumption of goods and services. Goods range from basic necessities to luxury items. Services include various activities that benefit others. Modern complex societies are the result of centuries of technological development and social change.

The Agricultural Revolution

Being 10-20 times more productive than hunting and gathering societies, agrarian societies produce considerable surpluses. The four factors of agricultural technology, productive specialization, permanent settlements, and trade have been important in the development of the economy. Economic expansion has also created greater inequalities.

In agrarian economies like that which existed in medieval Europe, many people living in cities worked at home, referred to as the "*cottage industry*." An example from England three centuries ago is discussed.

The Industrial Revolution

Five revolutionary changes are identified as resulting from the industrial revolution of Europe beginning in the mid-18th century. These include: new forms of energy, the spread of factories, manufacturing and mass production, specialization, and wage labor. Greater productivity steadily raised the standard of living. The **Social Diversity** box (p. 531) illustrates however that their were special problems facing women who worked in factories.

The Postindustrial Society

By 1950, further changes created the beginning of the *post-industrial society*, an economy based on service work and high technology. Machines have taken over many jobs previously done by humans, and many new jobs are part of the expanding bureaucracy of our economy. Most jobs now in our society are service related and not part of industrial production. A critical part of the post-industrial economy is the information revolution. Another significant factor regards the location of work, with more people today working at home.

Sectors of the Modern Economy

Three parts, or sectors, of society's economy exist and their relative balance shifts over history. The *primary sector* is the part of the economy generating raw materials directly from the natural environment. Today in the U.S. only 3 percent of the labor force is involved in this sector. The *secondary sector* is the part of the economy that transforms raw materials into manufactured goods. About one-third of the labor force is involved in such work. The *tertiary sector* is the part of the economy generating services rather than goods. About two-thirds of our labor force is employed in such work. **Global Maps** 19-1 and 19-2 illustrate important data.

COMPARATIVE ECONOMIC SYSTEMS

Capitalism

Capitalism is an economic system in which natural resources and means of producing goods and services are privately owned. This system has three distinctive features: private ownership of property, pursuit of personal profit, and free competition and consumer sovereignty.

However, even in the leading capitalist society of the U.S., the government affects our economy very significantly. The government owns and operates specific parts of our economy, for example Amtrak and the postal service. It also assumes economic responsibility in bailout situations, as in the case of the Chrysler Corporation. Many state and local governments also own and operate large businesses.

Socialism

Socialism is an economic system in which natural resources, as well as the means of producing goods and services, are collectively owned. Its distinguishing characteristics include: collective ownership of property, pursuit of collective goals, and government control of the economy.

Socialism and Communism

Communism is a hypothetical economic and political system in which all members of society have economic and social equality. Marx viewed socialism as a transitory stage on the way to communism. However, nowhere has this system been achieved. Such a society, even for Marx, is a *utopia*.

Democratic Socialism in Europe

Several western European democracies have introduced socialist policies through elections. *Democratic socialism* is a political and economic system that combines significant government intervention in the economy with free elections. Great Britain, Sweden, and Italy are examples.

Relative Advantages of Capitalism and Socialism

Precise objective comparisons are not possible. Many factors affect a society's economic performance, including historical and cultural patterns, variations in the size and composition of the labor force, available natural resources, different levels of technological development, and trade alliances. However, certain comparisons can be made keeping these factors in mind.

Productivity

Table 19-1 (p. 537) compares economic performance for different capitalist and socialist economies using the per capita GDP as a gauge. The average figure for the socialist systems was only 56 percent of that for capitalist systems.

Distribution of Income

Table 19-2 (p. 537) shows income inequality is greater in societies with capitalist economies. The United States had the greatest income inequality among the capitalist economies identified.

A society's economic system shapes its politics. In capitalist societies there are extensive civil liberties and political freedom. From the viewpoint of socialists, this market-based freedom translates into doing what you can afford. On the other hand, socialist societies attempt to maximize economic and social equality. This limits personal liberty.

Changes in Socialist Countries

The Solidarity Movement in Poland during the 1980s and the dissolving of the Soviet Union in 1992 are discussed to illustrate the significant changes occurring in these countries.

WORK IN THE POSTINDUSTRIAL ECONOMY

The American economic system has also been going through major changes during this century. In 1991 there were 125 million Americans, or two-thirds of those over the age of 16, in the labor force. Table 19-3 (p. 539) shows the participation rates by sex and race. For white males the participation rate was 76.4 percent, for black males 69.5 percent, for white women 57.4 percent, and for black women 57.0 percent. Age also affects labor force participation.

The Decline of Agricultural Work

Currently, less than 3 percent of the American labor force is involved in farming. Figure 19-2 (p. 540) graphically illustrates the rapid decline in this sector of the economy. Yet, American agriculture is more productive now than it was in the past. More and more production is occurring in corporate agribusinesses.

From Factory Work to Service Work

As indicated in Figure 19-2, by 1988 two-thirds of the labor force were in service jobs. In 1900, more than 40 percent were in blue-collar jobs. Many of the white-collar occupations are lower paying service jobs.

The Dual Labor Market

One way to describe the change which is occurring in our economy is to divide work into two different labor markets. The *primary labor market* includes occupations that provide extensive benefits to workers, while the *secondary labor market* includes jobs providing minimal benefits to workers. A growing proportion of new jobs in postindustrial economies fall into the secondary labor market. The **Sociology of Everyday Life** box (p. 541) relates the feelings of a factory worker and a service worker concerning their respective work. Both are suggestive of Marx's concept of alienation.

Labor Unions

In recent years there has been a significant decline in *labor unions*, or organizations of workers that attempt to improve wages and working conditions through various strategies, including negotiations and strikes. While union membership peaked during the 1970s, today only 17 percent of the non-farm labor force is unionized. Compared to other industrialized societies the United States has relatively low union membership. Several factors related to this decline. First, the blue-collar sector of the economy has been experiencing massive layoffs in recent decades. Second, most newly created jobs are found in the service sector, which is far less likely to be unionized. Third, the Reagan administration helped create a national climate of hostility toward unions.

Professions

A *profession* is a prestigious, white-collar occupation that requires extensive formal education. They share the following characteristics: theoretical knowledge, self-regulated training and practice, authority over clients, and community orientation rather than self-interest.

Besides traditional professions like medicine and law, "new professions" share these qualities, including accounting and architecture. Many new service occupations are seeking professional standing, a process known as professionalization. This process is initiated by members of an occupational category by labeling their work in a new way. This is followed by the development of a professional association, which develops a code of ethics and perhaps even schools to train members. In marginal cases, paraprofessional status may be obtained, denoting special training, but lacking extensive theoretical education.

Self-Employment

Self-employment refers to earning a living without working for a large organization. In the early 19th century, about 80 percent of the labor force was self-employed. By 1870, only about one-third was, and by 1940 only one in five. Today, about 8 percent of the labor force is classified as self-employed.

While the potential for earning good incomes is present, about one in three small businesses do not survive five years.

Unemployment

Some unemployment is found in all societies. In predominantly industrialized societies the unemployment rate rarely drops below 5 percent. Such a level is even viewed as natural. Currently, about 7 percent of the civilian labor force in the U.S. is unemployed. Unemployment is much more common in the secondary labor market than in the primary labor market. Rates vary by race, age, and sex also. Figure 19-3 (p. 545) illustrates these patterns for 1991. Black unemployment is more than twice that for whites. While white males and females have comparable rates, black males have considerably higher rates than black females. Rates though are typically underestimated because by definition a person must be actively seeking employment and many people are "underemployed."

The Underground Economy

In violation of government regulations concerning the "free enterprise" system is the *underground economy*, or economic activity involving income or the exchange of goods and services that is not reported to the government. Such activity ranges from having garage sales and not reporting the money generated, to illegal drug trade. The single largest segment of this underground economy is legally obtained income unreported on income taxes. Perhaps 10 percent of the economic activity in the U.S. is unreported.

Social Diversity in the Workplace

Major changes are occurring in the workplace in terms of its composition. Demographic shifts are dramatically increasing the proportion of minority group members in the work force. The **Decade of Change** box (pp. 546-47) looks at the workforce of the 21st century.

Technology and Work

The technological nature of the workplace is also affecting who is working. For example, with the rise of information technology, more women are working. Five ways in which the computer has changed the nature of work are discussed. These include: deskilling labor, becoming more abstract, limiting interaction, creating new standards for productivity, and enhancing the supervision and control of workers

CORPORATIONS

A *corporation* is an organization with a legal existence including rights and liabilities apart from those of its members. Of the approximately 18 million businesses in America, 3.4 million are incorporated. There are two primary benefits of incorporating, including the protection of owners from personal liability, and providing advantages under tax laws which increase profits.

Economic Concentration

While one-half of American corporations are small, with assets of under $100,000, the largest corporations dominate the American economy. Over this century there has been a tremendous concentration of national and international economic power. Several statistics are reviewed to illustrate this process. Table 19-4 (p. 549) shows the 20 largest corporations in the U.S. for 1990 as ranked by sales and assets.

Conglomerates and Corporate Linkages

A *conglomerate* is a giant corporation composed of many smaller corporations. RJR-Nabisco, Coca-Cola, and Beatrice Foods are discussed as examples.

Another type of linkage between corporations is called *interlocking directorates*, or social networks made up of people who simultaneously serve on the boards of directors of many corporations. This is an important part of the American economic system. It is not necessarily against the public interest, but does tend to concentrate power.

Corporations and Competition

The competitive market in America is actually limited to smaller businesses and self-employed people. Large corporation are part of the noncompetitive sector. *Monopoly*, or domination of a market by a single producer, was declared a century ago by the government to be against the public welfare. Monopolies have been limited, but *oligopoly*, or domination of a market by a few producers, persists.

The government's role is to protect the public interest. Yet capitalists ideally support minimal government intervention. Also, the government is the single biggest consumer of large corporations. Corporations and government really then work together to help make the economy stable and profitable.

Corporations and the Global Economy

The largest corporations in the world, most of which are American, now span the globe. Beatrice Food, exxon, and General Motors are discussed as examples. Such corporations are huge. Exxon, for example out-produces almost any Third-World nation. Advantages and disadvantages of multinational corporations are discussed.

THE ECONOMY OF THE TWENTY-FIRST CENTURY

Today's rate of economic change is comparable to that which existed at the turn of the last century. Socialism, representing about one-fourth of all humanity, will likely be very variable over the next century.

A critical turning point occurred for America in 1990, when for the first time, foreign corporations owned more of the U.S. than American corporations owned abroad. events around the world are therefore critical to the U.S. economic system. Our economic future is no longer a matter of the performance of national economies, but rather a global economic system.

PART IV: KEY CONCEPTS

Define each of the following concepts in the space provided or on separate paper. Check the accuracy of your answers by referring to the key concepts section at the end of the chapter in the text as well as by referring to italicized definitions located throughout the chapter.

capitalism
communism
competitive sector
conglomerates
corporation

cottage industry
democratic socialism
economy
interlocking directorate
labor unions
monopoly
noncompetitive sector
oligopoly
postindustrial economy
primary labor market
primary sector
profession
professionalization
secondary labor market
secondary sector
socialism
tertiary sector
underground economy

PART V: STUDY QUESTIONS

True-False

1. T F   The economy includes the production, distribution, and consumption of both goods and services.
2. T F   In medieval Europe, people living in cities often worked at home, a pattern called cottage industry.
3. T F   Most workers in the New England textile factories in the early 19th century were women.
4. T F   The terms primary, secondary, and tertiary, referring to sectors in the economy, imply a ranking in importance for our society.
5. T F   Socialism is both a political and economic system.
6. T F   Per capita GNP tends to be significantly higher in capitalist as compared to socialist economies.
7. T F   The income ratio, as a measure of the distribution of income in a society, tends to be higher in socialist systems as compared to capitalist systems.
8. T F   The secondary labor market includes jobs providing minimal benefits to workers.
9. T F   An oligopoly refers to domination of a market by a few producers.
10. T F   While the global economy is becoming very important, still, American corporations currently own about 35% more overseas than foreign companies own in the United States.

Multiple-Choice

1. That part of the economy that transforms raw materials into manufactured goods is termed the:

    (a) primary sector   (d) competitive sector
    (b) secondary sector   (e) basic sector
    (c) manifest sector

2. Which of the following is not a sector of the modern economy:

    (a) primary   (c) manifest
    (b) secondary   (d) tertiary

3. Which of the following societies is not an example of democratic socialism?

    (a) Great Britain   (d) all are examples
    (b) Italy   (e) none are examples
    (c) Sweden

4. A political and economic system in which free elections and a market economy coexist with government efforts to minimize social inequality is termed:

    (a) socialism   (d) democratic socialism
    (b) market communism   (e) oligarchy
    (c) world economy

5. Socialist economies have about _____ as much income inequality as found in capitalist systems.

    (a) one-half   (d) one-tenth
    (b) one-sixth   (e) one and a half
    (c) twice

6. How many people in the United States were in the paid labor force in 1991?

    (a) 75 million   (d) 125 million
    (b) 50 million   (e) 90 million
    (c) 200 million

7. What percentage of women over the age of sixteen have income-producing jobs?

    (a) 31.7   (d) 67.5
    (b) 44.6   (e) 81.5
    (c) 57.3

267

8. In 1940, one-fifth of all American workers were self-employed. Currently, what percentage of American workers are self-employed?

(a) less than 1   (d) 12.5
(b) 3.1   (e) 20
(c) 8.2

9. Which of the following is most accurate:

(a) white males have higher rates of unemployment than white females
(b) a higher proportion of black females are unemployed than black males
(c) unemployment is more common in the secondary labor market than in the primary labor market
(d) unemployment has risen significantly since 1982
(e) all of the above are accurate

10. Giant corporations that are clusters of many smaller companies are called:

(a) megacorporations   (d) monopolies
(b) multinational corporations (e) conglomerates
(c) oligarchies

Fill-In

1. _____ range from necessities like food to luxuries like swimming pools, while _____ include various activities that benefit others.

2. A _____ is an economy based on service work and high technology.

3. The _____ is the part of the economy generating raw materials directly from the natural environment.

4. The _____ is the part of the economy generating services rather than goods.

5. _____ is a hypothetical economic and political system in which all members of society have economic and social equality.

6. Among the societies with predominately capitalist economies, _____ has the highest per capita GDP at $_____.

7. While _____ percent of males over the age of 16 in the U.S. have income-producing jobs, _____ percent of the females do.

8. _____ are giant corporations comprised of many smaller companies.

9. The _____ sector of the economy is actually limited to smaller businesses and self-employed people. Large corporations fall within the _____ sector.

10. Our economic future is becoming less a matter of the performance of _____ economies and more a matter of a _____ economic system.

Definition and Short-Answer

1. What is meant by the term "cottage industry"?
2. What were the five revolutionary changes brought about by the industrial revolution?
3. Define the concept postindustrial economy.
4. What are the basic characteristics of capitalism as reviewed in the text?
5. What are the basic characteristics of socialism as reviewed in the text?
6. Differentiate between socialism and communism.
7. What is democratic socialism?
8. Comparing productivity and economic equality measures for capitalist and socialist economic systems, what are the relative advantages and disadvantages of each of these economic systems?
9. Differentiate between the primary and secondary labor markets.
10. What are the basic characteristics of a profession?
11. What is meant by the differentiation between the competitive and noncompetitive sectors of the economy?

PART VI: ANSWERS TO STUDY QUESTIONS

True-False

1.	T (p. 529)	6.	T (p. 537)
2.	T (p. 530)	7.	F (p. 537)
3.	T (p. 531)	8.	T (p. 540)
4.	F (p. 532)	9.	T (p. 550)
5.	F (p. 534)	10.	F (p. 552)

Multiple-Choice

1.	b (p. 532)	6.	d (p. 538)
2.	c (p. 532)	7.	c (p. 539)
3.	d (p. 535)	8.	c (p. 543)
4.	d (p. 535)	9.	c (pp. 544-45)
5.	a (p. 537)	10.	e (p. 548)

Fill-In

1. goods/services (p. 529)
2. postindustrial economy (p. 531)
3. primary sector (p. 532)
4. tertiary sector (p. 532)
5. communism (p. 535)
6. U.S./ 17,615 (p. 536)

7. 75.5/57.3 (p. 539)
8. conglomerates (p. 548)
9. competitive/noncompetitive (p. 550)
10. national/global (p. 552)

PART VII: ANALYSIS AND COMMENT

Social Diversity

"Women in the Factories of Lowell, Massachusetts"

Key Points: Questions:

Sociology of Everyday Life

"Factory and Service Jobs: The More Things Change..."

Key Points: Questions:

A Decade of Change

"The Workforce of the Twenty-First Century"

Key Points: Questions:

Health And Medicine $\boxed{20}$

PART I: CHAPTER OUTLINE

I. What is Health?
    A. Health and Society
    B. Historical Patterns of Health
        1. Health in Preindustrial Societies
        2. Health in Industrial Societies
    C. Global Patterns of Health
II. Health in the United States
    A. Social Epidemiology: The Distribution of Health
        1. Age and Sex
        2. Social Class and Race
    B. Environmental Pollution
    C. Cigarette Smoking
    D. Sexually Transmitted Diseases
        1. Gonorrhea and Syphilis
        2. Genital Herpes
        3. AIDS
E. Ethical Issues: Confronting Death
III. Medicine
    A. The Rise of Scientific Medicine
    B. Holistic Medicine
    C. Medicine and Economics in Global Perspective
        1.Medicine in Socialist Societies
        2.Medicine in Capitalist Societies
    D. Medicine in the United States
IV. Theoretical Analysis of Health and Medicine
    A. Structural-Functional Analysis
        1. The Sick Role
        2. The Physician's Role
    B. Symbolic-Interaction Analysis
        1. The Social Construction of Illness
        2. The Social Construction of Treatment
    C. Social-Conflict Analysis
        1. Unequal Access to Medical Care

2. Medical Care and the Profit Motive
3. Medicine and Social Control
V. Summary
VI. Key Concepts
VII. Suggested Readings

PART II: LEARNING OBJECTIVES

1. To show the ways in which the health of a population is shaped by society's cultural patterns, its technology and social resources, and its social inequality.
2. To know the differences in health among early societies, agrarian societies, and industrial societies.
3. To know the challenges that face the world in confronting the poor health of the Third World.
4. To explain how age, sex, race, and social class affect the level of health of individuals in our society.
5. To identify and describe the issues of environmental pollution, cigarette smoking, and sexually transmitted diseases to world health today.
6. To explain the ethical issues related to dying and death.
7. To distinguish between health care and medicine.
8. To compare and contrast scientific medicine with holistic medicine.
9. To compare and contrast medical care in socialist and capitalist societies.
10. To describe, compare, and contrast the three sociological paradigms and their contributions to understanding health and medicine.

PART III: CHAPTER REVIEW

A story of a female college student with *anorexia nervosa* opens this chapter. This health problem is both a biological and sociological issue. Ninety to ninety-five percent of people with this disease in the U.S. are female. Most are white and from affluent families. Cultural pressure is very much involved in creating this disease. It is an illustration of how social forces shape health in America.

WHAT IS HEALTH?

Health is being defined as a state of complete physical, mental, and social well-being. Therefore, it is viewed as much a *social* as a *biological* issue.

Health and Society

Health in any society is shaped by several important factors. These include: health related to a society's cultural patterns, health related to a society's technological and social resources, and health related to social inequality. Each of these is reviewed.

Historical Patterns of Health

Health in Preindustrial Societies

Health as a social issue is demonstrated by the significant increase in well-being over the course of history. The simple technology of hunting and gathering societies made it difficult to maintain a healthful environment. As many as one-half of the people in such societies died by age twenty, and few lived passed the age of forty.

The agricultural revolution increased surpluses, but also inequality, so only the elite enjoyed better health. Urbanization during medieval times created horrible health problems. Life expectancy was no better in Europe during medieval times than it was thousands of years earlier.

Health in Industrial Societies

Initially, there was little improvement in health due to industrialization. The increase in health conditions, often believed to be attributable to medical advances, were actually related to the rising standard of living with its better nutrition and safer housing. It was not until the second half of the 19th century that medical advances had any significant impact on health.

Table 20-1 (p. 560) shows the 10 leading causes of death in the U.S. for the years 1900 and 1990. Significant differences appear. Medical advances have significantly changed the patterns, but so have lifestyles. About 60 percent of the deaths in the U.S. are attributable to heart disease, cancer, and cerebro-vascular diseases. Chronic illnesses, rather than infectious diseases are the major threat today.

Global Patterns of Health

Health in the Third-World, due to poverty, is much worse than in industrial societies. The World Health Organization (WHO) estimates 1 billion people worldwide to be in poor health, mostly due to hunger. Infectious disease is very widespread. The **Cross-Cultural Comparison** box (p. 561) discusses hunger in the Third World. Focus is given to a disease known in West Africa as kwashiorkor. **Global Map** 20-1 focuses on medical care in global perspective, showing the scarcity of medical doctors in Third-World societies.

Improving Third-World health is very problematic due to the vicious circle of poverty and disease, and the fact that the introduction of medical technology, while reducing the deaths from infectious diseases also is related to a population growth which hinders development in such areas.

HEALTH IN THE UNITED STATES

Social Epidemiology: The Distribution of Health

Social epidemiology is the study of how health and disease are distributed throughout a society's population.

Age and Sex

Health of Americans of all ages has improved during this century, with the exception of young adults, who are victims of more accidental deaths. Most females (84.6%) and males (73.1%) born during the 1980s can expect to live to at least age 65. Gender distinctions explain significant differences in longevity between males and females.

Social Class and Race

There is a strong relationship between social class and health. Table 20-2 (p. 563) shows American's perceptions of their own health by different groups. A strong positive correlation between income and health is illustrated. Health also affects income, given missed school and work resulting from illness.

Table 20-3 (p. 564) shows the life expectancy for American children by race and sex. Significant differences again emerge. For example, for white males, 75 percent can expect to reach age sixty, while only 58 percent of African-American males are expected to live that long. Factors related to the relationship are again economic, with African-Americans being overrepresented among the poor, placing them in conditions of poorer diet and greater stress. Further, the homicide rate among African-Americans, particularly for males, is extremely high.

While wealth is no cureall, affluent people live longer and healthier lives on average than other Americans.

Environmental Pollution

Air pollution and industrial wastes are major concerns for Americans. Some 30,000 toxic waste dump sites exist in the U.S., and the EPA has identified 1,200 as being in need of urgent attention. The Love Canal neighborhood near Buffalo is perhaps the most well known of the residential areas devastated by toxic waste contamination.

The 111 nuclear power plants operating in the United States (1991) provide 20 percent of our electricity. These plants are reviewed as another concern of Americans. Numerous malfunctions in such plants around the world have occurred over the last decade or so.

Cigarette Smoking

Cigarette smoking is the leading preventable cause of illness and death in America. It has recently begun to be labeled as deviant, as laws mandating smoke-free environments have been enacted in many parts of the country.

Evidence of the health risks of smoking first appeared in the 1930s. It was not for another thirty years until the government actually began systematic research. Currently, about 430,000 people die each year as a result of the effects of cigarette smoking.

Today, 27 percent of our adult population smokes. The figure was 37 percent in 1970. A further reduction over the next decade is expected. Some smokers become addicted to the nicotine. Smoking varies by social class, with blue-collar workers more likely to smoke than white-collar workers. African-Americans smoke in greater proportions than whites. A greater percentage of males smoke than females.

As sales in the U.S. and other industrialized societies drop, tobacco companies have begun to sell more products in the Third-World.

Sexually Transmitted Diseases

Increased concern about *venereal diseases* occurred during the 1960s at the beginning of the "sexual revolution." They are viewed by many as not just an illness, but also a punishment for immorality.

Sexually transmitted diseases (STDs) represent an exception to the general decline in infectious diseases during this century.

Gonorrhea and Syphilis

About 1 million cases of gonorrhea are reported each year in the U.S., although the actual number is probably much higher. Approximately 78 percent of the cases reported involved African-Americans. Untreated gonorrhea can lead to sterility.

Syphilis is much more serious. It can lead to damage of major organs, and result in blindness, mental disorders, and death. About 76 percent of the cases reported involve African-Americans.

Both diseases cannot be easily cured with penicillin. Neither then currently carries the label of a serious health problem in America.

Genital Herpes

It is estimated that one-eighth of Americans are carriers of this virus. The infection rate among blacks is about three times higher than it is for whites. Although not as serious as gonorrhea or syphilis, there is currently no cure available.

AIDS

AIDS, or acquired immune deficiency syndrome, is a health problem which could potentially become the most serious epidemic of modern times. AIDS is incurable and fatal.

AIDS is caused by a human immunodeficiency virus (HIV). The virus attacks white blood cells, the core of our immune system. About 1 million Americans in 1992 were infected with HIV. The presence of the virus does not necessarily generate AIDS. About 205,000 people had AIDS in the U.S. in early 1992.

Transmission of HIV almost always occurs through blood, semen, or breast milk. AIDS is not spread through casual contact. There are specific behaviors identified which put people at high risk for getting AIDS. The first is anal sex. Two-thirds of the people with AIDS are homosexual or bisexual males. Other risk factors include sharing needles, having multiple sex partners, and using any drugs.

AIDS has been a major financial problem as well, costing over 4 billion dollars in 1992. During the early 1990s the economic cost will likely triple. The government was slow to respond to the crisis because intravenous drug users and homosexuals were the first groups identified as having the disease. Money for research has increased rapidly in recent years. One drug AZT has shown the ability to slow the progression of the disease. Educational programs remain the best method to fight the spread of the AIDS virus as right now the only cure is prevention. AIDS is identified as both a medical and social problem. **Global Map** 20-2 (p. 569) shows HIV infection of adults worldwide.

ETHICAL ISSUES: CONFRONTING DEATH

Ethical issues permeate health and medical concerns. Questions addressed include: When is a person dead? Do people have a right to die? And, what about mercy killing?

Medical and legal experts presently define death as an irreversible state involving no response to stimulation, no movement or breathing, no reflexes, and no indication of brain activity.

The Nancy Cruzan case, concerning a young woman who went into an irreversible coma after an automobile accident in 1990 is reviewed. The U.S. Supreme has ruled in this case that a patient has the right to die.

A presidential commission in 1983 issued guidelines outlining the rights of people in permanent vegetative states. Included is the suggestion that physicians honor a patient's living will, or a statement of personal intention regarding heroic treatment of terminal illness.

Euthanasia, commonly known as mercy killing, is the assisting in the death of a person suffering from an incurable disease. It can take two forms, *passive* and *active*. The passive form is illustrated by the Cruzan case. The active form is illustrated by a physician, Jack Kevorkian, who has assisted a number of people in taking their own lives with his "suicide machine."

MEDICINE

Medicine is an institutionalized system for combating disease and improving health. As such, it represents an aspect of *health care*, which is any activity intended to improve health. For most of human history, the individual and family were responsible for health care. In preindustrial societies, traditional healers, from herbalists to acupuncturists, provide for the health needs of their society's members. Medicine emerges within technologically complex societies as people fill specialized roles as healers.

The Rise of Scientific Medicine

Scientific medicine dominates health care in the U.S., meaning the logic of science is applied to research and treatment of disease and injury.

In colonial America, medicine was the domain of herbalists, druggists, midwives, and ministers. The ratio of such medical people to the total population is equivalent to the current ratio of medical doctors to the total population.

In colonial times here in America and in Europe, little formal medical training existed. Medical care was plagued by unsanitary conditions and ignorance.

During the early 19th century, medicine came under the control of medical societies. By 1900 there were 400 medical schools in the U.S. Licensing became the order in the second half of the 19th century. Medical standards were established and directed by the American Medical Association (AMA), which was founded in 1847. By the early 1900s state licensing boards would only certify AMA approved physicians.

The AMA established physicians as scientific professionals with high prestige and earnings. At the same time, it restricted the practice of medicine to an affluent elite, dominated by urban, white males. In 1992, 84 percent of physicians were men, while 97 percent of nurses were women.

Those supporters of alternative approaches other than scientific medicine, like midwives, herbalists, and chiropractors, have been defined as a fringe area of medicine, with much less prestige and earnings.

Holistic Medicine

Holistic medicine is an approach to health care that emphasizes prevention of illness and takes account of the whole person within a physical and social environment. They are critical of scientific medical specialists for being focused on symptoms and diseases rather than with people. They believe if drugs and surgery must be used, they must be incorporated into the broader perspective of a person's life. The following are identified and discussed as major concerns of the holistic approach: patients are people, individual responsibility for health is stressed instead of dependency on medicine, a personal treatment environment is sought, and the goal of holistic medicine is optimum health for all.

Medicine and Economics in Global Perspective

Medicine in Socialist Societies

In societies like the People's Republic of China, the Common-Wealth of Independent States, government directly controls medical care. Medical costs are paid for by public funds, and medical care is distributed equally among all.

The People's Republic of China is still a relatively poor agrarian society which is just beginning to industrialize. With over 1 billion people, reaching everyone within one system is virtually impossible. While attempting private medical care for a time, in 1989 China returned to a government operated system.

Barefoot doctors, equivalent to paramedics in America, bring modern methods to millions of rural residents in China. Traditional healing arts remain strong in China. **Global Map** 20-1 (p. 562) shows that medical care in China is quite adequate by world standards.

The former Soviet Union provided health care paid for through taxes. People have not chosen their own physician, but go to a government health facility near their home.

Physicians, 70 percent of whom are women, have lower prestige and income than American physicians. In the United States 20 percent of the physicians are women.

Equality in care was achieved in the former Soviet Union, however its rigid bureaucracy created a highly standardized and impersonal system.

Medicine in Capitalist Societies

In capitalist societies, citizens provide for themselves based on their own resources and preferences. Government assistance is provided to varying degrees.

In Sweden there exists a compulsory, comprehensive system of government medical care. The program is paid for through taxes. This type of system is known as *socialized medicine*, a health care system in which most medical facilities are owned and operated by the government, and most physicians are salaried government employees.

Great Britain has a dual system in which socialized medicine exists, but for those who wish, and can afford it, private care is available.

The Canadian system doe not offer a true socialized medicine. The government reimburses citizens for medicare according to set fees. Physicians operate privately.

In Japan, a combination of private insurance and government programs pay for medical costs. Large Japanese corporations cover their employees well. For those not covered, the government pays 70 percent of the medical costs. Physicians operate privately.

Except for the U.S., capitalist societies have three major benefits in common. First, basic medical care is available to all, regardless of income. Second, the government protects citizens from catastrophic medical costs. And third, the system's structure in each of these societies encourages "well" people to use medical facilities, often preventing more serious illnesses from occurring.

Medicine in the United States

While European governments pay about 70 percent of their citizens' medical costs, the U.S. government pays only about 40 percent. For the most part, the U.S. medical system is a private, profit-making industry. It is identified as a *direct-fee system*, or a medical-care system in which patients pay directly for the services of physicians and hospitals.

The combination of no comprehensive national medical care program, and greater economic inequality then found in Europe, poor Americans have less access to medical care than their counterparts in Europe. The relative health of Americans is worse than is found in European societies.

The U.S. has not developed a national health-care program for several reasons. Americans have traditionally not been open to government intervention in the economy. There is little support for national health-care programs by the public. Also, the AMA has worked hard against dismantling the direct-fee system.

The technological advances in medicine have caused tremendous increases in the cost of medical care. These rising costs are displaced in Figure 20-1 (p. 577). Currently, medical care absorbs 12% of our GNP.

In 1990, 61 percent of the population of the U.S. received some medical-care benefits from a family member's employer. About 14 percent of Americans purchased some form of private coverage. So, a total of 75 percent of Americans are covered by private insurance programs.

Public insurance programs also exist. Medicare and medicaid were created in 1965. Medicare currently covers a portion of the medical costs for 13 percent of the population, and medicaid covers another 10 percent of the population.

HMOs, or *health maintenance organizations* are organizations that provide comprehensive medical care for which subscribers pay a fixed fee. These have become popular over the last decade or so, with 14 percent of Americans being covered by such programs.

In all, a total of 85 percent of Americans have some medical-care coverage. Most is privately funded. Failures in the current medical-care system in the U.S. involve incomplete coverage in terms of costs for serious illness, exclusion of certain medical needs, and the fact that about 15 percent of our population have no medical coverage.

THEORETICAL ANALYSIS OF HEALTH AND MEDICINE

Structural-Functional Analysis

Given its focus on society as a complex system that is stable and well-integrated, structural-functionalism provides a view of illness that sees it as dysfunctional. Every society must therefore establish means of dealing with illness.

The Sick Role

The key concept in structural-functionalist analysis of illness is the *sick role*, or patterns of behavior that are socially defined as appropriate for those who are ill. As developed by Talcott Parsons, the sick role has four characteristics, including: (1) a sick person is exempted from routine responsibilities, (2) a person's illness is not deliberate, (3) a sick person must want to be well, and (4) a sick person must seek competent help.

The Physician's Role

The physician is expected to cure illness. According to Parson's, a hierarchy exists in which physicians expect compliance from their patients.

Cross-culturally, the physician's role varies. As illustrated in the **Cross-Cultural Comparison** box (p. 580), in Japan physicians are very likely to conceal from patients information about the patient's illness.

Criticism of the structural-functional view of society includes a failure to recognize the inequalities in medical care services in the U.S.. Also, Parson's physician's role concept fits contemporary scientific medicine, but not holistic medicine.

Symbolic-Interaction Analysis

A personal account by a woman who was informed she might have cancer is presented to illustrate the subjective dimension of illness. As it turned out, she did not have cancer and was actually quite healthy, yet for a time her whole life was turned upside down. The concept *psychosomatic disorder*, referring to how a person's state of mind affects physical well-being relates to this point.

The Social Construction of Illness

The health of any person must be put into the context of the general health of the society. The definition of health and healthy life-styles vary cross-culturally and historically. Further, research by David Mechanic is cited to illustrate how definitions of illness are negotiated within particular social situations.

The Social Construction of Treatment

Research by Joan Emerson involving gynecological exams is used to illustrate how physicians "craft" their physical surroundings to make specific impressions on others.

A problem with the symbolic-interaction approach is that it minimizes an objective sense of health and illness.

Social-Conflict Analysis

Unequal Access to Medical Care

Unequal access to medical care is the central concern of the proponents of this perspective. Inequality for social-conflict theorists is rooted in the capitalist class system, which does not equitably distribute its resources, including medical and health care.

Medical Care and the Profit Motive

According to social-conflict theorists, the medical system is comprised of multi-million dollar corporate conglomerates out to make a profit. It is pointed out that three-fourths of all surgery in the U.S. each year is elective, not prompted by medical emergencies. Ivan Illich's research suggests that perhaps 1 million people each year in the United States have an adverse reaction to a medical drug. Moving toward socialism is viewed as necessary in order to improve medical care.

Medicine as Social Control

The scientific model of medicine dominates our understanding of health. It is argued that even this approach can be guided by political motivations. The medical establishment, for example, has a history of racism and sexism. The **Critical Thinking** box (pp. 583) illustrates how medical knowledge, argued to be based on scientific research, was used to maintain a subordinate role for women in society.

Objections to this approach include the fact that it minimizes the improvements in medical care brought about by scientific medicine.

PART IV: KEY CONCEPTS

Define each of the following concepts in the space provided or on separate paper. Check the accuracy of your answers by referring to the key concepts section at the end of the chapter in the text as well as by referring to italicized definitions located throughout the chapter.

AIDS
anorexia nervosa
direct-fee system
euthanasia
health
health care
HIV
HMO
holistic medicine
kwashiorkor

living will
psychosomatic
scientific medicine
sick role
social epidemiology
WHO

PART V: STUDY QUESTIONS

True-False

1. T F The World Health Organization defines health as the absence of disease.
2. T F The top five causes of death in the United States have changed very little since 1900.
3. T F Gender distinctions explain significant differences in the longevity of the two sexes.
4. T F Research suggests affluent people live longer and suffer less from illness than do other Americans.
5. T F Venereal diseases first appeared during the colonialization of Africa and Asia by European nations.
6. T F Approximately 70 percent of Soviet physicians are women.
7. T F The United States is unique among the industrialized societies in lacking government programs that ensures basic medical care to every citizen.
8. T F Only about 25 percent of the United States population has some private medical insurance coverage.
9. T F Japanese physicians, due to the more holistic nature of their approach, tend to be much more "open" with their patients about medical matters than American physicians.
10. T F Most surgery in the United States is elective, or not prompted by a medical emergency.

Multiple-Choice

1. The health of any population is shaped by:

   (a) the society's cultural patterns
   (b) the society's technology and social resources
   (c) the society's social inequality
   (d) all of the above

2. In early societies, such as hunting and gathering societies, about one-half of the people died by age 20, and few persons lived past the age of:

   (a) 27   (d) 50
   (b) 32   (e) 60
   (c) 40

282

3. The improvement in health in the 19th century was due to:

   (a) the rising standard of living
   (b) medical advances
   (c) changes in cultural values toward medicine
   (d) increases in the number of medical personnel to treat people
   (e) all of the above

4. The study of the distribution of disease or relative health in the population of a society is called:

   (a) scientific medicine   (c) holistic medicine
   (b) social epidemiology   (d) epistemology

5. Which of the following is accurate?

   (a) a larger proportion of males smoke as compared to females
   (b) a larger proportion of blacks smoke as compared to whites
   (c) a smaller percentage of people in the U.S. smoke today as compared to 1970
   (d) all above are accurate
   (e) none are accurate

6. The institutionalization of scientific medicine by the AMA resulted in:

   (a) expensive medical education
   (b) domination of medicine by white males
   (c) an inadequate supply of physicians in rural areas
   (d) all of the above
   (e) (a) and (b) only

7. Holistic medicine is a reaction to scientific medicine. Which of the following is not an emphasis advocates of holistic medicine share?

   (a) an emphasis upon the environment in which the person exists
   (b) an emphasis upon the responsibility of society for health promotion and care
   (c) an emphasis upon optimum health for all
   (d) an emphasis upon the home setting for medical treatment

8. Approximately what percentage of our GNP is related to health care?

   (a) 2   (d) 18
   (b) 6   (e) 24
   (c) 11

9. A formal organization that provides comprehensive medical care for which subscribers pay a fixed fee is termed:

(a) WHO   (d) DFS
(b) AMA   (e) PIP
(c) HMO

10. Which of the following theoretical paradigms in sociology utilizes concepts like "sick role" and "physician's role" to explain health behavior?

(a) social-conflict   (d) exchange
(b) symbolic-interaction   (e) materialism
(c) structural-functionalist

Fill-In

1. The leading cause of death today in the U.S. is _____, while in 1900 it was _____ and _____.
2. Famine stricken children in Africa who have bloated bodies are suffering from a protein deficiency known in West Africa as _____.
3. _____ is the study of the distribution of health and disease.
4. National attention was drawn to the problem of toxic waste in 1980, when residents of _____, near Niagara Falls, discovered deadly dioxin seeping into their homes and years.
5. AIDS, acquired immune deficiency syndrome, is caused by HIV, or a _____ _____ _____.
6. _____ medicine is an approach to health care that emphasizes prevention of illness and takes account of the whole person within the physical and social environments.
7. About _____ percent of American physicians are women.
8. While European governments pay for about seventy-five percent of their people's medical costs, in the U.S. the government pays for _____ percent.
9. Between 1950 and 1990 expenditures for medical care in the U.S. rose _____-fold.
10. Medical experts have long noted the existence of _____ disorders, in which a person's state of mind affects physical well-being.

Definition and Short-Answer

1. It is pointed out in the text that the health of any population is shaped by important characteristics of the society as a whole. What are the three general characteristics identified? Provide an example of each.
2. How have the causes of death changed in the U.S. over the last century in terms of which one account for most deaths?
3. What is social epidemiology? Provide two illustrations of patterns of health found using this approach.

4. What is AIDS? How is AIDS transmitted?
5. What are the two types of euthanasia? Discuss the Cruzan and Kevorkian cases to illustrate. Relate these cases to the "ethical issues confronting death" as reviewed in the chapter.
6. What is meant by the "sick role"?
7. Describe the characteristics of holistic medicine. How do they differ from those of scientific medicine?
8. How do health care systems operate in socialist societies? Provide specific examples.
9. In what ways does the health-care system of the United States differ from health-care systems in other capitalist systems?
10. What are social-conflict analysts' arguments about the health care system in the United States?
11. Discuss how symbolic-interactionists help us understand our health care system and our sense of health and illness.

PART VI: ANSWERS TO STUDY QUESTIONS

True-False

1.	F (p. 558)	6.	T (p. 575)
2.	F (p. 560)	7.	T (p. 576)
3.	T (p. 563)	8.	F (p. 577)
4.	T (p. 564)	9.	F (p. 580)
5.	F (p. 566)	10.	T (p. 582)

Multiple-Choice

1.	d (p. 558)	6.	d (p. 574)
2.	c (p. 559)	7.	d (p. 574)
3.	a (p. 560)	8.	c (p. 577)
4.	b (p. 563)	9.	c (p. 578)
5.	d (pp. 565-66)	10.	c (pp. 578-79)

Fill-In

1. heart disease, influenza, pneumonia (p. 560)
2. kwashiorkor (p. 561)
3. social epidemiology (p. 563)
4. Love Canal (p. 565)
5. human immunodeficiency virus (p. 568)
6. holistic (p. 574)
7. 20 (p. 576)
8. 40 (p. 577)
9. 40 (p. 577)
10. psychosomatic (p. 581)

PART VII: ANALYSIS AND COMMENT

Cross-Cultural Comparison

"Poverty: The Leading Cause of Death in the Third World"

    Key Points:

    Questions:

"Breaking Bad News: Comparing Japanese and U.S. Physicians"

    Key Points:

    Questions:

Critical Thinking

"Medicine and Victorian Women: Science of Sexism?"

    Key Points:

    Questions:

Population And Urbanization

21

PART I: CHAPTER OUTLINE

I.   Demography: The Study of Population
        A.   Fertility
        B.   Mortality
        C.   Migration
        D.   Population Growth
        E.   Population Composition
II.   History and Theory of Population Growth
        A.   Malthusian Theory
        B.   Demographic Transition Theory
        C.   World Population Today
                1.   Industrial Societies
                2.   Less-Developed Societies
        D.   The Importance of Demography
III.   Urbanization: The Growth of Cities
        A.   The Evolution of Cities
                1.   The First Cities
                2.   Preindustrial Cities in Europe
                3.   Industrial-Capitalist Cities in Europe
        B.   The Growth of U.S. Cities
                1.   Colonial Settlement: 1624-1800
                2.   Urban Expansion: 1800-1860
                3.   The Metropolitan Era: 1860-1950
                4.   Urban Decentralization: 1950-present
        C.   Suburbs and Central Cities
        D.   Postindustrial, Sunbelt Cities
        E.   Megalopolis: Regional Cities
IV.   Understanding Cities: Theory and Method
        A.   European Theory: Urban Life Versus Rural Life
                1.   Ferdinand Toennies: Gemeinschaft and Gesellschaft
                2.   Georg Simmel: The Blase Urbanite
        B.   U.S. Research: Observing the City
                1.   Louis Wirth: Urbanism as a Way of Life
        C.   Urban Ecology

D.   Third-World Urbanization
      1.   Causes of the Third-World Urban Growth
      2.   The Future of Third-World Cities
E.   The Historical Importance of Cities
IV.   Summary
V.   Key Concepts
VI.   Suggested Readings

PART II: LEARNING OBJECTIVES

1. To learn the basic concepts used by demographers to study population.
2. To describe, compare, and contrast the Malthusian theory and the demographic transition theory.
3. To explain how populations differ in industrialized societies and nonindustrialized societies.
4. To suggest ways in which the study of demography will provide guidelines to understanding and dealing with the earth's large population.
5. To compare and contrast the first cities of the world, preindustrial cities in Europe and industrial-capitalist cities in Europe.
6. To trace the transformation of the United States into an urban civilization from colonial settlement through urban expansion and the metropolitan era to urban decentralization.
7. To compare and contrast the characteristics of rural and urban life by explaining the theoretical views of Toennies, Simmel, Park, and Wirth.
8. To describe the key ideas of urban ecology and the related models of city structure.
9. To understand the causes of Third-World urbanization and the future prospects of Third-World cities.

PART III: CHAPTER REVIEW

This chapter begins with a brief review of Cortes' discovery and destruction of the great Aztec city of Tenochtitlan in the early 16th century. In its place he began to build Mexico City, which is expected to have a population of almost thirty million by the year 2000. It is a city which is part of a Third-World nation in great crisis. This chapter focuses on the processes of population growth and urbanization.

DEMOGRAPHY: THE STUDY OF POPULATION

Demography is the study of human population, investigating the size, age, sex composition and migration patterns of given populations. It is a quantitative discipline, however crucial questions about the consequences of these variables are analyzed and have great qualitative significance. Several basic concepts central to demographic analysis are discussed in the following sections.

Fertility

Fertility is the incidence of childbearing in a society's population. A female's childbearing years last from the beginning of menstruation to menopause. But, *fecundity*, or potential child-bearing, is greatly reduced by health and financial constraints, cultural norms, and personal choice.

A typical measurement used for fertility is the ***crude birth rate***, or the number of live births in a given year for every 1000 people in a population. In 1990 4.2 million live births occurred in the U.S. (population 253 million) for a crude birth rate of 16.7. The term "crude" relates to the fact that comparing such rates can be misleading because it doesn't focus on women of childbearing age, and doesn't consider varying rates between racial, ethnic, and religious groups. It is however easy to calculate.

Mortality

Mortality is the incidence of death in a society's population. The ***crude death rate*** refers to the number of deaths in a given year for every 1000 people in a population. There were 2.2 million deaths in the U.S. in 1990, for a crude death rate of 8.6.

The ***infant mortality rate***, refers to the number of deaths within the first year of life for each 1000 live births in a given year. The infant mortality rate in the U.S. in 1990 was 10.4. Table 21-1 (p. 588) compares fertility, mortality and infant mortality rates for countries around the world. Significant differences exist between industrialized and Third-World nations.

Life expectancy, or how long a person, on average, can expect to live, is negatively correlated with a society's infant mortality rate. For males born in the U.S. in 1990 life expectancy is 72.1 years and for females 79.0 years.

Migration

Migration is defined as the movement of people into and out of a specified territory. Some is involuntary, such as the historical existence of slave trading, while most is voluntary and based on various "push-pull" factors. Various examples of such factors are discussed.

Movement into a territory is termed *immigration*, and is measured by the number of people entering areas for every 1000 people in the total population. Movement out of an area, termed *emigration*, is measured by using the number of people leaving an area for every 1000 people in the population. The differences between the two figures is termed *net-migration rate*.

Population Growth

Migration, fertility, and mortality each affect a society's population size. The *natural growth rate* of a society is determined by subtracting the crude death rate from the crude birth rate. This figure for the U.S. in 1990 was 8.1 per thousand, or 0.8 percent annually. The projected rates for different world regions during the 1990s are presented in **Global Map** 21-1 (p. 591). Industrialized regions, Europe, North America and Oceania have very low rates, while the Third-World regions- Asia, Africa, and Latin America have relatively high rates. An annual growth rate of 2 percent (as found in Latin America) doubles a population in 35 years. In Africa, the growth rate is 3 percent.

Population Composition

The *sex ratio* refers to the number of males for every 100 females in a given population. In the U.S. in 1990 the sex ratio was 95.0. A more complicated descriptive device is the *age-sex pyramid* which is a graphic representation of the age and sex composition of population. Figure 21-1 (p. 590) presents the age-sex pyramid for the U.S. in 1990. Figure 21-2 (p. 592) compares the age-sex pyramids for Switzerland and Bangladesh. For the U.S. the *baby boom* and *baby bust* birth cohorts are discussed.

HISTORY AND THEORY OF POPULATION GROWTH

Until relatively recently in human history, societies desired high birth rates as high birth rates meant more human resources for productivity. High birth rates were needed to offset high death rates. Also, until the development of the rubber condom 150 years ago, birth control was very unreliable.

The growth of the world's population from 6000 B.C.E. and projecting through to the year 2000 is portrayed in Figure 21-3 (p. 592). A critical point in world population growth occurred in the middle of the 18th century as the earth's population began a sharp increase, resulting more from a drop in the mortality rate than from a rise in the birth rate. In the 20th century alone the world's population has increased fourfold. Currently there are a little over 5 billion people on earth. Around 1850 the world population reached 1 billion, in 1930 it reached 2 billion, in 1962 it reached 3 billion, in 1974 it reached 4 billion, and in 1987, 5 billion. By 2025 the world's population is projected to reach 8 billion.

Malthusian Theory

In the late 18th century Thomas Malthus developed a theory of population growth in which he warned of disaster. He predicted population would increase according to a geometric progression, while food production would only increase in arithmetic progression.

Malthus saw positive checks, such as famine, disease, and war; and preventative checks, such as artificial birth control and delayed marriage as the only two limits to population growth. The former he felt was immoral, and the latter he was not optimistic about.

For several reasons his projections have not been realized. First, the birth rate in Europe began to drop in the 19th century as children became less of an economic asset.

He also underestimated human ingenuity, specifically in terms of technological applications in solving food production and population related problems.

But his warnings still need to be taken seriously. Technology has caused problems for the environment, and population growth in the Third-World nations remains very high. Even if their population growth rate is reduced, any rate of increase in the long-range can be dangerous.

Demographic Transition Theory

Demographic transition theory has now replaced Malthusian theory and is the thesis that population patterns are linked to a society's level of technological development. Figure 21-4 (p. 594) illustrates three stages of technological change, and the related birth and death dates. Stage 1 is represented by the preindustrial agrarian society with high birth rates and high death rates. Stage 2, represented by industrialization, marks the beginning of the demographic transition, with high birth rates continuing, but death rates dropping significantly. In stage 3, the fully industrialized society, birth rates begin to drop significantly and death rates remain stable and low.

The lower birth rate in the third stage is related to a higher standard of living, resulting in children being a greater economic burden. Smaller families are also more functional as a higher percentage of women work outside the home. Further, a higher level of technology makes birth control widely available and reliable.

This view provides far more optimism than Malthusian theory. It has been incorporated into modernization theory. Dependency theorists have therefore been critical of this view.

World Population Today

Using demographic transition theory important differences between industrialized and nonindustrialized societies can be noted in terms of population patterns.

Industrialized Societies

Shortly after industrialization began the population growth in Europe and America peaked at 3 percent annually. It has been generally declining since, and since 1970 has not been above 1 percent. Europe and America are near population replacement level of 2.1 births per women, a point known as *zero population growth*, or the level of reproduction that maintains population at a steady state. In certain European societies, a fourth stage may have even been reached where there is actually a population decline.

America is still a relatively young society, with a median age of 32.7 in 1989. We expect to experience a continuation of population growth for the next several decades. Several factors, including the increasing cost of raising children, working women, and delaying marriage, are discussed as reasons for low birth rates in industrialized societies. A very significant factor of course remains birth control technology and its availability. Even Catholics no longer differ from other Americans in their contraceptive practices.

Less-Developed Societies

Few societies are still represented by stage 1. Most Third-World nations, having a combination of agrarian and industrial economies, fall in stage 2. Figure 21-5 (p. 596) shows the population distribution, past and projected, in industrialized and less-developed societies from 1750-2000. The decreasing death rates in nonindustrialized societies has resulted in the population explosion in these countries.

Birth rates are high for age-old reasons, the economic asset of children to the family and high infant mortality rates, The cultural norm of patriarchy also is a factor in the continuation of high birth rates. The social position of women is addressed.

In China, the government instituted in 1979 a one-child policy. Birth control in China, which has one-fourth of the world's population, is addressed in the **Cross-Cultural Comparison** box (p. 597).

Infant mortality rates are still high, and life expectancy compared to industrialized societies is still relatively low, but improvements are being made.

The Importance of Demography

It is argued that demography is an important field of study because it helps us understand population growth, which is a critical social problem today. Population growth is described as a "great wave."

URBANIZATION: THE GROWTH OF CITIES

Urbanization is the concentration of humanity into cities. World history has been characterized by three urban revolutions, which are discussed in the text.

The Evolution of Cities

The first urban revolution occurred about 10,000 years ago with the emergence of permanent settlements. Two factors are discussed as enabling urbanization to occur, a changing ecology and changing technology.

The First Cities

The first city is argued to have been Jericho, just north of the Dead Sea, coming into existence about 8000 B.C.E. By 4000 B.C.E. there were several cities within the Fertile Crescent in present day Iraq and along the Nile in Egypt.

Cities emerged independently in at least three other areas of the world in present day Pakistan (about 2500 B.C.E.) in China (about 2000 B.C.E.), and in Central and South America (about 1500 B.C.E.)

Preindustrial Cities in Europe

Urbanization began in Europe about 1800 B.C.E. on Crete and spread throughout Greece in the form of hundreds of city states. Athens is the most well known. Ancient Athens, as an example of urban life, is discussed.

As Greek civilization faded, the city of Rome grew to almost 1 million by the 1st century C.E. The militaristic Roman Empire had expanded throughout Europe and Northern Africa.

The fall of the Roman Empire started a period of urban decline. Cities became smaller, surrounded by "defensive" walls. By the 11th century medieval cities began to remove their walls to facilitate trade. Personal and family ties were strong in such cities. These cities in Europe were characterized by "quarters," or areas in the city where particular occupational groups were represented.

Industrial-Capitalist Cities in Europe

The new trading class, affluent, urban, and middle-class or bourgeoisie steadily increased in power during the middle ages in Europe. The second urban revolution was under way by about 1750. Industrial productivity caused cities to grow rapidly. Table 21-2 (p. 600) illustrates the growth of several European cities during the 18th, 19th, and 20th centuries.

Besides population changes, cities were transformed in terms of their physical layout. Factories, businesses, and broad boulevards dominated the urban landscape.

Urban social life began to change as well as crowding, impersonality, inequality, and crime became more and more characteristic of cities during the 18th and 19th centuries.

The Growth of U.S. Cities

Native Americans established few permanent settlements. The Spanish made their first settlement in St.Augustine in Florida in the year 1565. The English founded Jamestown in Virginia in 1607. Today, more than three-quarters of the U.S. population lives in urban areas.

Colonial Settlement: 1624-1800

The changing face of settlements in the northeastern U.S. during the 17th century is discussed. Figure 21-6 (p. 601) contrasts the different urban development patterns of the early 17th and late 17th century, showing how the traditional European shape of winding and narrow roads were replaced by grid-like patterns.

The first U.S. census in 1790 counted 4 million Americans. Table 21-3 (p. 602) shows the change in the number and percentage of Americans living in urban areas between 1790 and 1990.

Urban Expansion: 1800-1860

Important transportation developments are discussed which influenced the development of cities in the East to the Midwest. By 1860 about one-third of Americans lived in cities.

The Metropolitan Era: 1860-1950

Table 21-4 (p. 602) illustrates the rapid growth of cities in the late 19th century. It further shows population changes in cities during the 20th century. By 1900, New York City had about 4 million inhabitants. Chicago had about 2 million inhabitants. The growth between 1860-1900 marked the beginning of the era of the *metropolis*, a very large city that socially and economically dominates urban areas. By the end of World War I most of the U.S. population lived in cities.

Urban Decentralization: 1950-present

Since 1050, people have been moving away from the central cities in America. Table 21-4 (p. 602) illustrates how many northeastern and midwest cities have been experiencing either stable or declining populations. Urbanization continues however with the growth of suburbs.

Suburbs and Central Cities

Suburbs, the urban area beyond the political boundaries of a city, have been expanding in recent decades. Suburbs first appeared in the late 19th century, as some of the well-to-do moved from the hectic cities. Racial and ethnic intolerance also increased the movement to the suburbs. The post-World War II economic boom, more affordable cars, and an increased birth rate all were factors in the rapid growth of suburbia. By 1970, more people lived in the suburbs than in the central cities.

Shopping and industry also began to move out of the cities to the suburbs during this period. The loss of tax revenue caused many cities to decay, some reaching the brink of bankruptcy. The government responded with *urban renewal*, or government programs intended to revitalize cities. Many inner-cities have been rebuilt, yet critics argue this has benefitted business, not the poor residents.

Postindustrial Sunbelt Cities

In 1940 the "snowbelt" contained 60 percent of the population of the United States. In 1988 the "sunbelt" contained 55 percent of our population. This regional migration is linked to the post-industrial economy. This demographic shift is portrayed in Table 21-5 (p. 604). Six of the ten largest cities (by population) are now found in the sunbelt. These sunbelt cities, developed after decentralization began, tend to be larger in areas than snowbelt cities. The **Decade of Change** box (p. 605) discusses this pattern.

Megalopolis: Regional Cities

Decentralization has created regional cities. The Census Bureau officially recognized 284 urban regions in the U.S. in 1990. These are called *metropolitan statistical areas* (MSAs). MSAs must include a city with a population of at least 50,000, plus densely populated surrounding counties. The largest MSAs are called *consolidated metropolitan statistical areas* (CMSAs). In 1990 there were 20 of these in the U.S.

When several of the CMSAs geographically meet, like on the east coast from Boston to northern Virginia, a *megalopolis*, or vast urban region containing a number of cities and their surrounding suburbs, is created.

UNDERSTANDING CITIES: THEORY AND METHOD

European Theory: Urban Life Versus Rural Life

Ferdinand Toennies: Gemeinschaft and Gesellschaft

This German sociologist of the late 19th century differentiated between two types of social organization. The first *gemeinschaft* refers to a type of social organization with strong solidarity based on tradition and personal relationships. It describes social settings dominated by primary groups and small villages. Its meaning is similar to Durkheim's mechanical solidarity. In contrast, *gesellschaft* is a type of social organization with weak solidarity caused by cultural pluralism and impersonal social relationships. This represents city dwellers, and is similar to Durkheim's concept of organic solidarity.

Georg Simmel: The Blase Urbanite

This German sociologist used a micro-level analysis of how urban life shaped the behavior and attitudes of people. He argued city dwellers needed to be selective in what they responded to because of the social intensity of such a life. They develop then a blase' attitude out of necessity.

U.S. Research: Observing the City

The first major sociology program in the U.S. to focus on urban development was at the University of Chicago. Robert Park is perhaps the most famous urban researcher to have worked at Chicago. His is introduced in the **Profile** box (p. 609). He saw the city as a highly ordered mosaic of distinctive regions. Cities were viewed as complex social organisms by Park.

Louis Wirth: Urbanism as Way of Life

As another of the Chicago urban researchers, Wirth identified three factors that define urbanism: large population, dense settlement, and social diversity. He saw cities as impersonal, superficial, and transitory.

Mixed support for Park's and Wirth's views on city life have been found in recent decades. While a greater sense of community exists in rural areas, the difference compared to cities can be exaggerated. Also, early sociologists were incorrect in their projection that urban life would neutralize the effects of class, race, and sex.

Urban Ecology

Urban ecology is the study of the link between the physical and social dimensions of cities. One issue focused on is why cities are located where they are. Another issue concerns the physical design of cities. Several models explaining urban form are identified and discussed, including the concentric zone model, the sector model, the multiple-nuclei model, the social area model, and integrated analysis.

Third-World Urbanization

Previously described were the first and second urban revolutions. A third urban revolution began about 1950. In 1950, about 25 percent of the Third-World's population was urbanized, by the year 2000 this figure is expected to reach 50 percent (it currently is at about 40 percent). Table 21-6 (p. 612) compares the world's ten largest cities in 1980 and the projected sizes of certain cities for the year 2000. In the year 2000 only four of the largest cities by population are expected to be in industrialized societies.

Causes of Third-World Urban Growth

As the Third-World continues through the second stage of the demographic transition, and migration to urban areas in these countries continues, their cities are expected to experience further conflict and hardships. The Mexico City situation outlined at the beginning of the chapter is further discussed as an example of this pattern.

The Future of Third-World Cities

Modernization and underdevelopment theories provide different answers to what is needed in order to stabilize and nurture the Third-World urban growth patterns. Jane Jacobs is cited as arguing that Third-World nations must break ties with rich societies and develop trading networks among themselves. This view remains controversial.

The Historical Importance of Cities

Thomas Jefferson in 1800 and Rudyard Kipling in 1900 each indicated a distaste for urban life. The ancient Greeks, on the other hand, saw cities as the only path to find the "good life." Cities, it is argued, seem to comprise the best and the worst social life has to offer.

PART IV: KEY CONCEPTS

Define each of the following concepts in the space provided or on separate paper. Check the accuracy of your answers by referring to the key concepts section at the end of the chapter in the text as well as by referring to italicized definitions located throughout the chapter.

age-sex pyramid
concentric zone model
crude birth rate
crude death rate
demographic transition theory
demography
emigration
fecundity
fertility
gemeinschaft
gesellschaft
immigration
infant mortality rate
integrated analysis
life expectancy
Malthusian theory
megalopolis
metropolis
migration
mortality
multi-nuclei model
natural growth rate
sector model
sex ratio
social area analysis
suburbs
urbanization
urban ecology
urban renewal
zero population growth

PART V: STUDY QUESTIONS

True-False

1. T F Demographers using what is known as the crude birth rate, only take into account women of childbearing age in the calculation for this figure.
2. T F The U.S., using the demographer's natural growth rate measure, will experience a decline in population between 1990-2000.
3. T F A significantly larger percentage of the U.S. population over the next two decades will be comprised of childbearing aged women than at any other period in our nation's history.
4. T F The dramatic increase in the world's population beginning in the middle of the 18th century had more to do with a reduction in mortality rates than an increase in the fertility rate.
5. T F According to demographic transition theory, population growth patterns are linked to a society's level of technological development.
6. T F Protestants are more likely than Catholics in the U.S. to use contraceptive practices.
7. T F Urbanization in Europe began in about 1800 B.C.E.
8. T F Today, more than three-quarters of Americans live in urban areas.
9. T F Most of the ten largest cities in the U.S. (in terms of population) are in the sunbelt.
10. T F Compared to Louis Wirth, Robert Park had a relatively negative view of urban life.

Multiple-Choice

1. Cortes reached the Aztec capital of _____ in 1519.

   (a) Cuzco   (c) Montezuma
   (b) Tikal   (d) Tenochtitlan

2. The sex ratio in the U.S., or the number of males for every one-hundred females is:

   (a) 85   (d) 100
   (b) 90   (e) 105
   (c) 95

3. China contains _____ percent of the world's population.

   (a) 15   (d) 30
   (b) 20   (e) 40
   (c) 25

298

4. The first city to have ever existed is argued to be:

   (a) Athens   (d) Cairo
   (b) Tikal   (e) Jericho
   (c) Rome

5. According to the text, the "second urban revolution" was triggered by:

   (a) the fall of Rome
   (b) the industrial revolution
   (c) the fall of Greece
   (d) the post-World War II baby boom
   (e) the discovery of the new world

6. The period of 1950 to the present is described in the text as:

   (a) urban decentralization   (c) the metropolitan era
   (b) urban expansion   (d) the second urban revolution

7. Ferdinand Toennies' concept referring to the type of social organization with weak social organization resulting from cultural pluralism and impersonal social relationships is:

   (a) megalopolis   (d) sector model
   (b) gesellschaft   (e) multi-nuclei model
   (c) gemeinschaft

8. One issue studied by urban ecologists is the physical design of cities. Which of the following is not a model used to explain urban form:

   (a) concentric zone   (d) social area
   (b) multi-nuclei   (e) all are used as models
   (c) sector

9. What percentage of the Third-World's population is expected to be living in urban areas in the year 2000:

   (a) 10   (d) 50
   (b) 25   (e) 67
   (c) 37

10. Which of the following is expected to be the largest urban area (in terms of population) in the year 2000:

    (a) Tokyo-Yokohama   (d) Shanghai
    (b) New York   (e) Buenos Aires
    (c) Mexico City

Fill-In

1. _____ is the incidence of childbearing in a society's population.
2. Malthus saw two limits to population growth: _____ checks, such as famine, and _____ checks, such as birth control.
3. _____ _____ theory is the thesis that population patterns are linked to a society's level of technological development.
4. Two factors are identified which set the stage for the first urban revolution. The first factor was a changing _____, and the second factor was changing _____.
5. The metropolitan era is characterized in the text as existing from _____ to _____.
6. A _____ is a very large city that socially and economically dominates an urban area.
7. The Bureau of the Census recognizes 283 urban areas in the U.S. which they call _____ _____ _____, or MSA's.
8. _____ refers to a type of social organization with strong solidarity based on tradition and personal relations.
9. The model of urban development established by Ernest Burgess is called the _____ _____ model.
10. Urbanist Jane Jacobs thinks that expanding trade may solve many Third-World problems, but only if Third-World nations _____ trading ties with rich societies and _____ trading networks among themselves.

Definition and Short-Answer

1. What are the three basic factors which determine the size and growth rate of a population? Define each of the three concepts.
2. Differentiate between Malthusian theory and demographic transition theory as perspectives on population growth.
3. What are the three stages in the demographic transition theory? Describe each.
4. What is the official birth control policy today in China?
5. Identify and describe the five periods of growth of American cities presented in the text.
6. Differentiate between the concepts of metropolis and megalopolis.
7. Differentiate between the perspectives of Louis Wirth and Robert Park concerning urbanization in America.
8. What factors are causing Third-World urban growth?
9. How are urbanization patterns changing worldwide?

PART VI: ANSWERS TO STUDY QUESTIONS

True-False

1.	F (p. 588)	6.	F (p. 596)
2.	F (p. 590)	7.	T (p. 600)
3.	F (p. 590)	8.	T (p. 602)
4.	T (p. 592)	9.	T (p. 604)
5.	T (p. 594)	10.	F (p. 609)

Multiple-Choice

1.	d (p. 587)	6.	a (p. 603)
2.	e (p. 590)	7.	b (p. 606)
3.	c (p. 597)	8.	e (pp. 609-10)
4.	e (p. 598)	9.	a (p. 610)
5.	b (p. 600)	10.	d (p. 612)

Fill-In

1. fertility (p. 588)
2. positive/preventative (p. 593)
3. demographic transition (p. 594)
4. ecology/technology (p. 598)
5. 1860/1950 (p. 602)
6. metropolis (p. 603)
7. metropolitan statistical area (p. 606)
8. gemeinschaft (p. 606)
9. concentric zone (p. 609)
10. break/build (p. 613)

PART VII: ANALYSIS AND COMMENT

Cross-Cultural Comparison

"Birth Control in China"

Key Points:

Questions:

A Decade of Change

"The Burgeoning Sunbelt"

    Key Points:

    Questions:

Profile

"Robert Ezra Park (1864-1944)

    Key Points:

    Questions:

Collective Behavior And Social Movements

22

PART I: CHAPTER OUTLINE

I.   Collective Behavior
    A.   Studying Collective Behavior
    B.   Crowds
    C.   Mobs and Riots
    D.   Contagion Theory
    E.   Convergence Theory
    F.   Emergent-Norm Theory
    G.   Crowds, Politics, and Social Change
    H.   Rumor and Gossip
    I.   Public Opinion
    J.   Panic and Mass Hysteria
    K.   Fashions and Fads
II. Social Movements
    A.   Types of Social Movements
    B.   Deprivation Theory
    C.   Mass-Society Theory
    D.   Structural-Strain Theory
    E.   Resource-Mobilization Theory
    F.   "New Social Movements" Theory
    G.   Stages in Social Movements
    H.   Social Movements and Social Change
III. Summary
IV. Key Concepts
V.   Suggested Readings

PART II: LEARNING OBJECTIVES

1. To identify the problems associated with studying collective behavior from a sociological perspective.
2. To explain the general characteristics of collectivities that distinguish them from social groups.
3. To distinguish among the concepts of crowds, mobs, riots, and panics.
4. To describe, compare and contrast contagion theory, convergence theory, and emergent-norm theory in terms of how each orients researchers in the study of collective behavior.
5. To describe the relationships of crowds to politics and social change.
6. To describe, compare, and contrast the various dispersed collectivities: rumor, public opinion, mass hysteria, fashion, and fads.
7. To identify and describe the four types of social movements.
8. To compare and contrast the four theories of social movements: deprivation theory, mass-society theory, structural-strain theory, and resource mobilization theory.
9. To describe the four stages of a social movement.
10. To explain the relationship between social movements and social change.

PART III: CHAPTER REVIEW

This chapter begins with the story of four black men, who as college students in 1960, sat at a "whites only" food counter at a Woolworth's in Greensboro, North Carolina. It is argued that their actions opened the way for the civil rights movement.

The focus of this chapter is *social movements*, or organized activity that encourages or discourages social change. Social movements are one of the most important types of *collective behavior*, referring to activity involving a large number of people, often spontaneous, and typically in violation of established norms.

COLLECTIVE BEHAVIOR

Studying Collective Behavior

Studying collective behavior is difficult for several reasons, including the *broadness* of the concept, its *complexity*, and the fact that it is often *transitory*. It is pointed out that this is perhaps true for all issues studied by sociologists. However, a particularly significant problem here is limited theoretical analysis of this domain of social inquiry.

A *collectivity* is a large number of people who interact little if at all in the absence of well-defined and conventional norms. Two types of collectivities are (1) localized collectivities, referring to people in physical proximity to one another, and (2) dispersed collectivities, meaning people influencing one another, often from great distances.

These collectivities are distinguished from social groups on the basis of three characteristics, including limited social interaction, unclear social boundaries, and weak or unconventional norms.

Crowds

A *crowd* is a temporary gathering of people who share a common focus of attention and whose members influence one another.

Herbert Blumer identifies four types of crowds, based in part on their level of emotional intensity. These include: the *casual* crowd, or a loose collection of people who have little interaction; the *conventional* crowd, resulting from deliberate planning of an event and conforming to norms appropriate to the situation; the *expressive* crowd, which forms around an event that has emotional appeal; and an *acting* crowd which is a crowd energetically doing something. Crowds can change from one type to another. A fifth type, or *protest* crowd, not identified by Blumer, is a crowd which has some political goal.

Mobs and Riots

When an acting crowd becomes violent it is classified as a *mob*, a highly emotional crowd that pursues some violent or destructive goal. Lynching is a notorious example in the history of the United States. The freeing of the slaves, which provided blacks with political rights and economic opportunities were perceived by whites as a threat. Lynching was used as a form of social control to exert white supremacy over blacks. Lynchings were at their peak between 1880 and 1930. Most of the 5,000 lynchings which were officially reported to the police during this time occurred in the deep South.

A violent crowd with no specific purpose is termed a *riot*, or a social eruption that is highly emotional, violent, and undirected. Throughout American history riots have resulted from a collective expression against social injustice. Examples from American history are reviewed. It is also pointed out that rioting behavior can result from positive feelings as evidenced by the riots involving college students on Spring Break.

Contagion Theory

The unconventional behavior of crowds has been a topic of sociological concern for many years. One of the first social scientists to try and explain such behavior was Gustave Le Bon, who developed *contagion theory*. This theory maintains that crowds can exert a hypnotic effect on its members. Anonymity of a crowd creates a condition in which people lose their identity and personal responsibility to a collective mind.

Critics claim that many crowds do not take on a life of their own separate from the thoughts and actions of their members. The tragic deaths at a Who concert in Cincinnati in 1979 is used as an example to illustrate.

Convergence Theory

This theory leads researchers to see the motives which drive collective action as emerging prior to the formation of a crowd. The argument is that people of like-mind come together for a particular purpose and form a crowd. As opposed to contagion theory, which focuses our attention on irrational forces, this perspective provides a view of rational processes creating a crowd.

Emergent-Norm Theory

Ralph Turner and Lewis Killian developed this theory, and argue like convergence theorists, that crowds are not merely irrational collectivities. However, they further suggest that patterns of behavior emerge within the crowds themselves. The New Bedford, Massachusetts tavern rape in 1983 is used to illustrate this process.

This view fits into the symbolic-interaction approach to the study of social life. Crowd behavior is seen, in part, as a response to its members motives, but that norms emerge and guide behavior within the development of the crowd itself. Critics of this view argue that not all members follow emergent norms.

Crowds, Politics, and Social Change

Crowds have historically been involved in the promotion of, and the protest against social change. The Boston Massacre of 1770 and the Boston Tea Party of 1773 are cited as examples in American history. It is argued crowds often spark controversy.

Rumor and Gossip

Mass behavior refers to collective behavior among people dispersed over a wide geographic area. *Rumor*, or unsubstantiated information spread informally, often by word of mouth is one example. Rumor has three essential characteristics, including thriving on a climate of ambiguity, being changeable, and being difficult to stop. The **Sociology of Everyday Life** box (p. 624) discusses the case of the rumored death of Beatle Paul McCartney in 1967.

Closely related to rumor is *gossip*, or rumor about the personal affairs of others. Gossip is referred to as being more localized than rumor. It can be an effective means of social control.

Public Opinion

Public opinion is a form of highly dispersed collective behavior. No one "public opinion" exists on key social issues, but rather is represented by a diversity of opinion. However, sharing particular traits in common with others can create certain patterns in attitudes.

306

A public grows larger and smaller over time as interest in a particular issue changes. The women's movement is used as an illustration. Certain categories of people are argued to have more social influence than others when it comes to shaping public opinion.

Propaganda is defined as information presented with the intention of shaping public opinion. It can be accurate or false, positive or negative. Various forms exist from politics to advertising.

Panic and Mass Hysteria

A *panic* is a form of localized collective behavior by which people react to some stimulus with emotional, irrational, and often self-destructive behavior. Generally some threat provokes a panic, as in the case of a fire in a crowded theater.

Mass hysteria is a form of dispersed collective behavior in which people respond to a real or imagined event with irrational, frantic behavior. The 1938 CBS radio broadcast of a dramatization of the novel War of the Worlds, is used as an example to illustrate how mass hysteria can emerge.

Mass hysteria often develops into a vicious circle, as illustrated in the **Critical Thinking** box (p. 626) concerning the Salem witch hunts of the last 17th century.

Fashions and Fads

Fashion is defined as a social pattern favored for a time by a large number of people. Fashions are transitory and occur for two reasons, the future-orientation of people in industrial societies and the high social mobility representing such societies.

American sociologist Thorstein Veblen originated the term *conspicuous consumption*, referring to the practice of spending money with the intention of displaying one's wealth to others.

A *fad* is an unconventional social pattern that is enthusiastically embraced by a large number of people for a short time. They are sometimes referred to as crazes. While fads are truly "passing fancies," fashions tend to reflect fundamental human values and social patterns that evolve over time.

SOCIAL MOVEMENTS

Three characteristics differentiate social movements from other types of collective behavior: a higher degree of internal organization; typically longer duration, often spanning many years; and the deliberate attempt to reorganize society itself.

While being rare in preindustrial societies, social movements are common in industrialized societies. They develop around a wide range of social issues.

Types of Social Movements

Social movements are classified along two basic dimensions, *breadth*, concerning the proportion of the population in society involved and *depth*, concerning the question of how superficial or extensive the change being sought is for the society.

Four types of social movements are identified based on these dimensions. Figure 22-1 (p. 628) presents a model of the different types identified along these two dimensions. These types include: *alternative social movements*, which pursue limited change for certain individuals (planned parenthood being an example); *redemptive social movements*, which focus on a limited number of individuals, but seek to change them radically (fundamentalist church organizations are an example); *reformative social movements*, which seek limited social change for the entire society (proponents of holistic health care are an example); and *revolutionary social movements*, which seek basic transformations of the entire society (the John Birch Society is an example).

Deprivation Theory

Deprivation theory holds that social movements arise as people react to feeling deprived of things they consider necessary or believe they deserve. This approach is implicit in Karl Marx's expectation that industrial workers would eventually organize in opposition to capitalism.

Relative deprivation is a perceived disadvantage based on some comparison. In the middle of the 19th century, Alexis deTocqueville studied the question as to why a revolution occurred in France and not in Germany in the late 1790s. What puzzled him was that social conditions in Germany were far worse than they were in France. His answer to this apparent paradox was that German peasants had known nothing but feudal servitude and thus had no basis for feeling deprived. Improving social conditions in France had raised the expectations of its people during the latter part of the 18th century.

Figure 22-2 (p. 630) illustrates the model developed by Jamie Davies predicting that social movements are more likely to occur in a society when an extended period of improvement in the standard of living is followed by a shorter period of decline.

Weaknesses with this perspective include its inability to help us explain why social movements emerge among some categories of people and not others, and the apparent circular reasoning involved in this approach. This latter point refers to the fact that deprivation is identified as a condition only if a social movement emerges.

Mass-Society Theory

This approach, first developed by William Kornhauser, suggests people who feel isolated and insignificant within a broad, complex society are attracted to social movements. Using this perspective, involvement in social movements is viewed as being more personal than political.

Research provides inconsistent support for this approach. The nazi movement in Germany; for example, primarily recruited people who were not socially isolated. Further, political goals of urban rioters in the U.S. have been shown to be part of the participants' purpose.

Structural-Strain Theory

This perspective was developed by Neil Smelser in the early 1960s. In this theory, six social conditions are identified as fostering social movements. These include: (1) structural conduciveness, (2) structural strain, (3) growth and spread of an expanation, (4) precipitating factors, (5) mobilization for action, and (6) lack of social control. Each of these conditions is explained in the text.

This approach is identified as being distinctly social, rather than psychological. This theory however contains the same circularity of argument as found in the relative deprivation theory. Further, it fails to incorporate the important variable of resources, such as the mass media, into a formula for explaining social movements and their relative success or failure.

Resource-Mobilization Theory

Resource-mobilization theory argues that social movements are unlikely to emerge, and if they do, are unlikely to succeed without necessary resources.

This theory's dual focus on discontent and available resources for the success of a social movement provides critical insight for researchers. However, critics argue that powerless segments of the population can promote successful social movements if they organize effectively and have strongly committed leaders. It is also pointed out that power struggles within the status quo of society itself must be taken into account.

"New Social Movements" Theory

A major question focused on by researchers using this approach concerns how and why many recent social movements are different from those of the past. Theorists using this view are concerned with issues such as global ecology, women's and gay's rights, and risks of nuclear war. Two features of this approach is a national (and sometimes international) scope and concern for the quality of life. This view also highlights the power of the state and the mass media.

Stages in Social Movements

While recognizing each social movement is unique, four stages are identified which most move through. These stages include: *emergence, coalescence, bureaucratization*, and *decline*. These are reviewed in the text. Figure 22-3 (p. 635) illustrates the stages.

A social movement declines for several reasons, including the accomplishment of its goals, poor political leadership, inability to counteract forces from the status quo, repression by leaders of their followers, and finally, some social movements may eventually become an accepted part of the system.

Table 22-1 (p. 633) summarizes the five theories of social movements: deprivation theory, mass-society theory, structural-strain theory, resource-mobilization theory, and "new social movements" theory.

Social Movements and Social Change

Social movements either encourage or resist social change. Social change is both a cause and a consequence of social movements. Many past social movements, though taken-for-granted by most people today, did much to affect our social lives.

PART IV: KEY CONCEPTS

Define each of the following concepts in the space provided or on separate paper. Check the accuracy of your answers by referring to the key concepts section at the end of the chapter in the text as well as by referring to italicized definitions located throughout the chapter.

acting crowd
alternative social movement
casual crowd
collective behavior
conspicuous consumption
conventional crowd
convergence theory
contagion theory
crowd
deprivation theory
dispersed collectivities
emergent-norm theory
expressive crowd
fad
fashion
gossip
mass hysteria
mass-society theory
mob
panic
propaganda
redemptive social movement
reformative social movement
relative deprivation
resource-mobilization theory
revolutionary social movement
riot
rumor
social movements
structural-strain theory

PART V: STUDY QUESTIONS

True-False

1. T F People gathered at a beach or observing an automobile accident are used in the text as examples to illustrate conventional crowds.
2. T F Using contagion theory, it is argued that people loose their individual identities and surrender personal will and responsibility to a collective mind.
3. T F Mass behavior refers to collective behavior among people dispersed over a wide geographic area.
4. T F According to the text, social movements are rare in preindustrial societies.
5. T F According to the text, reformative social movements have greater depth, but less scope than redemptive social movements.
6. T F Mass society theory focusing attention on the point that social movements are most likely to occur in areas with close social ties.
7. T F Using mass-society theory, social movements are viewed as more personal than political.
8. T F "New social movements" tend to focus more on economic matters than on the quality of life.
9. T F According to structural-strain theory, people form social movements because of a shared concern about the inability of society to operate as they believe it should.
10. T F According to our author, social change characteristic of large and complex societies is a consequence, but not a cause of social movements.

Multiple-Choice

1. Which of the following is not identified as a difficulty in researching collective behavior using the sociological perspective?

    (a) the concept of collective behavior is broad
    (b) collective behavior is complex
    (c) collective behavior is often transitory
    (d) all are identified as difficulties

2. Herbert Blumer identified several types of crowds based on their level of emotional intensity. Which of the following is not a type of crowd identified by Blumer?

    (a) casual   (d) acting
    (b) conventional   (e) emergent
    (c) expressive

311

3. A theory of crowds which claims that the motives which drive collective action do not originate within a crowd, but rather precede its formation if called _____ theory.

(a) contagion   (c) convergence
(b) reactive   (d) subversive

4. One of the first theories of crowds, developed by French sociologist Gustave Le Bon, is called _____ theory, which focuses on how anonymity in a crowd causes people to lose their identities and surrender personal will and responsibility to a collective mind.

(a) mob   (c) retreative
(b) convergence   (d) contagion

5. A theory which argues that crowds are not merely irrational collectivities is

(a) consensual theory   (c) structural theory
(b) emergent-norm theory   (d) reactive theory

6. The witches of Salem are used to illustrate:

(a) gossip   (c) mass hysteria
(b) rumor   (d) panic

7. What type of social movement seeks limited social change for the entire society?

(a) revolutionary   (d) alternative
(b) redemptive   (e) reformative
(c) deprivation

8. The pro-democracy movement in Eastern Europe is used to illustrate which theory of social movements?

(a) mass society   (c) resource-mobilization
(b) structural-strain (d) "new social movements"

9. The following points--people join social movements as a result of experiencing relative deprivation; social movement is a means of seeking change that brings participants greater benefits; social movements are especially likely when rising expectations are frustrated, best fit which theory of social movements?

(a) deprivation theory   (c) structural-strain
(b) resource-mobilization   (d) mass-society

10. Which of the following is not identified as a stage in the evolution of a social movement?

   (a) emergence
   (b) coalescence
   (c) decline
   (d) realignment
   (e) bureaucratization

Fill-In

1. Riots, crowds, fashions, fads, panics, mass hysteria, public opinion, and social movements are all examples of _____ _____.
2. A _____ is a large number of people who interact little, if at all, in the absence of well-defined and conventional norms.
3. Studying collective behavior can be difficult because it is _____, _____, and often _____.
4. _____ refers to information presented with the intention of shaping public opinion.
5. Thorstein Veblen defined _____ _____ as the practice of spending money with the intention of displaying one's wealth to others.
6. _____ are truly passing fancies, whereas _____ tend to reflect fundamental human values and social patterns that evolve over time.
7. _____ _____ is a perceived disadvantage based on some comparison.
8. Using mass-society theory, social movements are viewed as more _____ than _____.
9. "New social movements" have two distinct features, including being _____ in scope and focusing on the _____ of life.
10. The third stage of a social movement after emergence and coalescence is _____.

Definition and Short-Answer

1. What are three basic characteristics of dispersed collectivities?
2. Differentiate between the four types of crowds identified by Herbert Blumer on the basis of level of emotional intensity.
3. Differentiate between contagion theory, convergence theory, and emergent-norm theory in terms of how each explains crowd behavior.
4. Differentiate between the concepts rumor and gossip.
5. Using structural-strain theory, Smelser identifies six social conditions that help foster social movements. What are these social conditions?
6. What are the five theories of social movements? Compare and contrast each of these in terms of how they help us explain social movements.
7. What are the four stages of social movements?

PART VI: ANSWERS TO STUDY QUESTIONS

True-False

1.	F (p. 619)	6.	F (p. 630)
2.	T (p. 621)	7.	T (p. 630)
3.	T (p. 623)	8.	F (p. 632)
4.	T (p. 627)	9.	T (p. 633)
5.	F (p. 628)	10.	F (p. 635)

Multiple-Choice

1.	d (p. 618)	6.	c (p. 626)
2.	e (p. 619)	7.	e (p. 628)
3.	c (p. 621)	8.	b (p. 631)
4.	d (p. 621)	9.	a (p. 633)
5.	b (p. 621)	10.	d (p. 634

Fill-In

1. collective behavior (p. 617)
2. collectivity (p. 618)
3. broad/complex/transitory (p. 618)
4. propaganda (p. 625)
5. conspicuous consumption (p. 627)
6. fads/fashions (p. 627)
7. relative deprivation (p. 629)
8. personal/political (p. 630)
9. national/quality (pp. 632-33)
10. bureaucratization (p. 634)

PART VII: ANALYSIS AND COMMENT

Sociology of Everyday Life

"The Rumored Death of Beatle Paul McCartney"

Key Points:

Questions:

Critical Thinking

"The Witches of Salem: Can Whole Towns Go Crazy?"

    Key Points:

    Questions:

Social Change And Modernity

23

PART I: CHAPTER OUTLINE

I.   What is Social Change?
II.   Causes of Social Change
      A.   Culture and Change
      B.   Social Structure and Change
      C.   Ideas and Change
      D.   The Natural Environment and Change
      E.   Demography and Change
III.   Modernity
      A.   Ferdinand Toennies: The Loss of Community
      B.   Emile Durkheim: The Division of Labor
      C.   Max Weber: Rationalization
      D.   Karl Marx: Capitalism
      E.   Understanding Modernity: The Theory of Mass Society
            1.   Expanding Scale of Social Life
            2.   The Rise of the State
      F.   Understanding Modernity: The Theory of Class Society
            1.   Capitalism
            2.   The Persistence of Social Inequality
      G.   Modernity and the Individual
            1.   Mass Society: Problems of Identity
            2.   Class Society: Problems of Powerlessness
      H.   Modernity and Progress
IV.   Modernization in Global Perspective
V.   Summary
V.   Key Concepts
VI.   Suggested Readings

PART II: LEARNING OBJECTIVES

1. To know the four general characteristics of social change.
2. To explain the five sources of social change.
3. To understand the four general characteristics of modernization.
4. To compare and contrast the explanations of modernization offered by Toennies, Durkheim, Weber, and Marx.
5. To explain the difference between modern and traditional societies on the basis of: scale of life, social structure, cultural patterns, and social change.
6. To identify the key ideas in two major interpretations of modern society: mass society and class society.
7. To know the problems faced by individuals in class society and mass society.
8. To explain the relationship between modernity and progress.
9. To explain the key ideas of modernization theory.
10. To explain the key ideas of world system theory.

PART III: CHAPTER REVIEW

The radical transformation of the Kaiapo culture living in Brazil's Amazon region is discussed. Many profound questions concerning social change are raised.

WHAT IS SOCIAL CHANGE?

Social change, the transformation of culture and social institutions over time, is the focus of this chapter. Four general characteristics represent the process of social change:

    (1)   Social change is universal although the rate of change varies;
    (2)   Social change is both intentional and unplanned;
    (3)   Social change is often controversial; and,
    (4)   Social change has variable consequences.

Examples for each of these characteristics are discussed to illustrate. For example, William Ogburn's theory of *cultural lag*, which recognizes that material culture usually changes faster than nonmaterial culture, is discussed in reference to (1) above.

CAUSES OF SOCIAL CHANGE

It is being argued that the causes of social change are found both inside and outside of a given society.

Culture and Change

Cultural change results from three basic processes: *invention*, *discovery*, and *diffusion*. Examples for each are presented.

Social Structure and Change

Tension and conflict within a society can be a source of social change. The work of Karl Marx is briefly reviewed as an illustration of theory which links social structure and social change.

Ideas and Change

Max Weber's thesis concerning the influence of the Protestant work ethic on industrialization in Europe and America reflects the influence of ideas on social change. His argument was that the disciplined rationality of Calvinists was fundamental in this process of change.

The Natural Environment and Change

The controlling of the natural environment and its resources by colonists in America demonstrates the power human groups have in manipulating nature. However, examples from India and Crete are pointed out to demonstrate the devastating power of nature of humans and our social lives. **Global Map** 23-1 shows the energy consumption rates in different countries.

Demography and Change

Demographic factors are discussed to show their affect on how societies change.

MODERNITY

Modernity refers to patterns of social life linked to industrialization. *Modernization* is therefore the process of social change initiated by industrialization. Peter Berger has identified four general characteristics of modernization:

(1)   The decline of small, traditional communities;
(2)   The expansion of personal choice;
(3)   Increasing diversity in beliefs, and a future orientation; and,
(4)   Future orientation and growing awareness of time.

Examples for each of these characteristics are discussed to illustrate.
Peter Berger is cited as arguing that modern societies increase autonomy and personal freedom, but also offer less personal and enduring social ties.

Ferdinand Toennies: The Loss of Community

Ferdinand Toennies is introduced to us in the **Profile** box (p. 646). His classic book Gemeinschaft and Gesellschaft focuses on the process of modernization and his reaction to the impersonalization of the world. He did not see modern society as "worse" than preindustrial society, but he was critical of growing individualism.

His concepts of *gemeinschaft* and *gesellschaft* are discussed in some detail using changing conditions in America as illustrations.

One feature of gesellschaft is geographical mobility of a society's population. Table 23-1 (p. 648) shows the extent to which Americans changed residences between 1989 and 1990.

While synthesizing various dimensions of social change, Toennies's work did not clarify cause and effect relationships between the variables he studied. He also has been criticized for being a romanticist.

Emile Durkheim: The Division of Labor

Central to Durkheim's analysis of modernity is his view of the increasing division of labor in society. Durkheim did not see modernization as the loss of community, but rather as a change in the basis of community from *mechanical solidarity*, or shared sentiments and likeness, to *organic solidarity*, or community based on specialization and mutual dependency. These two types of solidarity are similar in meaning to Toennies' concepts of gemeinschaft and gesellschaft.

Durkheim was more optimistic then Toennies about the effects of modernity, yet he still feared anomie could result given increasing internal diversity of society.

Max Weber: Rationalization

Max Weber argued that ideas and beliefs are what caused social change. For him, modernity meant increased rationality and a corresponding decline in tradition. In this process bureaucracy increased as well. Compared to Toennies and Durkheim, Weber was pessimistic and critical about the effects of modernity. He was concerned that rationalization would erode the human spirit.

The **Critical Thinking** box (p. 649) illustrates anomie as a condition of urban life. The case of the murder of Kitty Genovese in Queens New York is discussed.

Karl Marx: Capitalism

While other theorists of the late 19th and early 20th centuries were concentrating their thoughts and research on moral consensus and social stability, Marx focused on social conflict. He agreed with Toennies' analysis of the changing nature of community. He was concerned with Durkheim's sense of the increase in the division of labor. His position also supported Weber's view about increasing rationality and declining tradition. However, for Marx, these processes were all changes which supported the growth of capitalism, and of this he was very critical. Such changes, for Marx, would eventually lead to social revolution.

Understanding Modernity: The Theory of Mass Society

As explained in the text, modernity is a complex process involving many factors. Table 23-2 (p. 651) summarizes the characteristics of traditional and modern societies along the dimensions of scale of life, social structure, cultural patterns, and social change. Sixteen different variables, including seven institutional domains and nine relating to social structures and social processes are focused upon comparing the two types of societies.

One approach to the study of social change is viewing modernization as a process which creates mass societies. A *mass society* is a society in which industrialization proceeds and bureaucracy expands while traditional social ties grow weaker. This approach draws on the work of Toennies, Durkheim, and Weber. Two points are stressed using this perspective. First, the expanding scale of social life creates impersonality and cultural diversity to an extent which is overwhelming for individuals, drawing meaning out of their lives. Second, the expanding role of the government dominates the regulation of people's lives through a complicated and impersonal bureaucratic structure.

Expanding Scale of Social Life

In preindustrial America and Europe, limited community size, social isolation, and a strong traditional religion created homogeneous cultural values (Dukheim's mechanical solidarity and Toennies' gemeinschaft).

Industrialization created geographical mobility, urbanization, and large organizations which provided greater opportunities for a variety of social groups. All of this created what Durkheim referred to as organic solidarity, and what Toennies called gesellschaft.

The Rise of the State

Preindustrial Europe was essentially governed by local nobility. As time passed, governments became more centralized; consequently power has come to reside in large bureaucracies. This has resulted in the depersonalization of human life.

Modernization is viewed both positively and negatively using the mass society approach. It is accepted by many social and economic conservatives who support conventional morality and oppose the expanding power of the government.

Understanding Modernity: The Theory of Class Society

This approach is largely derived from Karl Marx's analysis of society. A *class society* is a capitalist society with pronounced social stratification. The social inequality present is understood as producing feelings of powerlessness among the people.

Capitalism

For Marx, it was the growth of capitalism, not the industrial revolution which caused the increasing scale of social life during the 19th century in Europe and North America.

He saw the profit motive, which emphasized self-interest and greed, as forces which broke down social ties which bound small-scale communities.

Marx also saw advances in science as a reason for such change. He believed science and the technological solutions it offered gave legitimacy to the status quo.

The Persistence of Social Inequality

While many theorists argue that modernization began to break down rigid categorical distinctions, proponents of the theory of class society see a greater concentration of power and wealth occurring.

A criticism of this approach, however, is that it tends to underestimate the ways in which egalitarianism has increased in modern societies. The mass-society theory and the class-society theory are summarized in Table 23-2 (p. 654).

Modernity and the Individual

While mass-society theory and the theory of class society have been discussed to this point as perspectives focusing on macro-level issues concerning patterns of change, they also offer micro-level insights into how modernity affects individuals.

Mass Society: Problems of Identity

According to this view, establishing an identify becomes more difficult with the social diversity, atomization, and rapid social change which modernization brings about.

David Riesman developed the term *social character* to mean personality patterns common to members of a society. He views preindustrial societies as promoting *tradition-directedness*, or rigid personalities based on conformity to time-honored ways of living. This would be associated with Toennies' gemeinschaft and Durkheim's mechanical solidarity. In culturally diverse and rapidly changing industrial societies, another type of social character emerges. This type, called *other-directedness*, refers to highly changeable personality patterns among people open to change and likely to imitate the behavior of others. In the U.S., for example, people tend to conform to peers and easily become influenced by fads.

Class Society: Problems of Powerlessness

According to this view, individual freedom is undermined by the persistence of social inequality. Herbert Marcuse, using this perspective, challenges Weber's contention that modern society is rational. For Marcuse, because society is failing to meet the basic needs of many people it is actually irrational.

Modernity and Progress

Generally, people view modernity as progress, but this conception ignores the complexity of social change. The Kaiapo of Brazil, highlighted earlier in this chapter, illustrate this point.

An interesting perspective is offered in the **Sociology of Everyday Life** box (p. 658), in which the concepts of *honor* and *dignity* are discussed in relation to the idea of human rights.

The issue of individual choice and freedom versus social responsibility and social obligation is addressed. Social change does not proceed in a predictable, linear fashion, and cannot merely be understood as *"progress."*

MODERNIZATION IN GLOBAL PERSPECTIVE

Modernization theory and dependency theory, discussed in great detail in Chapter 11, are reviewed. Modernization theorists see modernity as increasing the standard of living among the people of a society. However, many problems are involved as well, including an increasing materialistic approach to life, which this approach tends to underemphasize.

Dependency theory, on the other hand, views social change as something which is not under the control of individual societies. Placing our understanding of social change within a global perspective is argued to be of vital importance.

PART IV: KEY CONCEPTS

Define each of the following concepts in the space provided or on separate paper. Check the accuracy of your answers by referring to the key concepts section at the end of the chapter in the text as well as by referring to italicized definitions located throughout the chapter.

class society
individualization
mass society
modernity
modernization
other-directedness
social change
tradition-directedness

PART V: STUDY QUESTIONS

True-False

1. T F Max Weber argued that technology and conflict are more important than ideas in transforming society.
2. T F By the year 2030, it is estimated that about 15% of the U.S. population will be over age sixty-five.

3. T F According to Peter Berger, a characteristic of modernization is the expression of individual choice.

4. T F Almost 20 percent of Americans change their residence annually.

5. T F According to our author, Durkheim's view of modernity is both more complex and more positive than that of Toennies.

6. T F Compared to Durkheim, Weber was more critical of modern society, believing that the rationalization of bureaucracies would cause people to become alienated.

7. T F A mass society is one in which industrialization and expanding bureaucracy have weakened social ties.

8. T F According to Reisman, a type of social character he labels other-directedness represents rapidly changing industrial societies.

9. T F Class-society theory maintains that persistent social inequality undermines modern society's promise of individual freedom.

10. T F According to the text, the concept of honor is diminishing in significance for most members of modern society, while the concept of dignity is becoming more important.

Multiple-Choice

1. The Kaiapo:

   (a) is a small society in Brazil
   (b) is a ritual among the Mbuti of the Ituri forest
   (c) is a sacred tradition involving animal sacrifice which has been made illegal by the Canadian government
   (d) are a people of Asia who represent the gesellschaft concept developed by Toennies
   (e) is a ritualistic war pattern of the Maring, a New Guinea culture of horticulturists

2. William Ogburn's theory of _____ states that material culture changes faster than nonmaterial culture.

   (a) modernity   (d) cultural lag
   (b) modernization   (e) anomie
   (c) rationalization

3. The rapid development of medical devices to prolong the life of seriously ill people has outpaced our ability to define death clearly. This situation is an illustration of:

   (a) modernity   (d) anomie
   (b) cultural lag   (e) gemeinschaft
   (c) mechanical solidarity

323

4. Which of the following is not a source of social change?

   (a) ideas
   (b) population
   (c) genetic heritage
   (d) the natural environment
   (e) social structure

5. As the power of tradition declines, a society's members come to see their lives as an unending series of options. Peter Berger refers to this process as:

   (a) modernization
   (b) gesellschaft
   (c) rationalization
   (d) alienation
   (e) individualization

6. Which of the following is most accurate?

   (a) Durkheim's concept of organic solidarity refers to social bonds of mutual dependency based on specialization
   (b) Toennies saw societies as changing from social organization based on gesellschaft to social organization based on gemeinschaft
   (c) Peter Berger argued that modern society offers less autonomy than is found in preindustrial societies
   (d) Durkheim's concept of mechanical solidarity is very similar in meaning to Toennies's concept of gesellschaft

7. Durkheim's concepts of mechanical and organic solidarity are similar to the notions of:

   (a) mass-society and class-society
   (b) tradition-directedness and other directedness
   (c) anomie and progress
   (d) gemeinschaft and gesellschaft
   (e) none of the above

8. _____ theory focuses on the expanding scale of social life and the rise of the state in the study of modernization.

   (a) mass society
   (b) social class
   (c) dependency
   (d) modernization
   (e) rationalization

9. Which social scientist described modernization in terms of its affects on social character?

   (a) David Reisman
   (b) Peter Berger
   (c) David Klein
   (d) William Ogburn
   (e) Herbert Marcuse

10. _____ suggested that those we be critical of Karl Marx's view that modern society is rational because technological advances rarely empower people; instead, technology tends to reduce people's control over their own lives.

(a) Emile Durkheim   (d) Herbert Spencer
(b) David Reisman   (e) Herbert Marcuse
(c) Ferdinand Toennies

Fill-In

1. _____ refers to the transformation of culture and social institutions over time.
2. Social change results from three basic processes: _____, _____, and _____.
3. _____ refers to patterns of social life linked to industrialization.
4. Durkheim's concept of organic solidarity is closely related to Toennies' concept of _____.
5. Max Weber held that _____ and _____ cause social change.
6. Mass society theory draws upon the ideas of _____, _____, and _____.
7. _____ is a society in which capitalism has generated pronounced social stratification.
8. _____ refers to personality patterns common to members of a society.
9. David Reisman argues that preindustrial societies promote _____, or rigid personalities based on conformity to time-honored ways of living.
10. Modernization enhances concern for people as _____, which is expressed in the concept of _____.

Definition and Short-Answer

1. What are the four general characteristics of social change?
2. Five general domains which are involved in causing social change are identified and discussed in the text. List these and provide an example for each.
3. Peter Berger identifies four general characteristics of modern societies. What are these characteristics?
4. Differentiate between Toennies', Durkheim's, Weber's and Marx's perspectives of modernization.
5. What factors of modernization do theorists operating from the mass-society theory focus upon?
6. What factors of modernization do theorists operating from the theory of class society focus upon?
7. What are the two types of social character identified by David Reisman?

PART VI. ANSWERS TO STUDY GUIDE QUESTIONS

True-False

1.	F (p. 642)	6.	T (p. 650)
2.	F (p. 644)	7.	T (p. 652)
3.	T (p. 646)	8.	T (p. 655)
4.	T (p. 648)	9.	T (p. 656)
5.	T (p. 648)	10.	T (p. 658)

Multiple-Choice

1.	a (p. 639)	6.	a (p. 648)
2.	d (p. 640)	7.	d (p. 648)
3.	b (p. 640)	8.	a (p. 652)
4.	c (pp. 641-42)	9.	a (p. 655)
5.	e (p. 645)	10.	e (p. 656)

Fill-In

1. social change (p. 640)
2. invention, discovery, diffusion (p. 641)
3. modernity (p. 644)
4. gesellschaft (p. 648)
5. ideas/beliefs (p. 649)
6. Toennies/Durkheim/Weber (p. 650)
7. class society (p. 653)
8. social character (p. 655)
9. tradition-directedness (p. 655)
10. individuals/dignity (p. 658)

PART VII: ANALYSIS AND COMMENT

Profile

"Ferdinand Toennies (1855-1936)

    Key Points: Questions:

Critical Thinking

"Modern Society: What Do We Owe Others?"

Key Points: Questions:

Sociology of Everyday Life

"Traditional Honor and Modern Dignity"

Key Points: Questions: